from Bad to Wurst

Bavarian Adventures of a Veggie Cook

Denise Barnes

© Denise Barnes 2008

First published in Great Brita
Pen Press Publishers Ltd
25 Eastern Place
Brighton
BN2 1GJ

ISBN 978-1-906206-06-2

Printed and bound in the UK

A catalogue record of this book is available
from the British Library

Cover design by Jacqueline Abromeit
Cover and text illustrations by Suzie Huntington
Photographs by Edward Stanton

www.denisebarneswriter.com
www.tannerhof.de

'A sparkling, hilarious read.'   Richard Milton

In *from Bad to Wurst*, Denise Barnes takes us on a zany tour as she grapples with life working in a Bavarian health clinic – learning German, becoming a vegetarian cook and dealing with amorous Bavarians are just some of the problems she encounters and overcomes with the customary ingenuity, determination and wicked sense of humour of an English girl abroad.

There are bittersweet moments, too, as Denise looks back on her youthful adventures and brings them up to date by revisiting Bavaria, this time as a guest rather than a naïve young kitchen maid.

Denise brings a sparkling, fresh and witty eye to her descriptions of young dreams and indiscretions that will strike a chord with everyone who has yearned for adventures abroad.

This book is a must-have for anyone who is thinking of visiting Germany – even if only in your imagination. It's a treat equally for those with the energy to board a train and for those whose travelling is done from the comfort of an armchair.

ACKNOWLEDGEMENTS

My biggest thank you goes to the original von Mengershausens who had the foresight to create Tannerhof, and especially Anneli von Mengershausen who had the foresight to hire me! Also, thanks to all the staff, then and now. To dear Mum who would have been so proud to have seen the finished book, and her sister Brenda, who I hope will be proud on her behalf! My sister and best friend, Carole, who had such a starring role. Edward Stanton, my husband, who took the photographs, and came up with such a fab title in all of five seconds. Richard Milton, my friend, for his professional advice and encouragement, and his late wife, Rosie Milton, my closest friend, who knew I was writing this book but never got to read it. I miss you, Rosie, and your wicked sense of humour. Del, Mieke, Lorraine and Gisela, who were on hand when the homesickness kicked in, and, of course, the inimitable Barry, who complained that I have not made him handsome enough in the book, though he probably wishes he still had his Brillo-pad hair as he is now closely-shaven! Don and Herman for providing romantic interludes—maybe I made a terrible mistake, Herman, by refusing to become a Hausfrau...am I too late? To Walter & Jenny Fliess for writing "Modern Vegetarian Cookery" – Penguin 1964. The book was a godsend, as all the Tannerhof recipes were in German. To Volker and Jutti Heil for their lovely sense of humour and for our conversations in all kinds of subjects, giving me a better insight into Germany both yesterday and today.

And finally to Suzie Huntington for her charming illustrations which perfectly capture my year at Tannerhof.

I apologise for any mistakes I may have made when writing in German.

To my long-suffering Tannerhof travelling
companion - my dear sister, Carole,
and my dear friend, Del.

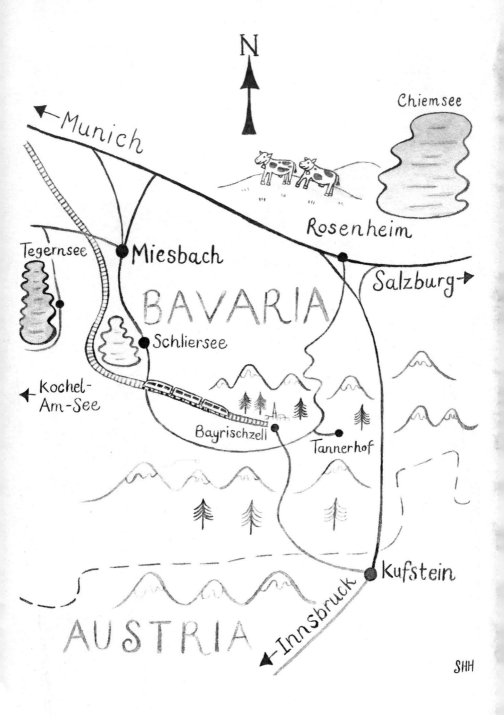

CONTENTS

Part I

Part II

Part III

PART I

MARCH 1973 - FEBRUARY 1974

'DEN, *PLEASE* COME home with me, *please*,' my sister Carole begged as we stood on the spotless platform of the little station of Bayrischzell in Bavaria, waiting for the train to take her away from me, and back to England. Pots of early-blooming flowers were precision-placed, just so many feet away from one another, and a light March breeze made them nod in agreement. 'Just look on it that we've had a lovely few days' holiday.'

'No, I've got to stay.' I have been stubborn since I was two years old, when I had my first tantrum. In despair, my grandmother, who was looking after me for the day, plonked my quivering bare bottom outside on her stone doorstep and told me not to move. I sat there sobbing, just long enough for an enormous boil to start growing, for which my grandmother never forgave herself. 'I've always wanted

3

to live abroad and this is my chance. And I'm not giving up before I've even tried it.'

'If it's awful, don't let pride stop you – promise?' Carole stamped her boots up and down in the snow as though to emphasise her point, but I knew her feet had gone numb like my own. She's always taken on the role of big sister, even though there's less than two years between us.

'I promise,' I lied.

'And why *Germany*?' Carole asked for the hundredth time. She still couldn't believe I intended to work at Tannerhof, a health clinic on the German/Austrian border. 'Why not Italy, where at least it's warm and the men are good-looking?'

'Maybe it's because of Mum's father being German. I'm just curious. It's a bit weird having a grandfather we've never met and who never even knew of Mum's existence, let alone ours. And for some reason, I fancy learning German.'

'He must've been dead for years now, so why bother?'

'Well, if it hadn't been for Nana Nelson having an affair with a German prisoner-of-war, *we* wouldn't be standing here on this platform.'

'Probably no bad thing.' Carole was her usual cynical self. 'All those Germans jangling their bunches of keys like they're prison wardens – *ugh!* I couldn't bear it.'

'You won't have to,' I replied. 'Your train's coming.'

Minutes later, after Carole had given me an awkward hug and a hasty, embarrassed kiss, the train took her further and further away until it was finally swallowed up in the hazy ring of mountains.

I was completely alone. Only Carole knew where I was but she, no more than I, had any idea what my job might entail. Was I completely mad for having answered an advertisement in *The Lady* – a magazine Carole always maintained was written for old ladies? I was addicted to its pages and pages of Sits Vac abroad.

Mostly, they were upper-crust mothers advertising for au-pairs to look after their little Tamaras and Tarquins six-and-a half days a week for meagre wages. Not my scene at all, as I was 27 years old, divorced, with no children, and other people's filled me with horror. You can imagine my excitement, then, when I read this advertisement that appeared just after Christmas:

Young lady required to help in kitchen of Sanatorium in beautiful Bavaria. Small wage and all found. Time off for skiing, ice-skating etc. Please contact Frau v. Mengershausen, Tannerhof, Bayrischzell, Oberbayern, Deutschland.

This was infinitely more interesting than cleaning Swiss loos in some posh ski resort, even though I had little cooking experience to offer. But I had just given up meat whilst tucking into a turkey sandwich left over from the Christmas festivities and devouring a book at the same time called *Why Kill For Food?* I'd only got to about page 20 when I put the not-quite-eaten turkey sandwich back on the plate and vowed never to touch meat again. And I never have.

I immediately applied for the job and as I dropped the letter in the post-box, I remember thinking: 'This could change my life.' Several weeks went by and I continued working in the office of a shop that sold radios and televisions, sorting out a six-month pile-up of VAT paperwork. VAT had only recently been introduced and many shopkeepers were afraid of it. Luckily, Sidney, my boss (dreadful name, but he got away with it as he was gorgeous – and knew it – with humorous brown eyes, the merest hint of a Roman nose, and a very definitely kissable mouth) was able to teach me the rudimentaries (unfortunately, only of VAT), but he was lazy. The office was in an appalling mess. It was a challenge, though a dull one, and the only way I kept from screaming with boredom was to fantasise about those sensuous lips…

As the weeks went by, my longing to work in the Bavarian Alps became more deeply buried under Sidney's own mountain of paperwork. So I had almost forgotten about health clinics when one evening, as I flopped into an armchair after a particularly frustrating day, my mother reluctantly handed me a letter post-marked Deutschland.

I will never forget the thrill of reading the hand-written letter.

Dear Denise,

I am delighted that you would like to stay by us. We would like you to start work in the kitchen in middle of March. You will receive 400 DM a month, and one day free a week. Please write you accept and I will send your train ticket. The weather is very cold. We have snow. Take warm clothes. I enclose a photograph of Tannerhof and the village of Bayrischzell. Another English girl is coming soon after, but you will be the first.

I hope you will enjoy your time by us. Herr Koch will meet the train when we know which one you take.

With friendly greetings,

Anneli v. Mengershausen

Mum picked up the postcard Frau Mengershausen had enclosed. It was a photo of a typical Bavarian-style chalet, laden with cheerful hanging baskets, rolling lawns and a half circle of mountains forming a magnificent backdrop under a quite unbelievably blue sky – or so it seemed to me that gloomy February evening.

'This must be their summer photo,' I said. Mum turned the card over.

'Sanatorium?' She was alarmed, and I could almost read her thoughts: I was going to work in a sanatorium where I would obviously contract TB like some young film-star in one of those black and white TV melodramas that she so enjoyed watching in the afternoons.

'It's just German for health farm,' I replied. It was only when I started work at Tannerhof that I realised nothing could be further from the truth.

Mum didn't sound convinced. Her pretty face tightened but I deliberately took no notice, and wrote back immediately to confirm I was coming on March 22nd. But a few days later there was a complication.

'Carole's coming over in March!' Mum was excited as she came off the phone. 'And you'll be in Germany.' I could tell she was pleased to throw another obstacle in my path by the way she said 'Well, I'd have thought it would be more important to be here to see your sister.'

I rang Carole, who lived in Georgia with her American husband Lamar, and Adam, her son, and she instantly had the solution.

'I'll come with you for a few days and see exactly what you're getting into. If it's awful, as I think it will be, we can both come back together.'

I wrote to ask Frau Mengershausen if I could possibly bring my sister so she could see where I was going to be living for the next year. This time she telephoned me.

'You may come with your sister and have five days' holiday,' she agreed. 'Then you will begin work and your sister will return to England.'

These words sound curt as I write them, but Frau Mengershausen was actually a very kind person and it was just her way of speaking English.

A fortnight later Carole arrived from the US and we began to plan the trip. She wanted to fly, but I insisted we go by train as I wanted to see as much of the countryside as possible. But the day before we were due to set off, I awoke with my throat on fire, eyes streaming, nose pouring, coughing, shivering... the lot.

'Well, *you* won't be in any condition to go to Germany tomorrow,' announced my mother triumphantly. 'It's bed for you for a few days.'

'If I can get out of bed in the morning,' I told her, 'I'm going.'

I could and I did.

CHAPTER 2
NIGHT TRAIN TO MUNICH

IT WAS EXCITING to find the right platform on Victoria Station amongst the swirl of people, even if the destination was the rather unromantic-sounding Ramsgate. But we nearly had a disaster. Carole couldn't find her nose spray. She panicked as she was addicted to it.

'I'll have to get some from Boots,' she said.

'But we're leaving in five minutes!' I was horrified.

'Seven,' she corrected. 'I'll be back in a few moments. Can you take my case?'

And without waiting for an answer, she sprinted down the platform. Five minutes later she was nowhere in sight. What could I do? She had her own ticket but I had her luggage. Did I stay behind or go off with the train in one minute and forty seconds?

I was saved from making a decision. Carole came flying along just as the porter blew his whistle.

'I was ready to go without you,' I said cruelly. 'Did you get your spray?'

'Last one,' she said at the same time as the train gave an almighty jolt, and as we were standing, trying to arrange our luggage, we both fell over like two old ladies.

Ramsgate. Then a-not-very-smooth crossing to Ostend, Carole just managing to stop herself from being sick, and finally a foreign station. Throbbing beasts bearing signs of Vienna, Moscow, Paris, Istanbul were impatiently waiting their turn like greyhounds on a race track. We needed the train to Brussels where we would change for Munich. There it was, not so groomed as it might be, but that, as far as I was concerned, only added to the glamour. Other passengers pressed and bumped into us as we searched for our reserved seats in the right coach. It was to be a long journey – twenty-four hours door to door.

'I've found my nose spray.' Carole triumphantly pulled out a little plastic bottle from the depths of her bag. 'Would you believe it?'

'Yes, I would.'

'It's actually quite smoky in here,' she said, carefully spraying up each nostril. 'I'm going to complain when the conductor comes.' She pulled out some knitting.

'What are you making?'

'A Bavarian hat to match the sweater I've already made you as a leaving-behind present.'

'You'll have to knit all through the night to get it finished,' I said, worrying about the expensive sleeper I'd booked for us on the next train to Munich.

'Here comes the ticket man,' Carole said. 'Oh, I love his shoulder bag. I wonder if it's old and worn, or if it's got a paint effect on it to make it look distressed.' Being an interior designer, she noticed things like that.

He came closer and proved to be… old and worn – just like his bag.

'Is there a no-smoking carriage?' Carole asked him as we handed over our tickets.

Of course, he didn't understand English. He kept gesturing towards the window. We didn't know what he was so agitated about, until he pointed to a tiny picture of a bottle with a red circle round it, which I had thought meant "Do Not Smash Your Bottles Through the Window".

But Carole said: 'It must mean "This is a Champagne Class carriage"!'

He wrote down 'Ghent' on a piece of paper and the number 2, which we took to mean that we should move to second class at the next stop. But I was definitely not getting off this train with my luggage to try and find the carriage – I'd had enough of people running along the platform just as the train was about to depart.

The conductor had already moved on and was talking to another passenger. I went up to him with my flirtiest smile, which may have lost its full effect, I realised later, when I saw my blood-shot eyes in the smeary mirror in the train toilet.

'Please don't make us carry our heavy luggage to another carriage. We've come from England this morning and we're really tired.'

He looked at me sternly, though it might have been that he couldn't understand a word I'd said. The other passenger asked what the problem was, and when I explained, he said the same thing had happened to him and he was also arguing the toss. Although he spoke immaculate English, I could tell by his slurred delivery that he had had a few too many. Not to mention that he was swaying out of synch with the train. I asked him his nationality.

'Belgian.'

I turned to the conductor and said, 'This gentleman is actually *Belgian* – he's in his own *country*, and even *he* didn't realise he was in a first-class carriage.'

My collaborator translated this to the conductor, who just shrugged. Then he explained that he was a sailor and not used to train transport. By this time, we were having a jolly little conversation, and the conductor (according to another translation) said, 'The English always have a good sob story to tell when they want their own way.'

I told him it was not because I was English but because I was a woman. It was lost on him, but I thanked him anyway for letting us stay in smoky first class, even though he still hadn't given his permission. Another blank look and he moved on.

But when we drew into Brussels, lo and behold, there was our conductor, smiling and helping us off with our luggage. He then, dear man, found our platform for the Munich train, and just as his own train was moving, he jumped on the step, swinging precariously on the outside as he waved us goodbye. And probably good riddance.

We had a half an hour to spare before we boarded but only dared stop for a quick drink.

'Pooh!' Carole's nose wrinkled. 'You know you're in France just by the smell of Gauloise and garlic.'

'Belgium, actually.'

'Same difference.'

The midnight coffee tasted like car oil when it's ready to be changed, but caffeine was just the job to perk up our cramped and exhausted bodies and find our way to the train bound for Munich. My cold, which hadn't been too bad throughout the day, now made a full come-back. I was beginning to shiver.

'*Vous êtes ici*,' said a moustached porter, as he checked our tickets, indicating our sleeper, which had four bunks, stacked two on either side.

'Will we be on our own?' Carole asked him in her best school French.

He frowned, trying to work out Carole's question, which I thought was perfectly clear, and then produced a torrent of indecipherable French, so we couldn't work out whether we would have our privacy or not.

There was about enough space to accommodate a family of fig-wasps. Every inch was used for storage: a hidden wash basin that doubled as a dressing-table, a folding ladder – it was all there if you could find it. In the bathroom cabinet, disguised as a perfectly-flat mirror, were two sealed paper cups, already filled with water. We were just wondering whether we dare drink from them when a new porter tapped on the door to explain the workings of our quarters. He was German.

'Do you speak English?' I asked.

He nodded. 'A little.'

'Is this drinking water?'

'They are for putting your teeth in,' he answered, without a trace of irony.

Still in her trousers and T-shirt, Carole tucked herself into her sheet on the lower bunk, but I knew I wouldn't sleep unless I got into my nightdress. The ladder in the sleeper was absolutely impossible. If you didn't get it hooked on properly it was dangerous. I hate ladder-work at the best of times. Once, between jobs, I helped our local window cleaner called Alan Bucket – I swear that was his name! He was so impressed with my window cleaning that by the afternoon he had offered me a partnership! Reluctantly, I turned him down. I don't do ladder-work.

Carole says she will never forget the picture of my thin white legs under a ghostly nightdress climbing the bunk ladder and hauling myself over the bar to my narrow little bunk – every bit as wide as a park bench. A light glared in my eyes but I couldn't find the switch and assumed it was down that ladder, which I couldn't face again. It was only the next morning that I found the switch right by my bunk. I pulled the blanket over my head to block out the light, and the lint must have set off a coughing fit, which made my nose run, which made me sneeze a dozen times without stopping.

'For goodness sake, Den!'

'I can't help it,' I whimpered.

'Well, I hope *I* don't catch it, that's all. Good thing we're on our own.'

With that, the train rattled to a halt, doors slammed open and shut all the way up the train and back again, and so did ours. A small brown man climbed in under the weight of a suitcase the size of an American fridge.

'You can't stay here,' Carole warned him in a very firm tone. 'My sister has a shocking cold.'

'I have *too*, sorry for *you*,' came a powerful Pakistani accent, thickened by nasal infection, and to our horror he proceeded to undress and join me on the other top bunk. When he lay down and faced me, his head was so close, he might as well have rested it on my own pillow. I turned my back to confirm I wasn't interested.

Several hours later and a couple of stops before Munich, our little Pakistani poet silently slipped away.

'That was the worst night I've had in my entire life,' Carole grumbled. She's prone to exaggeration. 'The two of you sneezing and spluttering and blowing your noses. Groaning, sniffing, sighing, turning – I thought I'd go mad!'

Of course, that made us start laughing, and by the time our porter brought us two builders' mugs of coffee and we had dug out a couple of old airline refresher towels, and cleaned our teeth by using our fingers and rubbing toothpaste on our gums (we failed to find any running water in the secret wash-basin), we revived like forgotten plants who had just been given a life-saving drink .

Our train slid into Munich. We heaved our luggage over the 'gap'. How we managed not to fall to our deaths on the electric lines below – the 'gap' being three times the width of our English ones, and with no warning voice over the speaker to mind it – I'll never know, and struggled to the nearest café; this was twenty years away from the wonderful invention of suitcases on wheels. It wasn't even 6 am but almost every beer-barrel-shaped table was packed with mostly men chattering in a strange gutteral language. I had to remind myself that this was to be my nearest city for the next year… and my new language. It was a sobering thought.

We tried to order eggs and coffee, thinking people would understand English in a capital – though I wonder how many people would understand German in London. But the bleached blonde behind the bar shook her head, her dangly earrings telling us she had no idea what we were on about. In the end, a tall businessman ordered for us and bowed his fair head slightly as we thanked him. He asked where we were going and then pointed to the last platform at the far end of the station.

'It only goes so far as Bayrischzell,' he told us. 'When ze train stops, so do you.'

For an hour-and-a-half, Carole madly clicking her needles trying to finish my hat, we trundled through the most beautiful countryside I had ever seen. White-covered mountains you could almost reach from the open train window, cosy wooden houses tucked into the valleys or clinging on to the side of steep hills, and swathes of fir trees leading the way. And everywhere… snow.

It was funny to watch passengers alighting with their skis nonchalantly flung over their shoulders. And even more strange when we stopped at a little town called Miesbach for a couple of minutes and then began moving backwards. No-one in the carriage took the slightest notice, so we guessed it must be normal. Another half hour rolled by, Carole's needles clicking in time with the train's wheels. Then:

'Bayrischzell!' A porter shouted the name, and I felt a little shiver that was nothing to do with my cold. I wasn't sure if it was excitement… or apprehension.

We tumbled onto the platform with our luggage and a red-faced man with a Tyrolean hat complete with badger brush stomped towards us. There was no smile of welcome.

'Fräulein Barnes?' He pronounced it Barn-es.

I nodded, and he swept up our baggage in one movement. My sister and I, lungs amazed at the pure crisp air they were drawing in, followed his snowy footprints. Herr Koch threw our cases unceremoniously into the back of his van, looking as though he would like to hoist us up with them, but instead opened the side doors and in we got. There was a blur of mountains, a smudge of village, and a road that churned our stomachs at every bend. I didn't dare look at Carole, but I could see her grim white face out of the corner of my eye.

And then… Tannerhof. I recognised the main house from Frau Mengershausen's photograph. It stood out from a complex of chalets, glittering in the early morning sun. This is where I'm going to live, I thought. It's like a dream.

As Herr Koch pushed open the front door with his sludgy boot, I smelled a smell I will never forget – a bewitching blend of cinnamon, apples and candle-wax against a background of smoked wood came drifting through the hall to greet us. Seconds later, a middle-aged lady with neat grey hair and an endearing buck-toothed smile hurried towards us.

'Good morning. You are ze Fräulein Barnes sisters, *ja*? I welcome you. I am Frau Weilland, the housekeeper.'

Carole and I returned the beaming smile, but Herr Koch, taking absolutely no notice, tossed our bags down by the umbrella stand and gestured Carole to wait while he took me down some steps to a snow-covered dwelling called the *Gochel-Hütte*, which was topped by a weather-vane of a cockerel. It was a wooden hut which, I later discovered, held five Tannerhof workers. I was taken aback to see that although we all had our own bedrooms, we had to share a wash-basin, which was out of sight behind a piece of curtain that looked like an old cut-up bedspread. No loo in the building. All very primitive. I hadn't expected these sorts of conditions in Germany and wondered how Carole was faring.

She told me she had been led halfway up a mountain behind the main house to a small wooden hut. After she had unpacked and was struggling down on her own, she met a man well in his sixties running *up* the mountain. He was kitted out in *Lederhosen*, with embroidered braces over a white shirt, the sleeves rolled up, can you believe, in minus degree weather, complete with feathered hat, as though he were performing in a show, and it took her a few seconds to realise this was his everyday outfit. She wished him *Guten Morgan* and he replied, '*Gruss Gott, Fräulein*'. (That's 'Greetings to God' in Bavarian.) 'You are English. When do you come here?'

She admitted she had only just arrived, and was impressed with the beauty of the place, but that it was very steep getting up to her room, to which he gave her a stern look and said, 'It is a *privilege* to stay here and climb up ze mountain, *Fräulein*.' With that, he hurtled out of sight.

The five days Carole and I spent together felt rather odd. We didn't exactly feel as though we were on holiday because we were trying to make sense of the place and the people I would be working with. All the staff knew I'd come there to work, and everyone was polite, but we had a suspicion that some of the dining room staff in particular couldn't really see why they had to wait on us as though we were paying guests. We didn't have any idea what the kitchen staff thought, as we had no direct contact with them. But Frau Mengershausen always greeted us with a warm smile whenever she spied us.

'You are settling in?' She would ask. 'Is all to your satisfaction?'

That was quite difficult to answer truthfully. I'd like to have said, 'It would be nice not to have to go outside in the snow to get to the lav' and 'Why are the two older waitresses so severe?' But of course I didn't say any such thing.

'I'm settling in well,' I would reply, 'and everyone's very kind to us.'

'Goot, very goot,' she'd nod, and hurry on.

We occasionally saw the four other workers who had rooms in my hut, but John, the assistant gardener, was the only one we could have a conversation with, as he was American, so roughly spoke our language.

'What's it really like here?' Carole managed to pin him down one day as he was just about to clean up for lunch.

'Well, I've been here for six months… got another six to go. They're not a bad bunch… bit serious… but so long as they see you're working your butt off, they're okay. The dialect is hard to understand.'

'Did you know German before you came?'

'A bit, but it didn't help that much. It's better now. But I didn't come for that reason. I wanted to take some time off before uni, and I like the big outdoors.'

A girl who was too big to be an advert for a health clinic lived in the far corner of my hut. She wasn't German. We couldn't place her nationality – Greek, maybe, with her long black hair and matching eyebrows that topped tired brown eyes. She would smile shyly and, without pausing, unlock her door and disappear into her room.

We recognised the pretty Bavarian girl with a cap of shiny brown hair, who introduced herself as Traudl, as she sometimes waited on us at lunch and dinner in the guests' dining room without any hint that she shouldn't have to do this. She, too, was always in a hurry so we didn't have much conversation, and there was the language barrier, though we suspected she knew more English than she let on.

The fourth room was occupied by Gisela, a masseuse.

In spite of everything – that is, neither of us being certain I would stay – we decided to make the most of our five days. With the March sun glancing on and off the terrifyingly-beautiful mountains, and warming our backs as we tried skiing for the first time (not at all a success, as we spent more time *in* the snow than on top of it), we breathed in air that ought to be bottled and sent to England. We went ice-skating, walking, shopping in the darling little village of Bayrischzell, had saunas, massages and wonderfully-healthy food, giving no thought as to its preparation. We treated ourselves to a day of culture in Munich, and admired paintings, buildings and the sophisticated shops. We learned Bavarian dancing at the local hop called the *Heuboden* (hayloft). We guiltily ate huge portions of *Kuchen* (cake). We slept like babes. We looked and felt as though we could jump over the moon. And still Carole was reluctant to leave me behind.

I stood on the platform for several minutes, feeling sick. I *had* to see this through. Why did it now seem like a prison sentence? I reminded myself that this was my choice. And that it would expand my life experiences. It was time for me to say *auf wiedersehen* to my old life, report for duty, and show those Germans what we Brits were capable of. It didn't take me long to realise that nothing could be further away from that little fantasy.

I turned from the station and squelched and slipped up the hill to Tannerhof, wondering what the hell I'd let myself in for.

Chapter 3

Start as You Mean to Go On

First day in the kitchen. This was an enormous room off the main hall, and if the hatch, which was as wide as an up-and-over garage door, was open, you could see three women bustling about. I had felt a bit guilty during my five days with Carole, as when I would glance through the hatch out of curiosity, they always looked as though they could do with some extra help: well, here I was, aproned-up, nervous, but ready to be welcomed with open arms.

Normally, the kitchen staff had their breakfast at 7 o'clock, but this first morning I was told to report to Frau Cygan (pronounced Seegan), the head cook, at 6.45 am.

Frau Cygan was a little bird-like woman who barely came up to my shoulder. She had cropped grey hair wisping out from her snowy cap, and bright intelligent eyes that saw the best in everyone.

Her skin was soft and pink, just like my grandmother's, and immediately I relaxed. She was the only one who spoke a few words of English, which she told me she'd learnt at school, but that was 60 years ago.

'Come, Denise. Zis is Emmi, ze assistant cook.'

Emmi shook my hand with her square, rough-red one, which had obviously never collided with any handcream. '*Gruss Gott*,' was all she said with a little nod of her fair head. No smile. She was much younger than Frau Cygan, with a curvaceous figure, and her apron seemed to bristle with efficiency. Oh, dear.

'And Anita,' continued Frau Cygan. 'She does all.' This was better. A girl in her early twenties, with short dark hair and brown eyes. At least she smiled at me as she shook hands.

'And Suna.' Frau Cygan took me into the adjacent scullery and introduced me to another member of the kitchen staff. 'She is from Turkey and does all washing.'

Suna was great, both in size and warmth. My hand disappeared in her large fleshy grasp, and she grinned so widely that for a second you could glimpse her cheekbones which would usually sit unnoticed.

The five of us sat round a wooden table, already laid. Different coloured breads – dark rye, light rye, linseed, whole grain (Mother obviously didn't have any Pride here) – lay on a wooden board, overlapping like slates on a roof. A glass bowl, filled with home-made müesli, was placed in the centre, next to a ceramic blue bowl of quark. (Later, I found out that quark is a very low-fat sheep's cheese that can be used in cooking savoury and sweet dishes, or simply as an alternative to yoghurt or fromage frais. The Germans mix it with milk to make a soft, creamy texture.) A plain white teapot exuded unrecognisable hedgerow smells, and a slab of butter the colour and gloss of Magnolia paint (unlike our bright yellow dyed stuff at home) sat on a stainless-steel plate next to a bowl of honey. Slices of cheese, thin as playing cards, and tomato chunks topped

20

with herbs, were laid out with the artistry of a still-life painting. All the plates and cups and saucers were hospital white, but there was something that lifted this from an ordinary staff breakfast - lighted candles. Several were dotted around the table. I don't know why, but I instantly cheered up. Was this for my benefit, being the new girl? I learned later that, like the guests, we had candles on our table at every mealtime. For the moment, I was simply charmed. But the feeling didn't last.

We sat like cloistered nuns, passing things to one another in response to a grunt or a gesture, and helping ourselves to the müesli. I couldn't believe they didn't need to discuss the day's menu, or just generally have a chat. It was unnerving.

Seven-fifteen. Suna cleared the table and Frau Cygan and Emmi finally had a little conflab. I heard my name mentioned. Then Emmi led me over to one of the worktops, pulled out a chopping board almost the size of our breakfast table-top, set it 'just so' and dumped a small forest of parsley in the middle.

'*Petersilie,*' Emmi said to me. I had no idea what she was talking about.

'*Nicht verstehen.*' (I don't understand.) I was to use that expression an awful lot in my first few weeks.

'Chop the *Petersilie,*' Emmi repeated a little louder, only all the words she used were German. I gave my usual blank stare when I don't understand something. She grabbed the chopper and hovered it over the green mass, rocking it backwards and forwards in the air, pretending to chop.

'Oh.' I cotton on fast. 'What is it called? *Pe-pe-t…*'

'*Pe-ter-si-li-e.*' Emmi emphasised the last syllable.

'*Pe-ter-si-li-e,*' I returned.

I was rewarded with a faint twitch of Emmi's mouth. This was quite exciting. 'Your German word for today is *Petersilie.*' Not the most urgent word for most people trying to learn German, I admit, but essential for me.

By 11 o'clock I realised that no-one had stopped for a break, not even a sip of water; we had been working solidly for three-and-a-half hours. This was obviously the German worker in action. My throat was parched, as I imagined it would be in the desert with the last slug of the water accidentally spilt – by me, of course. I needed a coffee… anything. Eleven-fifteen. I could either seethe and continue working, or I could start as I meant to go on. Bravely, I chose the latter.

I finished mixing 25 cartons of quark with milk in an enormous stainless-steel bowl, and furtively looked around. Everyone was busy. Frau Cygan was putting some decorative tomato slices on the millet pudding she'd made, Emmi was making cakes for someone's birthday, Anita was scrubbing carrots and Suna was already in the scullery facing the first pile of dishes.

I sauntered over to the island in the middle of the big square kitchen that housed the various hobs and ovens, holding a mug and tin of dandelion coffee. This was the closest I could find to real coffee. Come to think of it, I'd never smelt any real coffee wafting through the house. It was obviously *verboten* at Tannerhof. All that dangerous caffeine.

I tipped boiling water into my mug and stirred, which brought the kitchen to a halt. No scuffling shoes, no odd murmur, no sounds of scraping and washing and chopping… just silence. All eyes on me. They were staring with undisguised astonishment. Then Frau Cygan must have said something like: *'Don't take any notice – she's English – that's what they all do.'*

And Emmi snorted, *'Well, if that's how the English behave, taking breaks all the time, I still cannot understand how they won the war!'*

A few moments later they silently resumed work – without me. I sat with my drink, allowing myself ten minutes, but couldn't enjoy it with everyone rushing about, and was almost relieved when the time was up. Would I have the nerve to go through that ritual every morning?

Wonderful savoury herby smells were beginning to emanate from the ovens, but I'd hardly had a chance to appreciate them when Anita ushered me to a corner of the room to slice a barrel-load of her scraped carrots.

'Like so.' She deftly cut both ends off a carrot, cut it down the middle length-wise. 'Like so,' she repeated, and chip-chopped her way along the carrot, forming crescent-shaped pieces as she went. Every slice was exactly the same thickness as its neighbour.

I tried it.

'Nein, nein, Denise – you complete English twit.' Or words to that effect.

'OK,' Anita nodded at my next attempt and there was a flicker of approval in those dark eyes. Before I could hug that tiny morsel, Emmi was back with my bowl of *Petersilie*. With irritation, she pushed the bowl in front of me, knocking the carrots to one side, and said, *'Nicht fein genug*, Denise.' (Not fine enough.) She made a see-saw motion with her red-knuckled fists to demonstrate the chopping utensil and bustled back to her work station.

I wasn't sure if I should finish the carrot chopping or the parsley chopping. Maybe they needed the parsley right away. So I took the chopper and threw the offending greenery onto another board. I chopped and chopped until the parsley spewed parrot-green juice, and took the bowl over to Emmi for inspection. She looked at it with contempt, her face dangerously red. Perhaps this was the result of bending down to check progress in the ovens, but I felt she was cross with me. She shook her head again and took the bowl. Really, there was no pleasing the woman. Frau Cygan was engrossed, so didn't witness this little scene. Of course, I had never cooked in a professional capacity before, so I wasn't used to the importance of presentation and the stress of getting everything timed to perfection that was part and parcel of feeding so many people.

My next job was to prepare apples (the excitement builds!). Anita was elected to show me what to do. It's actually easier than you'd think. She washed a bucket load, took one in her left hand, and with a sharp knife in her right, simply quartered it and threw the lot into an enormous saucepan.

'Don't you take out the core and pips?' I asked her.

'*Nicht verstehen.*'

Makes a change, I thought. So far this morning *I* hadn't understood a word. I de-cored and de-pipped one to explain.

'*Nein, nein,*' she said. (Why do they always say it twice?) She cut another apple the same way as the first. I shrugged. I didn't have to eat it.

She decided to help me, but it was disconcerting having her watch how I was cutting them, making sure they were done to her satisfaction. We worked in silence. When the pan was filled, she poured in some water, scattered a few cinnamon sticks on the top, and put it to boil. While we were waiting for them to soften, she took some cauliflowers and showed me how to make cauliflower soup. She used a technique similar to the one she'd used for the apples, putting all the stalks and green leaves into a pan, with water and vegetable stock – not the kind you buy in little cubes, but all lovingly home-made.

Pretty soon, an enticing smell of apple and cinnamon assailed my nostrils, and I recognised the delicious combination I had smelt when I first came through the front door of Tannerhof. No time to stand and inhale. Anita was brandishing a sieve that she set over a stainless steel bowl you could bath a baby in, and ladled out the cooked apples with all their cores and pips. With a pestle the size of a baseball bat, she pounded the apples through the sieve until a golden pulp plashed into the waiting bowl. She handed me the pestle, which almost broke my wrist. These German women were jolly strong. She muttered something that I gathered meant I was to carry on.

I laboured for what felt like hours. Finally, and proudly, I surveyed my beautiful bowl of *Apfelmus,* as I was to call it. My arm was aching and I had come to the conclusion that watching paint dry would be quite an interesting pastime by comparison, but thank heavens I'd finished. Would it pass the test? Anita came over.

'*Gut*, Denise,' she said. I beamed. The beam left as quickly as it had come when Emmi appeared with the saucepan of cooked cauliflowers and a fresh sieve. Oh, no. Oh, yes. My last half hour in the run-up to lunch was spent pushing more food through those miserable little holes.

Miraculously, and no thanks to me, we were ready at dead on twelve-thirty. The guests, who had been hiking, skiing, ice-skating, swimming, and sauna-ing, were already in the dining rooms, gripped with the pangs of hunger.

It was an hour later when we had ours. I, who had been so hungry, had now lost all interest in food, but as soon as dear little Frau Cygan set a plate of her millet rissoles and veg before me, all casually sprinkled with parsley as though it had chopped itself, I devoured the lot. I did wonder what had happened to the soup – not that I could have tackled any – and was pleased when Frau Cygan informed me that it had been the main event of the Light Diet Room.

'*Köstlich*,' I declared. (Delicious.) I had asked Frau Cygan how to say that word during the morning session, as I was determined to get on the right side of Emmi. Emmi simply nodded.

I staggered to my room, worn out. Gone was my plan to study German grammar, gone was the idea of a brisk healthy walk, gone was the temptation to wander down to the village to look at the shops. I collapsed into bed. My last flicker of brain activity was wondering if the Germans, like the Italians and Spaniards, had a siesta – or was this only in hot countries? I was asleep.

'We meet again *halb fünf*,' Frau Cygan had told me.

Fine – I had several hours until the evening shift. I slept through most of them. Groggy with tiredness and sleep, but dead on half-past five, I opened the kitchen door surprised to see everyone already in full action. Saucepans were bubbling, plates were clattering. Emmi, who was stirring something on the hob, just looked up and sniffed. She reminded me of my Aunt Edna when she didn't approve of someone. Frau Cygan hurried over.

'It is late, Denise.' She didn't say it unkindly.

I glanced at my watch. 'It's exactly half-past five.'

Frau Cygan looked puzzled. Then her anxious face cleared. '*Halb fünf* in German is half-past *four*.' It made no sense to me, but when I studied my German lesson the following day, I discovered it meant half an hour *before* five, that is, half-past four in *my* language. I had better remember this in future.

We prepared a simple supper of potatoes in their skins (unusual in the seventies when the English used to peel everything) which had been oiled and rolled in seeds, and looked like baby hedgehogs, then baked in the oven, and served with a little individual pot of yoghurt, quark and parsley dressing. A salad completed the meal.

At half-past six we in the kitchen sat down for our supper. Frau Cygan and Emmi, who I guessed didn't always see eye to eye, were conversing and I was desperately trying to get the gist of it, when Anita, without any warning, stretched right over me and threw her arm across my face to grab the bowl of quark. I was just about to put a forkful of food in my mouth, and her arm pushed the fork down the back of my throat. Choking, I glared at her. I longed to say, 'Haven't you got any manners? All you need say is "Please pass the quark," ' but a) she wouldn't have understood me and b) she wouldn't have taken any notice of me anyway. It had been a long day.

'*Gute Nacht*,' I said coldly to everyone, as I gathered up my plates.

'*Gute Nacht*,' said Frau Cygan and Emmi together.

'*Bis Morgan*,' from Anita. (Until tomorrow.)

I ignored her and shut the kitchen door behind me with a faint slam. Suna, already bent over her sink like a giant comma, her long black hair lank with steam and about to trail in the water, took my dishes with a happy smile and plunged them into the boiling suds, her eyes saying, 'We foreigners have to stick together.'

It might not be enough, Suna. Maybe Carole was right. Maybe I wouldn't be able to survive this for a *week*, let alone a year.

CHAPTER 4
'SHE MUST HAVE NOTHING BUT GRATED APPLE AND GRUEL'

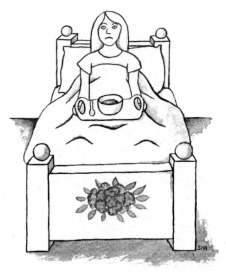

I HAD ONLY been at Tannerhof for two weeks when I woke up one morning, even earlier than my usual 5 o'clock, feeling terrible. I had stomach pains and felt nauseous and dizzy when my feet touched the wooden floorboards. Instantly, I knew I had to rush outside to the loo. I had the runs. Tottering back through the snow that had not yet been cleared by Herr Koch, I crawled into bed and pulled the duvet up to my chin. At first, I thought I'd just got a bug. It certainly wouldn't be food poisoning as the kitchen shone like an operating theatre and the food was fresh from the organic gardens every day.

Frau Mengershausen instructed me to eat very lightly with plenty of herbal teas and assured me it would clear up in a couple of days.

But it was now the third day and I wasn't getting better – in fact, I was worse. I think they started taking me seriously when I didn't even try to go to work that morning. I felt guilty that I was letting the team down – they would have to cover for my duties – not to mention feeling embarrassed that I should be ill at a health clinic.

I groaned again as I shivered under the thick bedclothes.

The following morning – day number four – I demanded to see a doctor.

'I will send Frau Doktor Kruger,' promised Frau Mengershausen. I was by now alarmed. I understood Doctor Kruger was a homeopathic doctor and not a 'real' one. And it was a real doctor I wanted to see.

Doctor Kruger came to my room later that morning. She seemed unconcerned but not unkind as she took my temperature and prodded my bruised and empty stomach. She then pronounced in halting English:

'You eat only *Apfel und Haferschleim*. Drink only water and herb tea.'

'How long?' I asked through dry, frightened lips.

'A week, maybe.'

A week! I'd probably be dead by then!

'You take zis, four times a day. I show you.'

As she spoke, she produced a small phial of blue tincture from a carpet bag and made me open my mouth to put a drop on my tongue, which by now had furred up like the inside of a tossed-out kettle. Then I had to turn over on my left side facing the wall and take another drop, then over on the right side facing her for the third drop, and then onto my stomach for the fourth drop. I did not have any confidence at all in this procedure, I can tell you – it smacked of quackery – but I was too weak to argue. I have always been deeply suspicious of any food or medicine that is blue, with the possible exception of blueberries. In the Deep South, where I lived for several years, they produce a blue cereal that I could never bring myself to eat. But I kept reminding myself that Tannerhof was a *health* clinic and they *must* know what they were doing.

Then it was time for my first bowl of *Haferschleim*. Perhaps before I continue I should explain what *Haferschleim* is. Imagine a bowl of porridge made with milk, a pinch of salt, a little swirl of cream and dob of butter, and a spoonful of treacle, or if you prefer, brown sugar, or even maple syrup. *Well, it's not that. Haferschleim* (brilliantly named to rhyme with 'slime') is a thin beige gruel made with water, pukingly bland. I somehow had to swallow it twice a day, plus a saucer of grated apple, brown-free from a sprinkling of lemon juice, but no more appetising for it.

Four times, religiously, through the day, I would administer the blue drops. Mostly, I was in such a semi-hallucinatory state that I didn't question it – until day six. Then, I actually began to wonder if they were trying to poison me to get their own back on the British. I know this sounds crazy but I just wasn't getting any better and the lack of food was having an effect on my brain. Frau Doktor Kruger never appeared again and the only human I saw was a young waitress as expressionless as the gruel she brought me. She never smiled or, for that matter, spoke. She simply dumped the tray on my table and scuttled out the door, terrified, I suppose, that I might speak to her with a furry foreign tongue. And all I could do was just lie there, watching the light grow dim in my spartan room, the painted furniture that looked so arty and cheerful in the day becoming claustrophobic.

My fevered mind strayed to Don, my American ex (I suppose he was now) boyfriend. I kept reliving our romance, and asking myself why it had ended so abruptly in Vienna in the middle of a planned six-month European trip. Surprisingly, I had had a letter from him before I left home, and although the postmark was Atlanta (his hometown), he'd told me the stunning news that he had accepted a job with the army in Augsburg. I couldn't believe the coincidence. Augsburg is only about an hour's drive from Bayrischzell. And neither of us had known the other was going to be working in Germany, let alone Bavaria. Surely it had to be fate.

A knock at the door rudely interrupted my hallucinatory dreaming, but this time it was quick and light – different from my usual waitress.

'*Kommen Sie hierein*,' I tried to call out, but it sounded to my ears like the pathetic mew of a last-born kitten.

The door opened and in walked a vision. A girl of about twenty with gorgeous coppery-brown hair that swung straight and shiny below her shoulders, merry eyes and a wide, smiling lipsticked mouth.

'Hello, I'm Lorraine, and I've brought you your supper.'

Her English accent startled me into a sitting position, but I was speechless.

'Are you feeling better?' she asked, with friendly concern.

'I am now. I don't see anyone all day except one waitress and she doesn't know a word of English. So you're the English girl they told me was coming. When did you arrive?'

'Yesterday.' Lorraine set a tray in front of me. I stared in disbelief and delight. A boiled egg (not in an egg-cup, but who cared?) with some delicious rye bread and butter, and a cup of tea. All right, it was *herbal* tea… but I was in heaven.

'Do you want to eat quietly on your own?'

'Oh, no, please stay.' I wasn't going to miss this opportunity of having a proper English conversation for the first time in three weeks.

Lorraine shifted a straight-backed chair from the table I used as a desk, stood it by my bed, and sat down, tucking one slim leg under her bottom, leaving the other to dangle gracefully.

'You eat while I talk,' she said.

She told me she'd just been working in Trieste where she'd been an au pair to what sounded like a ghastly Italian family. There were three very spoilt brats who refused to behave, and a

31

matriarchal harridan who ordered Lorraine to do housework, as well as child-minding, plus teaching them all English. And as if that wasn't enough, she was constantly having to ward off the husband's advances. The wife was beginning to get suspicious – why, Lorraine could never understand, as he was not in the least bit attractive with his greasy thinning hair and expanding paunch – and began treating her with contempt. After three months of misery, Lorraine packed her bags and fled.

She'd been given the name of Frau Mengershausen through a friend, and Tannerhof sounded intriguing, mainly, I suspected, because there were no children. She'd applied as a cleaner and was immediately accepted.

'What rotten luck,' I sympathised through a mouthful of runny yolk clinging to my soldier.

'Well, at least I can get around Italy on my own now,' Lorraine said cheerfully. 'I certainly didn't speak Italian before – not that I know any German. Do you?'

'Not much, but it's surprising how quickly you learn when you're forced to. Though I've only been in the kitchen a couple of weeks. The rest of the time I've been ill.'

'Poor you,' said Lorraine. 'But I think you're on the road to recovery now.'

She stayed a few more minutes, then took my tray with a 'See you tomorrow' and disappeared.

I was on the mend.

Lorraine brought me all my meals over the next two days – delectable dishes such as steamed trout and boiled potatoes – and as I got my strength back, I got to know Lorraine. She was only nineteen and, like me, had always wanted to live abroad but didn't have any languages. It seemed that she'd chosen Italy on the basis of pure romantic appeal, and even looking after children with no previous experience had sounded good to her, as they would be *Italian* children. To me, children were the same the world over. But

Lorraine's romance with Italy had soon dwindled, and her starry eyes now settled on a beautiful Bavarian clinic surrounded by mountains. Another romance that was sure to disappoint the first time she sank to her pretty knees – not in the pew of the dear little overblown Catholic church in the village below, but over a Tannerhof toilet. I didn't say anything as the last thing I wanted was for this butterfly to flit away, denying me my new companion.

'I'm getting up tomorrow,' I announced. 'But I don't think I can go back to work straight away. I still feel so weak.'

'I'll tell them you're getting better and should be back by Sunday,' said Lorraine.

That would make it nearly a fortnight. What would they say to me? Had they missed me? I needn't have worried. I managed to report for duty at 6.45 am on Saturday, erroneously thinking they would be glad to see me a day earlier than expected, and would ask me how I was.

Emmi merely said, '*Gruss Gott*, Denise. *Wir haben viel Arbeit heute. Schnell! Schnell!*' (We've got loads to do, so buck up and get moving!)

It was obviously going to take a lot more work on my part to feel like one of the team, but I was prepared to die trying… Well, I almost had, hadn't I?

Chapter 5
Del

'We have another English girl to come today,' Frau Mengershausen informed me one morning as I was clearing the breakfast dishes. I always seemed to be clearing away breakfast dishes when anything interesting or important was being said to me. She looked enchanting in her simple blue dirndl with its white apron as she laid a basket of mushrooms on the worktop.

It was a beautiful day in early May; the sun was just beginning to have some real warmth to it, and you felt that spring was here to stay after the long white winter. Snow lasted much longer in Bavaria with the air being so dry, and there were still some stubborn bits around, but now you could sit outside on your three-hour break between shifts, and it was even worth putting a dab of sun-screen on your face.

'How old is she?' I asked.

'Twenty-nine. She is called Dulcie Walker. She arrives zis evening.'

I was delighted with this news as although I had the company of Lorraine and Mieke (Mieke being the third English girl to join our merry band), both of them were quite a bit younger than me. Lorraine was a sweet girl but her conversation was pretty much boyfriends and make-up (can't fault that!) and she wasn't particularly interested in learning German. This was in direct contrast to Mieke, who was already fluent in Dutch, Russian and French, and was hoovering up German like it was her mother-tongue. But Mieke found it difficult to communicate with people. She was twenty-three and had spent long years studying languages at university. Not content with her degree, she had then gone on to further study, so she had very little experience of talking to people who were not students, or not as highbrow as herself. It had the unfortunate effect of making her introspective and consequently very serious, and she was the first to admit this.

I just hoped the new girl would be a friend.

Dulcie arrived late while we were in the kitchen having our supper. After helping to tidy up, I opened the door to the staff dining room, which was decorated in the same way as the guests' dining rooms: linen napkins, candles, flowers, and brightly-coloured hand-sewn rag rugs, and there sat the new arrival, completely alone, looking slightly bemused.

The first thing I noticed was her hair. It was the colour of sand, obviously not natural, but then, neither was mine, and it fell beyond her shoulders. Her chin, which jutted determinedly, just stopped her from being conventionally pretty, but she had a small neat nose and rosebud mouth that smiled at me, showing even white teeth. I smiled back.

'Denise.' I held out my hand to her.

'Dulcie,' she responded, 'but everyone calls me Del.'

We chatted for a few minutes and I detected a northern accent. 'You sound like a Geordie,' I said.

'That's right. Straight from Newcastle. Actually I've been working in Jersey for the last couple of years.'

'Doing what?'

Dulcie, or rather Del, wouldn't elaborate. Her eyes clouded over as was to often happen when you started asking her too many questions. She brought the conversation round to the present and told me she was to be one of the cleaners, like Lorraine and Mieke. I didn't envy her job but of course didn't say so. Nothing would have induced me to clean.

'Have you met the other two English girls yet?' I asked her.

'Just Lorraine, as I'm sharing with her upstairs. She seems nice, though I thought I'd have my own room. Not quite my scene.'

I had only been in Lorraine's room once. There were two large single rooms that were interconnecting, so you had a private space of sorts, though Del was looking doubtful at the prospect. I tried to be positive.

'That's great,' I said. 'You'll be in the main house. Much better than my room in the *Gochel-Hütte*.'

'Where or what is that?'

'It's a large wooden hut where five of us live – me, John, the assistant gardener, who's from California, and…'

'Really?' Del interrupted, looking at me with slightly more interest.

'No, nothing like that,' I said hastily. 'He's too young. He's only twenty.'

'So what? The younger the better, I always say.'

'I could never fancy him – he only eats raw food and he's full of spots.'

Del raised an eyebrow.

'Then there's Gisela,' I went on, 'the masseuse, who's half Dutch and half German - she's lovely - Hadji - she's Turkish - and a cleaner, and Traudl, one of the waitresses. The hut's very primitive – there's no inside toilet. Reminds me of when I was youth-hostelling in Europe.'

'I'd hate that,' Del said, regarding me with bright blue eyes. 'The hut *and* the youth hostelling. Do *you* mind?'

'I'm used to it. At least I can come and go without everyone watching me. So I s'pose there are compensations.'

'Did you know German before you came here?' she asked.

'None. How about you?'

'None whatsoever. I just fancied working in Germany for some nutty reason.'

'You'll soon pick it up,' I assured her. But she never did. She simply refused to learn, although in time she understood the gist of what they said. But she would always answer them in English. It drove them mad.

'I think I'll go and unpack,' Del said. 'I'm pretty tired. It's been a long day.'

Like all of us, she'd arrived by train.

'See you tomorrow then. *Schlafen Sie gut.*' I wanted to let her know that I could easily slip into the language. Del looked unimpressed.

'Goodnight then.'

'Goodnight,' I returned, and as she walked out the door, her back straight as a ruler, I thought, Mmm. Not sure about her, after all.

My feelings were confirmed a day or two later when I asked Lorraine how she and Del were getting on. She said, 'Fine' but I thought I detected a hesitant note. Then she surprised me by saying that the two of them were going off to a Bavarian evening that night, and no mention was made of my joining them. I was more upset than I would have thought. Lorraine was *my* friend and she'd been taken over. I felt jealous and angry and homesick all in one go. That morning, I'd received a letter from Carole, who had returned to the US, asking, 'Aren't you ready to go back to England yet?' Quite honestly, I was tempted.

The kitchen staff had still not really accepted me and were often, it seemed, overly critical, though this was most likely due to misunderstandings on my part because of the language barrier. German was an enormous effort even though I was studying every day, and I missed my family and friends back home. I was physically tired; emotionally, too, as I had not heard from Don except for a couple of postcards, and he was only fifty miles away. He had said he was very busy and would try to get down as soon as possible, but the weeks were going by and there was no sign that we were going to renew our love-affair. Everything seemed against me. And now I wasn't even wanted by the two English girls who were going to some crummy Bavarian evening.

I decided to go and visit them as they were getting ready to go out. Was I so pathetic as to shame them into inviting me? I knocked on their door, colourfully decorated by a basket of flowers, with some stray petals here and there, and all crackled with age. Carole would give her eye-teeth to achieve this effect when she's painting furniture. I heard their voices over the hum of the hairdryer.

'Come in,' from Lorraine.

She was in the far room sitting at a little table that was being used as a dressing table. Lipsticks were spread out, along with jars and bottles and hair-slides. She was waving the hair dryer over her long, shiny chestnut mane.

'Hello,' I sauntered through, nodding to Del. 'Just wondered if I could borrow your phrase-book this evening.'

'Here.' She tossed it over. I noticed Del was curling her eye lashes. Curling your lashes is a dangerous process which my sister and I go through every day of our lives. We have to be critically ill in bed to forego this ritual. You use a scissor-like instrument, open the curler and guide your lashes in between the protective rubber pad and the top. You squeeze the curler very gently as though you have your hands round someone's neck (not that I would know how that felt, you understand) and hold it for a few seconds – then *voilà!* Eyelashes that curl up to your forehead. I had never seen anyone use an eyelash curler before except Carole, so was faintly annoyed that Del had tapped into the secret of how to resolve the straight lash.

'So where are you off to?' I asked, my voice suitably casual.

'It's a festival in the next village,' Del said. (How on earth did she know what was happening in the area? She'd only been here five minutes.) 'Lots of beer and Bavarian music. Not your cup of tea, I wouldn't have thought.' Her eyes, now a cool blue, met mine in the mirror.

How would Del know what my cup of tea was? I'd only spoken to her twice. I watched as she applied black liquid eyeliner – too dark for her fair skin, I thought cattily, but she did it with such skill, I had to admit it suited her.

'I told Del you loved classical music,' Lorraine called through the interconnecting door. She had switched off the hairdryer and had caught some of our conversation.

'I like different kinds of music,' I said, going over to the doorway and noticing she looked worried. I hoped it was on my account…because they hadn't invited me. She was sweeping her hair up, and I realised her profile was exactly like the painting of Madame X by John Singer Sargent. I tore my thoughts away from this fascinating discovery. 'Bavarian included. Well, have a nice evening.' I turned to go before they saw my eyes well up.

'Wait!' from Del. 'You're upset. Do you want to come with us?'

'I don't want to spoil your evening.' By now I was feeling very childish.

'Don't be daft. We'll see you in twenty minutes outside the main door.'

And that was that. Del and I became close friends from that evening, and way beyond our Tannerhof days.

Del didn't go out of her way to make herself popular. The Tannerhof workers resented her refusal to speak German. She confided that she enjoyed annoying them, but I think it was because she didn't want to make a fool of herself. As I guessed would happen, she hated her cleaning role. But that swiftly changed one day when she actually had a row with one of the kitchen staff. I can't remember what it was about, but one of them – Emmi, I think – asked her to shut the door behind her as she marched off in a huff, and Del gave it an almighty slam, to their amazement. I couldn't help but admire her. I'd wanted to do just that on many an occasion.

The next day she was sent to the laundry room. We English girls had always said we never wanted to work there. The place was stifling, with enough steam to take you on the Trans-Siberian Express over the Gobi desert. There were no automatic washing-machines at Tannerhof in those days; just old-fashioned coppers where you heated up the water to nearly boiling point, and then threw in the dirty washing, and twirled it around for about ten minutes with a special long wooden stick. Then it had to be rinsed in huge vats of water, and finally put through the mangle and aired. It was also Del's job to help with the ironing. She told me she loathed that chore at home, so I bet her Tannerhof days of ironing put her off for life! I noticed her delicate skin become reddened with the heat and her eyes flashed in temper on many a morning.

But Del had a great sense of humour. I remember one evening at the *Heuboden*, she was being twirled round and round by my young Irish friend, Barry, (more about him later) who had quickly learned the rudiments of Bavarian folk dancing, having once been a ballet dancer. Gisela and I saw Del throw back her head and roar with laughter: she was still laughing when she stumbled back to our table, and Barry was on the point of collapse.

'I got *so* hot as Barry was flinging me round like a spinning top; the sweat was pouring off me. Luckily, I'm wearing a sleeveless dress. Barry said I was like a living sprinkler system and could have watered all the gardens in the village if he'd only just twirled me outside.'

But her folk dancing wasn't always fun. One night she was on her third date with a tall, fair-haired Bavarian called Kylan, who literally swept her off her feet. He was whirling her around in time to the music, and then, as part of the dance, he swung her exuberantly towards the beamed roof. One moment she was laughing as she soared upwards, and the next, as Kylan brought her down, blood was pouring from her head and running down her face, her mouth in the shape of The Scream, and her eyes full of shock. Poor Kylan. He was almost as shocked himself.

'I cannot imagine zat somesing so terrible will happen,' he kept saying, over and over.

'It's not your fault,' I tried to reassure him. 'But we need to get her to the hospital straight away.'

'*Ja*, someone is asking for a car.'

They got her to the hospital pretty quickly. By now, she looked as though someone had been interrupted whilst attempting to murder her. She managed not to faint, but Kylan fussed over her as though she were not long for this world. I must say, we were all worried to death until he brought her back from the hospital an hour later, complete with stitches, bandage and plaster. One hour… from the time she was picked up in Bayrischzell and taken to the nearest hospital in Hausham, about ten kilometers away, until the time she returned.

'Ze doctor, he say poor Del's head will soon be normal.'

Del, looking whiter than usual, managed to quip, 'I think he was being a bit optimistic. He was assuming I was normal to start with.'

CHAPTER 6
SUNA IN THE SAUNA

I FELT SORRY for Suna. She had the worst job of all. Washing all the huge saucepans and oven trays – anything, in fact, that didn't fit into the dishwashers. After we women in the kitchen had finally wiped down the last worktop around 2.30 in the afternoon, Suna would still be out in the back scullery, surrounded by piles of dirty pans and huge sinkfuls of hot soapy water, her thick black hair scraped back from her sweating forehead into an unforgiving rubber band. But I never heard her grumble once.

Sometimes, when I wasn't too exhausted, I'd help her. I'd marvel at her slowness. She was a big Turkish girl, in her early twenties, I was told, but her expression was much younger, and although she'd been working at Tannerhof for a year before I arrived, she hardly spoke any German. I don't think it was because she was too lazy or not bright enough to learn – it was more that no-one bothered to engage her in any real conversation; maybe because she worked on her own so much and merely carried out orders. This lack of contact made her shy but I was determined to break through the language barrier as I felt she was worth knowing. We would converse in French – hers being only marginally better than my dredged-up school French. But we managed.

Suna was so pleased whenever I stayed behind to give her a hand. Her moon-face would light up with a grateful smile, and one day she said: 'After, you come to my room for coffee? I make you real Turkish coffee.'

I was astonished. How was she able to smuggle coffee onto the premises? But as my French stopped short at the verb 'to smuggle', I simply replied that I would love to.

Her room was in the main house, but as soon as she unlocked the door, I entered another world – the world of the concubine – except there was no man for her to concupisce. A mysterious fragrance emanating from several incense sticks in little clay holders hit my unseasoned nostrils. Suna lit some candles that barely enhanced the dim light from the one beaded table lamp, and stooped to put on a record, her generous bottom challenging every stitch of her white overall, the whiteness seeming harsh against the soft colours of her surroundings. She began humming along with the singer – the music, to me, was as unfamiliar as the room – as she took what looked like a pepper-mill from the shelf above, spooned in some ground coffee beans and vigorously rotated the handle.

'Make very fine for good Turkish coffee,' she swung round and held the container under my nose. Mmmm. It smelled wonder-ful. She poured some cold water into a pretty little copper pot about four or five inches tall, wider at the base, with a long brass handle, and set it on the gas ring, gradually adding the contents of the coffee grinder, and alternating with sugar. When the mixture came to a boil, and just as it started to froth, she scooped off the bubbles and gave it two further boilings. What a procedure for a mere cup of coffee!

'Pas de sucre, merci,' I said, but Suna took no notice and added enough sugar to make jam. She handed me a cup the size of a thimble, delicate bubbly grounds still visible on the surface, and gave a little salutation with her own thimble. It looked and smelled as rich as melted chocolate but I couldn't see how drinking such a minute drop could possibly enliven that large frame. The instant I took the first sip, I knew. First of all, it was the strongest coffee to ever pass my lips; second, it was the sweetest; third, it was absolutely the best coffee I had ever tasted. I'd burnt my tongue in my eagerness to try real Turkish coffee, so I let it stand a few moments. Three swallows and the dolls-house cup was half empty. I tipped my head back for another intoxicating slurp, and got a throatful of sand. Suna had been waiting for this moment. She broke into a smile and then a giggle as I stuttered and coughed.

We celebrated with a second one. It had more power than any alcohol. Suna chuckled over nothing, and I joined her. The caffeine was obviously kicking in, and all the more invigorating because our bodies – well, mine anyway – had been deprived of the stimulant for several weeks. We sat for over an hour, Suna every so often changing the record, but I couldn't tell when one singer ended and the other began. Suna knew though. She wailed along with most of them and looked perfectly at ease for the first time since I'd met her.

I looked round the room, seduced by the way the light fell upon the rich red curtains shot with gold, the dazzling cushions and embroidered throws, and all the photographs, mostly of men and women dressed in Turkish clothes, looking to me as though they were going to a fancy-dress party. I thought I spotted Suna in one or two of them, but it was difficult to distinguish her features as the portraits flickered in the candlelight. Everything was strange and alluring.

'Your family?'

Suna nodded. Using sign language and odd bits of French, she let me know she couldn't go out and spend any money, as nearly every Mark she earned had to be sent home. I tried to ask her how it was she had come to work in Germany.

It was too complicated for her to explain, though I later read that in the sixties, the economic boom created half a million new jobs in Germany, but there were not enough European workers to fill them. Turks were attracted to Germany because in their own country work was often seasonal, and didn't pay very well, and although we foreigners at Tannerhof only earned pocket-money, it probably made all the difference to her family's survival. Unfortunately, the German government's plan was to invite the Turks over as *Gastarbeiter* (guest-workers) and ask them to leave when they were no longer needed. Only a year after I knew Suna, in 1975, the government stopped recruiting them.

What must it have been like for her as a child and then a young girl in Turkey? I tried hard to visualise her large family and their life, but I knew so very little about her country, it was impossible. I only knew it was as far away in similarity as it was in distance to my own comfortable upbringing and freedom of choice in career or marriage. Poor Suna – she never went to Munich, never even to the *Heuboden* for a spot of Bavarian dancing. It seemed to me as though her youth was slipping away.

We fell silent for several minutes, under the spell of the east. Suna's heavy black eyes dreamed. My senses were reeling.

I told the other English girls about my coffee afternoon, and how nice Suna was when you took the time to get to know her. I was also intrigued by Hadji, another Turkish girl, just turned twenty, whom we'd only been able to say hello to, as she didn't even have the smatter-ing of French that Suna could call upon. We could only communicate by smiles. Hadji was a cleaner and lived in the *Gochel-Hütte*. I'd seen her in the guest rooms, languorously dusting and sweeping, another bountiful female, though not nearly the size of Suna.

I decided to invite the two of them to a girls' sauna evening, just for the foreigners. Before I go on, I'd like to explain what a German sauna is like. It's quite different from an English version, although I'd never experienced either until one Thursday evening at Tannerhof when for once we'd had a fairly easy day in the kitchen and rats had momentarily stopped gnawing my feet.

'Tannerhof *Frauen* can go Tuesdays and Thursdays from seven until nine in the evenings,' Frau Mengershausen had explained when I told her I was planning to try the sauna. 'You will love it, Denise.'

I shuffled my way across the snow-bound lawns, and inched down a flight of icy steps that Herr Koch had either forgotten to sweep or they had already iced over, to the refuge of a little wooden building.

'Take a towel,' Mena, a pleasant-faced waitress whose generous curves made her look matronly before her time, commanded in German. 'Go in the shower, dry thoroughly, and you are ready for the sauna. At the top is hot, at the bottom is not so hot.'

I hadn't a clue what to expect, only that I must carry out her instructions. I had seen Mena go into the sauna baring all, but the English don't normally peel off their clothes in public with quite that lack of embarrassment. Personally, I think the German attitude is more healthy. After all, this was the females-only evening.

The sauna was like an inferno – where you'd be sent if you hadn't been good. '*Shnell! Schnell!* Shut the door,' Mena called from the dimly yellow interior. She was already roasting on the top shelf, her awe-inspiring breasts now flopped on either side of her as though they needed their own shelf to sit on, making her look positively flat-chested. Beads of sweat were finding their way down her face, trickling along her body and collecting in the folds of her stomach. I had a horrible vision of lying below, with Mena's fluids splashing onto my own body until I slipped off my perch in a drench of our combined perspiration.

I looked around curiously, trying to stop my modesty towel from slipping before I could get discreetly into position. The sauna was large enough to hold about eight clammy bodies, but I was thankful there was only Mena and myself. I could already smell Mena's odour – not unpleasant, but times eight… I wouldn't have relished being in a full house.

I unfolded my towel, the size of a tablecloth, and spread it out on the bottom rung to one side of her, stretching out in quite a Germanic way. A second later, the back of my throat prickled like I'd swallowed the contents of a pepper pot, and the hairs in my nostrils shrivelled and singed as though someone was holding a flare under my nose. Mena, above me, was still and quiet, so I didn't like to scream that I was being burnt at the stake, in case I interfered with some saunic meditation.

She had already warned me to stay in the sauna for only a few minutes on the first session, so I kept my eyes riveted on the sand in the foot-high egg-timer. Mena began to move above me, and eventually I saw two bright pink sturdy legs, crying out to be de-fuzzed, thump beside my own feet. I watched as she picked up a saucepan and tossed the contents onto the coals so they spat like a trapped cat. The smell of a forest… Eucalyptus. My nose cleared even though I hadn't been aware it was bunged. The timer crept to five minutes. All in all, I had relaxed for about twenty seconds, I thought, as I staggered up, longing to be so *au fait* with saunas that I, too, could casually toss a bowl of water over the coals and make them sing.

Mena had already been cooking for fifteen minutes before I went in, so she followed me into the shower-room. She turned the taps onto cold, but I was so worried about a violent strawberry mark on my chest that people at a fair would pay good money to gawp at, that it didn't register. To my relief, Mena's stupendous bosoms, when I openly inspected her, were just as red and mottled, and resembled a map of the old British Empire. She appeared unconcerned so I could only presume it was all normal. Bloody Hell! That burst of icy water wasn't normal! I was told later that because your body is thoroughly heated inside, rather like a convenience dinner heats up in a microwave, you don't notice the cold. What a lie!

'Now you come with me,' Mena said, and grabbed hold of my shivering arm before I could squeal, 'I'm not dressed, yet.' She flung open the door and tossed us both into the snow. *Aaaaaaaaaaaagh!* I was so disorientated, she might as well have been dragging me down into the Siberian wastelands. She was actually rolling naked in the snow and *laughing*. Thankfully, none of my English friends had spotted me. They would have laughed their heads off along with Mena, but I don't suppose any stray German would have taken any notice. Rolling naked in the snow after a sauna is, to them, a perfectly normal ending to the treatment.

She gestured me to follow suit. I gave a weak little roll like a new-born foal who hadn't yet found its legs, struggled to my feet, frozen, and dashed back into the heavenly heat of the changing room. And *that* was my first sauna. But I had to admit I had never felt so invigorated and so *clean*.

The English girls often went for a sauna but their session was... well... English. Warm showers and no frolicking in the snow. Pathetic.

But to get back to Suna. She and Hadji were thrilled to be included in a girls' evening, and on the next Staff Only night, we filed in, complete with shampoo, body lotion, shaving cream and razors. Del swore it was a perfect place to de-fuzz.

Both Turkish girls sauntered out of the sauna, not bothering to cover their ample bodies, just as we four English girls had showered, and were sitting on the bench, swaddled in virginal towels, chatting away. I longed to ask them if a German sauna was anything like a Turkish Bath, but as usual, my French was too superficial for this kind of discussion. Very frustrating. I had to wait thirty years before I experienced a real Turkish Bath (in Turkey), and it is the exact opposite – steamy heat, rather than the dry heat of the sauna. They're both great.

I'm not sure who started, Suna or Hadji, but they began humming and crooning. Then their voices changed in pace and pitch, as if they were calling the faithful. Very similar, I thought, to the recording I had heard in Suna's room the other afternoon. It was probably nothing like it, but you needed eastern ears to tell the difference. The girls were glowing like horses, tossing their long dark treacle-shiny manes, and fascinatingly, they had no bush between their thighs. Was this a Turkish custom? My school French definitely didn't run to this. They started to sway seductively to their own music, dimpled fingers stretching and circling above their heads, as though they were luring the gods. And we... we were being treated to a Real Live Belly Dance! Right here in the barn... I mean sauna.

We all stopped talking, eyes now on the two women. Mountains of flesh, most of it stockpiled around their bottoms and bellies, began to quiver in time to their humming. Then Hadji sank to the floor in one liquid movement, and Suna, not to be out-done, unhesitatingly followed, sensually gyrating her lower parts. They rose as one, their movements becoming more vibrant and abandoned, breasts flying to a far-off beat, blurring into one, bellies almost caving in and then thrusting out like proud pregnant mothers, but there was nothing maternal about their expressions. This was a lusty, magnetic dance for grown-ups, and I had a fleeting thought that it was a pity there were no appreciative males in the audience. But in a way, it was marvellous that they wanted to belly dance just for us. After the first astonishment, we started to smile and then to laugh and clap to their rhythm. They began to laugh as well, holding out their arms to invite us to join them, but we knew we would look like schoolboys at their first dancing lesson, so we shook our heads. Bad move.

'Shaking your head in Turkey means 'yes',' grinned Mieke, looking positively pretty and relaxed for once, as they triumphantly hauled us onto the floor, our towels slipping from us like Salome's last veil.

We did our own version of soulful wailing, which almost stopped our exotic dancers in their tracks – we must have sounded like female foxes on the make – but undeterred, we clapped and sang, shuffling about in a nondescript manner, arms flailing as though we were calling for help. How could they be so agile? And so graceful? Their weight only seemed to emphasise the skill and incredible muscle control of their bodies. Actually, the other Turkish name for 'belly dance' is 'muscle dance'. And for that extra snip of useless information, belly dancing has probably been around since around 1400 BC, when Egyptian tomb paintings were discovered depicting scantily-clad dancers in callisthenic positions. But this was 1973, in the sauna of a Bavarian sanatorium and we were hypnotised. They looked incredibly beautiful; chubby necks now elongated as they threw back their dark heads, jewelled eyes flashing, hair cascading, skin glowing, full lips smiling… If Frau Mengershausen had happened to put her head round the door, she would not have found any trace of her Turkish maids. Whilst we English girls looked exactly the same – only without clothes!

I've had hundreds of saunas since that evening, but somehow they've all seemed – oh, I don't know – just a little bit dull.

Chapter 7
Bosom Pals

Prost

One of my problems at Tannerhof was how to address people. In the early seventies the Germans were very formal, and I think they still are, but to a lesser degree. I knew that Frau Cygan wasn't married, even though she was addressed as Frau, rather than Fräulein, but this was due to respect for her age. Why calling someone 'Mrs' should be a mark of respect I'll never know, unless it's for putting up with a man at close quarters over a long period of time. Yes, on thinking about it, that *would* command respect.

We have a similar problem at home these days when we try to decide whether couples are husband and wife or 'partners', and the confusion is exacerbated when they are actually *business* partners. When you ask the question, 'Are you a sleeping partner?' you can get some funny looks. In my career as an estate agent, I had to ask applicants their names dozens of times a day, but in the last ten years there was no point in bothering to ask if they were Mr and Mrs, as they often weren't.

But in German it's extra confusing as you have two ways of addressing a person – *Sie* (the formal 'you') or *Du* (like the French '*tu*' or 'thou', which is our nearest translation but of course has fallen out of use). '*Du*' is more intimate, and as such is not to be used lightly. Not to be used without the other person inviting you to do so. Usually it would be the older person giving permission to the younger one, as in the case of Maria, my favourite waitress. One early morning she beamed at me through the kitchen hatch, her wholesome face lighting up under her severe bob, unflatteringly caught up at one side with a kirby grip.

'*Gruss Dich*, Denis-e. *Wie geht's?*' (Hello, Denise. How are you?)

I was thrilled that she used the familiar voice, instead of the usual and more formal *Gruss Gott* so I answered her in the same vein.

'*Gut, danke,* Maria. *Und Dich?*' (Well, thank you, Maria. And you?) Normally, I would have used the formal '*Sie.*'

'*Gut, danke,* Denis-e.' She stretched out a sturdy arm to take the tray of müesli, leaving me delighted that she had decided to bestow this honour upon me. Little did I realise quite what a step it was until Traudl, the pretty young waitress who loved correcting my German, asked me to have tea in her room that same evening after work.

She also had a room in the *Gochel-Hütte*, and like my room, it was typically Bavarian, with its heavy painted furniture and multi-coloured oval-shaped rag rugs. The rugs always reminded me of when I lived in Georgia, and several of my US friends had early-American style homes, built of wood, with folksy interiors. Hand-made rag rugs on a bare wooden floor would make an entrance hall look cosy and welcoming, and my friends often put them in living rooms, kitchens and bedrooms for a casual country look.

I noticed Traudl had fresh Alpine flowers in a painted vase (the Bavarians paint everything they possibly can that doesn't move), and all was fresh and neat, just like Traudl herself.

'Come, Denise, sit,' she said in English, gesturing me over to an easy chair.

I plonked down gratefully after another hard day. If I don't end up with varicose veins, I'll be very lucky, I thought grimly, tucking one aching leg under the other.

I watched Traudl as she busied herself with a tray, and was surprised when she opened a bottle of wine as though she had been doing it all her life, and not been holed up in a sanatorium where alcohol was condemned.

'I thought we were having tea,' I said, as she handed me a glass of pale gold liquid, her slender fingers curved round the stem. 'But this is much nicer. I didn't know we were allowed to drink wine.'

'Oh, yes,' Traudl answered, 'when it's a special occasion.'

I was intrigued.

'I think we know ourselves now to use the '*Du*' form of address. And in Germany, we have a celebration when that happens.' She smiled across at me from the opposite straight-backed chair (she had given me the comfortable one), hazel eyes sparkling, altogether a picture of health. The chestnut hair, normally pulled back from her face when she was working, was loose this evening, and her face, bereft of any make-up, glowed even before she had taken the first mouthful.

'What do you say in England – cheers?'

Can you believe there is actually a celebration with wine just to let someone know that from now on you are prepared to be friends? I'm all for opening a bottle of wine to toast the cat to the Queen, but this was amazing. It really does emphasize the difference between our cultures – or rather it did in those days. Traudl looked so pleased I couldn't help smiling back and repeating her enthusiastic '*Prost*' as we clinked our glasses. Then I remembered that Maria had got away without the ceremony of the wine when she'd spoken to me so familiarly that morning. I would have to give her a strong word. This blood-brother business definitely required a few glasses of wine to seal a relationship.

'How long do you have to know each other?'

'Sometimes weeks, sometimes years,' Traudl replied seriously. 'Sometimes never.'

It was all a bit strange to me, but what the heck. I'd been accepted as a friend by Traudl, and I'd broken away for one evening from the usual herbal leaf and flower concoctions. I tipped back my glass and savoured the soft, sweetish but never cloying Moselle, letting it linger on my tongue, before it slipped ecstatically down my throat. Of course it went straight to my head. Goodness, was that Traudl coming over to top me up?

Sadly, I didn't see much of Traudl for all our *Du's* and *Dich's*, as she left Tannerhof two months later to finish her degree in Hotel Management. I was disappointed as she was such a lovely person, and I will always pronounce *München* (Munich) properly because of her insistence.

But I still had Gisela. And Gisela didn't ever bother with celebratory wine. We were friends from the start. She was half Dutch and half German and, true to her education, spoke fluent French and excellent English, so we never bothered with any formalities – she always wanted the opportunity to practise her English and that was fine by me after a few headaching hours speaking kitchen German. She loved to have fun and giggle with we English girls, except when her exotic boyfriend Parvis, who was from Persia (as Iran was called in those days) but now lived in Munich, was playing her up by seeing other women. Then she would become very angry, though she always defended him when we used to tell her he wasn't worth it and to ditch him. She would make all sorts of complicated plans to entice him back, usually by trying to make him jealous by flirting with other men.

Parvis was dishy with his dark flashing eyes and coal-black hair, though I personally could have done without the swagger (as if I had any say), but he treated Gisela like dirt most of the time. We couldn't understand why she was so intent upon keeping hold of him until she told us that he was the best lover in the world. Wouldn't it be marvellous to be made love to by the Best Lover in the World? But all the time you'd be worrying that maybe... just maybe... there was some Adonis out there who was even better. But Gisela had eyes for no-one but Parvis, and when he was around she would more or less dump us. We didn't worry too much as we knew it wouldn't be long before they would have another bust-up and she'd be back with her girlfriends.

She was a masseuse – just the right profession for her tall, statuesque figure. And she was stunning. Her wide-set eyes were huge, and the colour of melted toffee; she had a nose that tilted upwards, and full sexy lips, exactly the same shape as Diana Dors', that parted to show white even teeth. Men couldn't take their eyes off her when she walked into a room or passed them on the street. I had to accept this, even though I was used to a fair bit of male attention myself with my thick blonde hair, which I wore to my collar-bone (unless I was working, when I scraped it back in an unflattering ponytail). Gisela always grumbled about her fine, flyaway hair, even though it was a pretty colour, like matured polished oak, and compared it unfavourably with mine. Let me have one decent feature, Gisela.

She did have an unusual secret. I never thought it was anything to be ashamed of, or particularly hide, but Gisela did.

'Shall I have the operation?' Gisela asked me for about the dozenth time.

'No – you look great, just as you are.'

I stared at her with a mixture of affection, and... well, jealousy. She was almost beautiful. To men, there was no 'almost'.

'What does Parvis say?'

At the mention of his name, her eyes became brilliant and clear, accentuated by her incredible fasting – not just a twenty-four hour detox as we all did now and again, but twelve to fourteen days at a time, living only on herbal teas and juices. The fast was mainly to lose weight although she was so tall, she could carry an extra stone or two. But she was determined to squeeze into her new tight white jeans, which she had deliberately bought one size smaller. She was on one of those starvations now to try to win back the errant Parvis. Amazing how she had the strength to give her Russian-style massages, but her capable unlined hands seemed born to the work.

'He wants me to have it. So would *you*, Denise, if you are me?'

She snatched her sweater and bra upwards in one angry movement to reveal a voluptuous breast – but the other was the size of a new potato.

'Do you want that I give you a special massage, Denise?' Gisela asked me one afternoon when we were both off duty. I glanced at my watch. In England it would be dusk, but here at Tannerhof there was so much white outside that it reflected the light and the effect was not at all gloomy.

'I'd love one, but you're tired.'

'No, I'm not tired. I can do a strong massage for you. It is hard work in the kitchen. Come to my treatment room in five minutes. I go to prepare.'

Fabulous. I adore a massage. One of the best things in life. Even better when you have a masseur. But Gisela's hands were every bit as strong as a man's, so I knew I was in for a wallow in hedonism. The treatment rooms were on the lower floor where they have since built a swimming pool, although they didn't have one when I worked there. I arrived in the requested five minutes, but Gisela wasn't around. I heard her call from the room next door, which I had never been in. I realised why when I followed her voice. It was a large room, tiled from top to bottom, with no windows, and in the middle stood a gigantic raised pool filled almost to the brim, gently steaming like a lazy volcano.

'I give you a special under-water massage,' she told me.

I didn't like the look of it. I don't care for large quantities of water at the best of times. I didn't even swim in those days and it would be another ten years before I managed to conquer my fear.

This geyser looked positively menacing – steely-grey and very *very* deep.

'I'm not sure, Gisela...' I stared at it.

'You *vill* like it,' she said, her German side coming to the fore. She pressed a button, and the pool became agitated, then angry. I'd never seen anything like it. This was before jacuzzis had been invented, don't forget.

In a flash I was undressed and into the bath, as she euphemistically called it. At least the water was warm. Looking very professional in her white uniform, she bent over me with a hose the size of a rattlesnake and proceeded to massage me using the pressure of the water rather than her friendly, warm, caring hands.

She'd told me she was going to give me a strong massage, but nothing could have prepared me for this. Ouch! But after a minute I began to get used to it, and both nerves and joints unstiffened as the water pressed into my aching limbs and back and shoulders. Don't let her use it on my breasts, I prayed silently, oh please don't let her use it on my breasts or they'll be torn off in an instant. She didn't, and I emerged completely intact; even my nipples were still in place, I was relieved to see. Red and spent, I stood before her like a child with her mother while she patted me dry.

'Was it good, Denise?' Was it good? It was bloody marvellous.

CHAPTER 8
BIRTHDAY GIRL

JUNE. LIFE WAS pretty good, all in all. I had begun to love working in Germany, and found Tannerhof endlessly fascinating. I was beginning to pick up the language and was sure Emmi and Anita had gone a step or two towards accepting me as an integral part of the kitchen team. It had taken a great deal of patience on my part and very little on theirs, that I could see. I never had any problems with Frau Cygan – she was kind to me right from day one.

As I said – life was pretty good. The sun was shining and the next day was going to be my birthday. Now, I'd made a rule when I was seventeen never to work on my birthday. And I was determined to stick to this rule. I had asked Frau Mengershausen if it would be all right to take the day off, especially as it was on a Friday, and I thought she might let me have a long weekend. She did!

The only small cloud was that I didn't know where to go. Twenty-eight tomorrow. It would be lovely to go somewhere quite different, just for a change. After breakfast, I was clearing the table when the telephone rang. Emmi answered, and said to whoever it was, '*Ein Moment, bitte…* Denise, *für Dich.*'

I took the phone and was taken aback to hear a soft southern accent say, 'Hi, Denise. How are you? It's Don.'

He didn't have to add the last bit. I knew perfectly well who it was. Except for a couple of postcards, I hadn't heard from him for several months; not since I'd had the letter from him telling me he had a job in Augsburg , which crossed with my letter telling him I had a job just south of Munich. But he'd done nothing about it. Until now.

'I'm fine,' I replied cautiously. 'And you?'

'Real good, I guess. Well, it's a special day tomorrow.' He'd remembered. 'So I thought I'd take you away for the weekend. Can you get the time off?'

'I have tomorrow and the weekend off,' I said, desperately trying not to sound too eager. Don had let me down too many times in the past. I didn't need any more hurt.

But his voice made me feel like wax melting. It was the southern accent – not the drawling whine you hear in Oklahoma or Texas, where the word 'yes' has two syllables (yay-es) – but an educated, Rhett Butler sort of voice, a voice I can rarely say 'no' to.

'Wonderful,' he said. 'I'll pick you up tomorrow at 9.30.'

'Where are we going?'

'Ver-nice.'

I was puzzled. It sounded a bit like Venice, yet he'd pronounced it to rhyme with my own name. Well, I wasn't going to show my ignorance by asking.

'Sounds wonderful,' I said. 'I'll be ready.'

Back in my room I got the maps out and studied Germany particularly carefully. No sign of any name remotely like Venice or

Ver-nice. Austria also failed to throw any light. But when I looked at Italy, Venice, of course, nearly jumped off the page and bit me. 'He *must* mean Venice.' I was really excited by now. We had never included Venice in the Grand European Tour we'd made two years ago, youth hostelling by *car*, which had not gone down at all well with the various wardens, who had sometimes tried to stop us from actually checking in. Unless you arrive by foot, you are not a serious youth hosteller, in their book. Sometimes, we used to leave the car at the end of a lane, and trudge the rest of the way to the youth hostel, so that we wouldn't risk the warden's contempt, me carrying the box of fresh vegetables that I intended to cook that evening (I was in charge of our vitamin intake), and Don acting as porter.

This grand travel took place six months after we had fallen madly in love, given up our jobs at the Board of Regents in Atlanta, which is a governing body controlling all the universities in the state of Georgia, and decided to go travelling. I was more or less going home, as we also planned to drive around Britain, but Don was actually *emigrating,* much to the chagrin of his Momma and Daddy and brother Byron. He had found a new tenant for the flat he was renting, and packed several suitcases and a rucksack with books and cameras and walking boots (though very few clothes), all weighing a ton, not to mention his guitar, which he'd half slung across his shoulder and which dangled alarmingly. He looked a very sorry figure when we met at Atlanta Airport for the flight to New York and could only take about five trembling steps before toppling over.

'Didn't you realise you'd never be able to carry all that stuff?'

'I practised it at home in the sitting room, and it seemed okay.'

'Not quite the same as walking to the gate, miles away, in a busy airport,' I said, trying not to laugh.

Don wasn't amused. And even less amused when, at Kennedy Airport, he told me to take care of all the luggage while he went to find a cab, and the moment his back was turned, a very cheerful young man came up to me and said, 'Can I help you with your bags?'

'It's not all mine,' I returned. 'I'm waiting for my boyfriend to come back. He's just ordering a cab.'

'Let me take some of it,' he said, and bending down and whisking up two cases at a time as though they were stage props, he dashed off in front of me.

How nice these New Yorkers are, I thought. Totally unlike the rude and brash people we're always told about. I hurried after him, my own cases firmly in my grip.

'Where're my bags?' Don suddenly shouted from behind me.

'Perfectly safe,' I said. 'A nice young man is helping us carry everything.'

'You fool!' Don was now screaming at me. 'Where'd he go? He's a god-damned thief!'

He bounded after my nice young man, who was by now outside the terminal. The NYM looked startled at the sight of Don, racing towards him, red with rage and exertion, and he crashed the cases to the ground.

'I was only trying to help the young lady,' he said. 'She looked like she could do with some.'

He walked away in a huff. Don and I forever argued whether he was a thief or not. I thought he was innocent, but Don labelled him guilty right from the start. I suppose that's the difference between our two countries' laws. In England, you're innocent till you're proven guilty. In America, it's quite the other way round.

Oh, well, back to Tannerhof – and birthdays.

Even though I wasn't on duty the next day, I decided to get up at the usual time, 5.30 am, and have breakfast with the kitchen staff. I didn't have to. I could've gone in later, and taken my breakfast in the staff dining room where Del and Mieke and Lorraine ate. But they were always later than me, so I would have probably sat on my own anyway. Might as well be with my work-mates.

What a surprise when I walked in the kitchen and saw Frau Mengershausen sitting on a chair, with Frau Cygan, Emmi, Anita, and Suna, and Irene from the adjoining salad room, standing in a line by the side of her. Immediately they saw me, Frau Mengershausen began strumming, and they all burst into what I assumed was a German version of Happy Birthday. It was a different tune from ours and very pretty it sounded.

'Viel Glück und viel Segen auf all deinen Wegen,
Gesundheit und Freude sind auch mit dabei.'
(Good luck and all blessings wherever you go,
May joy and good health also always foll - ow)

That is not the best translation but I am determined to make it rhyme. A very nice German couple, Herr and Frau Heil, kindly wrote the words out for me on another visit to Tannerhof (more of that later), as I would never have remembered them. I'd forgotten the tune so Herr Heil sang it and immediately I knew that was what the kitchen crew had sung thirty-two years earlier. He told me that Germans actually sing our English Happy Birthday nowadays, but this one is more traditional.

Back to the kitchen at Tannerhof in 1973 – everyone was smiling and singing, Anita's gruff voice a bit out of tune, and when I looked at Emmi, she gave me a nod and a rare smile. After they finished, Frau Cygan led me over to one of the side tables, which was piled with presents.

'For you,' she said, her little birdlike face creased in merriment. 'In Germany, ze birthday is very important. Many presents.'

They'd given me writing paper and envelopes, beautifully boxed; two LPs (long-playing records – this really shows my age now!), one of a band of folk singers, and the other, a Bavarian pop star famous for his yodelling; a thick green candle smelling like pine trees, massage oil, and *Strumpfhosen* (tights). I can't remember all of the presents, but I do remember feeling quite overwhelmed, especially when Herr Koch appeared at the back door with a trug of fruit just for me. His face was red as he handed me the basket, but I wasn't sure whether it was embarrassment or sunburn.

'*Viel Glück zum Geburtstag.*' (Many Happy Returns.)

'*Danke schön,* Herr Koch,' I replied. 'How kind of you. I'd give you a kiss if I didn't think you'd take it the wrong way.' I didn't actually say this last bit, as he wouldn't have understood a word, but he turned an even more alarming shade and made a hurried departure. Frau Mengershausen wished me a lovely day, and hoped I would enjoy my weekend. Was I going anywhere special?

'My boyfriend is taking me away for the weekend,' I said. 'I think we might be going to Venice.'

'How romantic,' she smiled, as she packed her guitar in its case, and hurried off.

It was time for breakfast. I was hungry. We always had breakfast rolls when it was someone's birthday – all the other days we had the different breads, and wonderful though these were, the Tannerhof rolls were even more delicious. Oven-warm, crisp and white, would you believe, in this healthiest of places? One of those rolls would be split in half and spread with that ever-so-slightly-rancid-tasting Continental butter, which takes some getting used to, then some honey, and finally topped with quark. Mmm, I could go for one this very moment.

Anita had placed extra candles on the breakfast table and she now set a pile of birthday cards at my place-setting. I wanted to tell them I felt quite spoilt, but as usual, my *Küche Sprache* (kitchen language) was lacking. I decided to make the most of all the attention, as I guessed it would be back to normal on my next shift. But before that, there was Venice...I hoped.

At 9.30, punctual as always, Don pulled up in his little red two-seater. The wind had ruffled his sun-streaked hair and his pale but very blue, intelligent eyes flicked over my face and looked approvingly at my slim-fitting jeans and open-necked white shirt as I struggled to look elegant while trying to cram my legs into such a small low space.

'Lovely,' was all he said, as though he'd seen me yesterday, even though it had been almost a year. We didn't kiss. We had this little game: when we hadn't seen each other for ages, and were both keyed up with excitement, we pretended to be very casual. We'd never discussed this; we just both knew we did it. The kiss, when it finally happened sometimes not until hours later – was then explosive.

'So how do you like working in Augsburg?' I asked him.

'It's okay. You know me, I try not to have to work too hard. It isn't terribly interesting, but I just like being in another country. So it's fine. How about you?'

'I love it,' I said, without hesitating. 'I feel I'm helping people, especially when they arrive and they're overweight, and then after a month, they've lost a stone or two and they come to the kitchen and thank me.'

'Well, I'm glad *you* haven't been dieting,' he glanced at me. In fact, I noticed that he was doing quite a bit of glancing.

'If anything, I've put on a few pounds. Can't stop eating, the food's so good. I hope it's not becoming an obsession. Anyway, where are you whisking me away to?'

'I told you – Venice. We never did go, did we?'

'We thought it would be too cold. We chose Berlin instead – and froze.'

'Well, the weather in Venice is supposed to be about seventy-six degrees, so it should be perfect. I want us to have a perfect weekend – no fights, no arguments – just romance… all the way.

'Sounds wonderful,' I said, with a shiver of anticipation.

Chapter 9
Escape to Venice

I WAS A bag of emotion being with Don in an open-top sports car speeding along in Germany just like we'd travelled nearly two years before. There were some wonderful memories but there were also too many nightmarish ones when I was not far from smothering him with a smelly old youth-hostelling blanket while he lay innocently sleeping. But that was because we had been cooped up in a small car all day long, Don doing all the driving (I don't think he trusted me to drive on foreign roads) and always arriving in an unknown city during the 5 o'clock rush hour when we couldn't understand the road signs and had no time to look at the map to get our bearings with all the hooting going on behind us. It had been nerve-racking, and would have put the most passionate relationship (which ours was) in jeopardy.

We were much more experienced this time, I reasoned, and more relaxed because we hadn't seen each other for a year or so, and this was only to be a long weekend, rather than our old tour of several months getting on each other's nerves.

Don seemed in a particularly good mood. He started to sing some German songs and I joined in with the ones I knew. That made us laugh, as Don knew he sang completely off-key, but somehow he got away with it, and occasionally, by fluke, it sounded like a planned harmonisation. Fired by such prowess, we went straight into the famous White Horse Inn song. Famous, that is, if you're my mother's age and saw the film starring… well, I'm too young to remember who starred in it… or are weird like we were and have somehow picked up such obscurities.

'Im weissen Rössl am Wolfgangsee
Dort steht das Glück vor der Tür…'

I studied his hands on the wheel. A little thick-set, but well-shaped – the fine golden hairs giving a decidedly masculine look. Hands that I loved, hands that had spent what seemed a lifetime caressing me. I couldn't wait to feel them again.

We stopped for a break in a small family restaurant off the main road, and as usual, were greeted politely and efficiently by a dirndled waitress.

'Everywhere's so clean in Germany,' I remarked. 'It's not just at Tannerhof.'

'Wait till you get to Italy,' Don said. 'You'll notice a big difference.'

Later, we trundled along for several hours, leaving the Alps behind.

'We're just coming up to the border,' said Don. 'Have your passport ready.'

It was really exciting in those days travelling from country to country. There were proper sentry boxes with gun-toting guards scrutinising passports, and sometimes making you get out of the car so they could search for counterfeit money or drugs or bodies, or whatever it was they were looking for. But on this occasion, there were just a couple of laid-back Italian soldiers, both gorgeous but too short for my taste, who flashed sparkling smiles at me when I greeted them with a '*Buon giorno.*' I like to think it was my blonde hair that gave me away, and not my dreadful Italian accent when they both said, 'Eengleesh?' and then went off into a torrent of Italian that left us completely baffled. It didn't matter. They cheerfully waved us through, and from that moment, we realised what a formal place we had been living in for the past few months. Even though we both loved Germany, this was like escaping out of prison. Wherever we stopped, people were smiling and friendly and full of *joie de vivre*. No matter that you didn't order a full meal, or if you only wanted a coffee. You were always ushered in and treated like an old friend.

This, of course, would be unimaginable in an English restaurant at seven-thirty. Picture it.

Indifferent reception. 'Have you booked a table?'

'No, I'm afraid not. But we only want a coffee.'

Sneery look from waiter. 'We're serving dinner, so that's not possible. Good evening.'

And you'd be swiftly ushered out the door.

But in Italy, waiters sang like opera stars as they rushed about carrying trays outside where people were enjoying the late afternoon sun. Though you paid for it. Sometimes, literally. For instance, they didn't mind over-charging the unsuspecting tourist, and we noticed that nowhere was as clean as the country we had just left. Toilets were often filthy (there is a much better standard of hygiene these days – probably due to tourists' demands) and there was litter everywhere. The exteriors of people's houses were almost always old and peeling, and there were no DIY shops like those that had sprung up all over England to help DIYers ruin their houses. Italians obviously didn't go in for house maintenance and renovation and extensions. They (the men) were too busy preening themselves for the evening *passeggiata* – the evening stroll where everyone promenades up and down the streets and around the *piazzas* flaunting themselves so as to catch the attention of someone (usually, though not necessarily, of the opposite sex) that they have their eye on.

If you're not promenading (and our clothes were definitely not of the quality and fashion you would want to promenade in), you have to sit at a table outside a café, sipping a dry martini, and indulge in one of my favourite pastimes – people-watching. You have to try not to look too enviously at all the slim-bummed, beautiful young things who completely ignore you. Little do they realise that they will one day be the onlookers, battling with wrinkles from too much sunbathing and the first ugly grey hairs. But you're prepared to put up with these minor irritations as they are such a happy bunch and not afraid to show emotion – sometimes too much of it – totally unlike the Germans, who are much more reserved until they know you. The British used to be like this, but have made a complete about-turn since the advent of the mobile phone, which has put discretion and privacy right out the window – usually of a train.

It was the first time either of us had visited Venice. Nothing prepares you for your first glimpse of Venice, no matter how many guide books you've read and photographs you've seen. For one thing, it was much bigger than I had imagined. And there was more water. In fact, Venice was awash with water. I thought there would be *some* roads around and between the canals, but it was all bridges and boats. I fell instantly in love.

We had to leave the car outside the city itself in a vast car park on the mainland (not *quite* the ingress I'd expected), and then take a *vaporetto* to enter Venice proper by water. Don, determined that things would go smoothly, had already booked a room with a balcony in a sweet little hotel with a view of one of the side canals.

We dumped our luggage and set off to find the perfect place to eat. When I say 'perfect', I really mean it. A lot of our past troubles were due to Don having to have everything the best. The best place to eat, the best hotel, the best service, the best holiday or day out, and, of course, the best relationship. Which meant the best sex – every time! And we all know how often that *doesn't* happen. If anything didn't come up to Don's expectations, he would be irritable and envious of people around him who he thought were having a better time. Obviously, that didn't have 'the best' effect on me, and I'd be in a permanent state of nerves as we walked for hours before Don spotted a restaurant or whatever we were looking for, which he hoped would be *the* one. Often, we'd passed it ages before, and we'd have to retrace our steps, me tottering on my high-heeled sandals, and arguing, which was not surprising with our blood sugar dangerously low. Not the best start to a romantic date.

Luckily, that first evening in Venice, after only a cursory glance at a few restaurants where waiters stood outside, trying to entice us in with their '*Buona sera*, pretty lady – you like eat in my *ristorante?*', Don picked a beautiful *trattoria* right on the Grand Canal, 'where we can watch all the comings and goings on the water', he said.

We ate outside, and as it grew darker, more candles were lit and placed on our table. Gondolas slid by – the backdrop of churches and a hundred palaces lined up on both sides of the canal like some fantastic piece of theatre – their owners singing to their customers who had paid vast sums for the privilege. Even if they didn't have any passengers, they would sing anyway. We were entranced. The wine flowed, and I was glad to see Don sitting back, his eyes bluer than the hazy lagoon he was scanning, more relaxed than I had seen him in ages. He caught me looking at him and grinned.

'Well, darling, are you ready for a gondola ride?' (Actually, he probably didn't call me 'darling' as he rarely used that endearment, but for the sake of such a setting, I'm leaving it in.) 'Even though they're a rip-off.' But I could tell he was as keen as I was to experience the most romantic ride in the world.

I picked up my handbag and jacket. 'Just choose a good-looking one who can sing,' I told him. I was amused to see him flag down a gondola as though it were a London taxi and attempt to haggle over the quoted price, though not very successfully. The gondalier, not in his first flush of youth, was a good salesman and wasn't budging.

'Can you sing?' I heard Don ask.

'*Si, si, signore*, I sing *molto bene.*'

Well, he was hardly going to say, 'Actually, I'm a lousy singer and can't remember words let alone hold a tune', was he? Not when he'd quoted several billion lire for a forty-five minute trip.

'He ought to be an opera star for that price,' Don grumbled, too embarrassed to pursue the knocking-down-of-the-fare, and to the Italian's delight, we agreed. The two of them helped me in and sat me on a plush red velvet seat, leaving just enough space for Don to join me. Our gondolier, who stood at the back of the gondola behind us so we were all facing forward, took up his oar. A slight push and we were off.

I read once that to row three people, including himself (and it always is a man – I have never heard of a woman gondolier, and I don't suppose a woman would ever rush for that equality), a gondolier only consumes the same amount of energy as he does when he is walking. And that the degree of curvature of the boat is based on his weight. So what happens if he becomes fat? Presumably, he's out of a job unless he can afford to have a new one built at great expense. Isn't that amazing information? And there's more. Before the gondola was used for tourism, it had a removable cabin that came into its own in winter and at night. It had a door and sliding windows fitted with Venetian blinds (what other kind?), curtains, a mirror and a charcoal burner! The cabin was there to protect passengers a) from the cold, and b) from nosy-parkers.

I like that idea of a private cabin, but Don and I would not have been aware of any prying eyes from our rower or anyone else that night, as we drifted for hours, it seemed, through the canvas of a Canaletto. It was a perfect time for Don to turn and kiss me – his lips gentle at first, then growing more amorous as his hands explored the contours beneath my top. For a brief second I wished I was wearing a floaty dress like a fifties' filmstar, but by now my senses were floating. I was vaguely aware of someone singing – probably something incredibly sentimental, but he could have been crooning 'Just One Cornetto' as far as I was concerned. I was in heaven. I can't imagine what on earth our gondolier thought as he plashed us through mysteriously-lit canals, away from the main tourist ones, but I expect he'd seen it all before. As for me, I doubted I'd ever get another chance to make love in a gondola. And do you know, thirty-odd years on, I can say with absolute honesty that I was right!

The next day was as sunshiny and as fluffy-clouded as you could wish. Our guide books and maps accompanied us to breakfast, and we made a plan of the various sights we wanted to see – St Mark's Square (who said it was the most beautiful drawing-room in Europe? – whoever it was, was right); the Doge's Palace; the enchanting Gothic *Ca'd'Oro,* which looked as though it were made of lace; the Grand Canal with its *Rialto* Bridge; the Bridge of Sighs – all offering the excited tourist (me!) fascinating vignettes whichever way I looked. Churches and galleries hiding paintings by Tintoretto, Titian, Mantegna, Bellini, Veronese, and, of course, the incomparable Caneletto – I was eager to see them all. And we did. Worn out and with cricked necks, not to mention being slightly tipsy from long, lingering late lunches, we drank in Venice.

Our last day – time just fell into a dream. I remember us walking over hundreds of bridges; coming across an equestrian statue by Verrocchio; admiring the four famous bronze horses now housed in the Museum of the Basilica, a beautiful Renaissance or Gothic church; flopping in a chair outside an inviting café for a pastry and coffee (maybe not Florians, but still the price of a main meal in most towns in Italy); and my favourite of all – stone-carved lions holding open books in their paws with the words *Pax Tibi* (Peace be unto thee). These are the lions of St Mark the Evangelist and they are the city's emblem. We spotted them in niches of palace walls, on columns or high up over portals in sculpted relief – they were everywhere, reminding Venetians at every turn and corner they still rule. Wonderful stuff.

We caught the *vaporetto* to Murano, island of glass factories, and Burano, island of lace. My initial thought was: seen one lace tablecloth, seen them all. But it was a joy to wander along, admiring the little pastel-coloured artists' cottages, and think how simple life could and ought to be. But we couldn't delay any longer. It was time to head for home. Home? Were we actually calling Germany *home*? It certainly seemed like it as Don pointed his little red two-seater northwards.

We'd had no arguments – only Sighs!

Chapter 10
You *will* have fun

Summer took its toll on me in the kitchen. It can get incredibly hot in Bavaria, and this summer was no exception. Flies dive-bombed onto the central island and inquisitively hung around the saucepans and dishes ready to sample the food and let us know the verdict before we cooks had a chance. They drove me mad but no-one took any notice. I kept waving them away (the flies, that is) but as soon as they flew off, they were back with a few more friends. Why didn't the staff deal with the flies? Everyone in the kitchen was so spotless in every other way. Surely they knew how filthy flies are. I remember when I studied the fly at school in biology class, I couldn't eat for a week, their habits were so disgusting. But hang on – we were in Germany – of course, these were *German* flies. That's why Frau Cygan and the team ignored them. There's always a logical answer if you look hard enough.

The kitchen crew also took no notice of the heat and didn't even stop for a glass of water. Maybe if Frau Cygan had had one, the others would have followed. But I was not about to wait and see what the others did; I simply continued with my morning coffee break (as I laughingly named it) and drank sips of water throughout the morning. The dieticians and health magazine journalists would be horrified today as they constantly tell us we must drink several litres of water every day. I can only hope my insides didn't get too dried up in the seventies; as for the Tannerhof kitchen women, one really wouldn't want to think too deeply.

It was hard to know what to do with our free afternoons when you knew you had to be at work two-and-a-half-hours later. If you wanted a change from Bayrischzell, you could go to the neighbouring village, but by the time you got a bus, which came once an hour, you didn't have time for more than a cup of tea and a slice of cake – that is, if you could eat it without feeling guilty (we usually could) before turning round and coming back. So we had to do things closer to home. That was when I discovered a little shelter half-way up a hill behind the main house; it was a wooden three-sided structure with no roof and a dividing wall down the middle, and I wondered what it was for.

'It's to do sunbathing without clothes,' Gisela told me. 'One side for women, the other for men.'

I was quite impressed, as I had never attempted nude sunbathing – it was pretty much frowned upon in England in those days, and if you did it you were considered wild and weird – and I was also impressed that it was obviously so normal in Germany, they had actually built a special place for it. I definitely had to try it out.

'I'll come with you,' Del said, so we climbed the hill the following afternoon armed with suntan lotion, drinks and towels, and I had my book as I hate going anywhere without one. My idea of total relaxation is to be in the open air, very quiet, with nobody about, just my book. Del was more than happy just to lie in the sun drinking it up; in those days we didn't know how dangerous sunbathing was but we could never stay out too long as we all had to work the late afternoon shift.

'Trouble is, my skin's so fair I go pink,' Del grumbled as she slapped some oil on her white legs before turning over onto her stomach. 'Can you do my back, Denise?' This was the life.

Mieke and Lorraine had declined to join us; I think they were both too shy to strip off. And Gisela would never nude-sunbathe in front of anyone as she had her secret to contend with, which she never shared with anyone except me, as far as I was aware. Mena had beaten us to it, so it was just as well that Lorraine and Mieke didn't want to come, as the shelter was barely(!) big enough for three.

I'd forgotten about the dividing wall until I heard male voices on the other side. Whoever was there must have been asleep when we first arrived because I had happily stripped off without any self-consciousness and settled myself into a corner with my paraphernalia. So their voices came as a shock. I looked over at Mena. She didn't flicker. Her oily body was completely stretched out, pubes to the sun, and nothing and no-one was going to disturb her.

It all quietened down – the men must have fallen asleep again, and so did Mena and Del. I read, and the only attention I got was a fly that insisted upon diving back onto my book every time I told it to shove off. I could hear its chums gently buzzing in the distance but for me it was the sound of summer, which had finally arrived in Bayrischzell after a long cold winter and short coolish spring. A soft breeze every now and then puffed over my exposed body, which was loving every moment, and I gave myself up to it all.

After half an hour, Del woke up. Mena was still asleep and was looking dangerously red. I wondered if I should wake her, but she stirred and opened her eyes when we started talking. There was no sound from next door.

'What are these for?' Del turned her head to Mena. She looked to see what Del was peering at and smiled. I had already noticed some small holes in the dividing wall.

'Oh, it's just woodworm,' I said.

'Woodworm, my foot,' Del said, looking closely at the holes. 'The worms would have to be the size of baby snakes. No, these have been made properly with a drill.'

'*Die Männer,*' Mena said, smiling as if to say, *Boys will be boys.*

Del immediately put her eye to the largest hole.

'It's Herr Koch,' she informed us, saying it like 'cock' as she always did, in spite of my telling her over and over how it was pronounced. 'Not a pretty sight. He's certainly named appropriately.'

We giggled and didn't care if Herr Koch wondered what we were laughing at. Mena didn't understand our joke as she scarcely spoke a word of English. Just as well, when we were being so rude about him. How were we to know that one day, a decade later, she and Herr Koch would get married?

Nude sunbathing was not the only fun thing to do at Tannerhof that summer. There was the annual staff outing. Everyone on the domestic side was expected to go – the cleaners, laundry workers, gardeners, waitresses, and kitchen crew. The professionals such as the doctors and therapists and people who worked in the office were not invited. They had to stay and look after the guests, and the office workers would have to set out the lunch (which we in the kitchen had, of course, worked twice as hard the day before to prepare). I was disappointed that Gisela wouldn't be joining us but she said she couldn't go as she was on one of her fasts. She didn't normally mix with the domestic staff; one of the reasons why we became friends so quickly was because I was from England and she could practise her English.

As usual, preparations began taking place the day before. The cleaners piled dozens of cushions and ground-sheets and rugs into Herr Koch's van, and Emmi was in charge of the picnic early in the morning of the day itself, which was very promising, weather-wise.

I don't remember us going in cars, so presumably our walk started from Tannerhof itself. But I *do* remember a long tiring walk up the mountain, and people twice my age or more leaping on ahead, occasionally stopping to admire the wild flowers. Don't ask me to name them, but they were Alpine flowers you just don't see in England. All that mountain climbing didn't half keep those Bavarians fit. There must have been about twenty of us and although there were several plump figures marching ahead, no-one except the Turkish girls was particularly overweight, unlike the lumps you see today in England and America, a result of all our fast foods and no exercise.

It took about three hours to get to the place where we were headed, and I was at the point of losing consciousness, what with the lack of oxygen, the sun burning the back of my neck which my hair didn't seem to be protecting, the distinct dearth of coffee breaks (I should have been used to that by now, but I wasn't), and the fact that it was way past our normal lunchtime. We must have brought water with us on that three-hour hike, but I can't remember stopping. Then, finally, *Gott sei dank* – we'd arrived.

'Okay?' I asked Suna, who was by now struggling at the rear.

'Okay,' she answered, tears of perspiration pouring down her face, which was red from sun and exertion. Her lips were set in a determined manner, reminding me of my mother when she was having to do something she didn't really want to do, such as taking part in a picnic.

We spread out the rugs and picnic by a clear stream that was somewhat reduced in depth by the onset of the sudden hot weather, and our little spot began to give the impression that a meal might soon emerge. We laid out blue-checked tablecloths as flat as you could on the side of a mountain, and plates and cutlery clattered and jangled (no plastic plates and forks for us) as Emmi and Anita served the food. We'd made our usual salads, though we had a treat today with potato salad as only the Germans can make it – not swamped in mayonnaise as it is in England, but with olive oil that glazes the potatoes while they are still warm, and chopped up gherkins and onions to give flavour and texture. There were vegetable flans and stuffed eggs and fresh fruit and yoghurt. We had cold juices to drink, though I remember thinking how a glass of chilled wine would have slipped down nicely. Most of the time we never gave a thought to having wine with our meals – it wasn't there to tempt us and so we forgot about it. Until we ventured beyond the Tannerhof boundaries, that is.

I was sorry Frau Cygan hadn't joined us, and I supposed her arthritis must be playing her up, but it was rather nice for the rest of us to be together that day, for once with no chores to do. I leaned my back against a tree, one of the many thousand pines, breathing in its scent and enjoying the shade, and listened to the *shhhhh* of the stream. I looked round at everyone, their Bavarian accents a pleasant drone in my ears and thought: they have begun to accept me and I am closer to accepting them, even though I don't agree with everything they do. I can't help admiring their incredible capacity for hard work – we're like an over-grown family – there's occasionally some bickering, and a bit of gossip goes on, but so far as I'm aware, never anything malicious, and you can see there's a genuine fondness amongst them. Maybe they really do know how to have fun after all.

Chapter 11
Herman

It didn't take me long to notice there was quite an attractive male guest who always gave a slight inclination of his head whenever he passed me in the hall, and occasionally, it would be accompanied by a slight smile. As there had been very little communication from Augsburg since the Venetian weekend, I decided he might be fun to go out with (I was too new in Germany to understand that German men take dating very seriously), but it would be difficult to attract him, dressed as I was every day in my kitchen overalls and thick-soled shoes. I felt like an eighteenth century serving- wench longing to be rescued from all this domesticity by the son of the lord of the manor.

Luckily for me, the rule in those heady seventies days was that guests were required to book a minimum of three weeks at the sanatorium, unlike the English spas nowadays, where a week is regarded as a luxuriously long stay, and three nights or even a day is considered perfectly normal, and of perceived benefit to our stressed minds and bodies. At the sanatorium, they believed the body needed at least three weeks of fresh air, fresh food, exercise, relaxation and treatments to change bad habits, both mental and physical. I think they were right, but people today are looking for instant results, and the spa owners (I can only speak for my own country) are looking for their money.

I say this because in the last twenty years or so, my mother and I have been to many health spas in England and Scotland. The food is usually good to exceptional, although one or two don't seem to worry about cooking with sugar and fat, and they are usually the ones who offer real coffee and alcohol. But what makes me really upset is that the waitresses and therapists do not eat the same food as the guests. If the spa was *really* concerned about health, then the first thing they would provide would be healthy food for the staff. Waitresses have told me more than once that they have to go to the canteen, which serves pizzas, chips, sugary desserts and fizzy drinks and so on, with nary a salad leaf in sight. Whereas at Tannerhof, all the staff eat exactly the same food, and I think this demonstrates the sincerity of the owners. 'A healthy life for all' seems to be their motto.

I have mentioned the Tannerhof concept to a couple of English health spa owners, but they come back with a feeble excuse about hygiene, and one even said it would encourage the staff to steal food!

Getting back to the attractive guest. Frau Uffort (who everyone called 'Ooffey'), one of the masseuses, told me that his name was Dr Herman Bedelmaier and that he came to Tannerhof regularly three times a year, sometimes four, mostly for stress, and there were still over two weeks left on this occasion for him to see that I had a brain, as well as a good figure (in those days). Yes, he was quite a lot older than me – but what did age matter? Yes, he was shorter than me – but only by an inch or two. And yes, he was going thin on top – but you can't have everything. He was nice-looking and spoke good English. After speaking nothing but poor German from a starting point of only '*Auf wiedersehen*', my throat was raw from all those gutteral noises – not helped by Traudl who, on my second week at Tannerhof, forced me to repeat '*München*' at least fifty times until she was satisfied that I had pronounced it properly. So you can imagine my joy at being able to converse in English.

Küchesprache, as I called kitchen language (not sure if it is one word, but it never hurts in the German language to run a couple of nouns together – several if you're feeling really playful) is pretty limiting. I could name all the pots and pans and crockery, utensils, ingredients, herbs, different dishes, physical aspects of the kitchen itself… but there, my prowess ended. Not only was my conversation limited, but I wasn't learning particularly good grammar from my kitchen mates, and my pronunciation was certainly not *hoch Deutsch* (high German). I didn't realise this until I finally left Tannerhof to study intermediate German at the *Goethe Institut* in Kochel-am-See. When I made a tape-recording from an extract of *Der Kleine Prinz,* our tutor roared with laughter. 'I've never heard an English girl speak German with a Bavarian accent,' she told the class – in German, of course.

Herman would be just the one to help me expand my vocabulary.

'*Guten Tag*, Herr Bedelmaier,' I gaily greeted him each morning if I spotted him going off walking or to the sauna.

'*Guten Morgen*, Fräulein,' he would reply, using the more formal salutation, which, of course, made me more determined than ever to break that German resolve.

But how to attract his attention? The answer came quite naturally one day. It was lunchtime and the kitchen, still spotless, was like a wasps' nest – all the workers choreographed, knowing exactly what they had to do to get the meal served at exactly one o'clock. And exactly twenty-five minutes later, the dirty dishes, piled straight and tall as soldiers at the wide kitchen hatch, were whisked away to the washing-up room. Time for the sweet course, which *I* was in charge of. I bent down to extract a baking tray the size of a small raft from the oven, admiring my dozens of baked apples that I'd carefully filled with raisins and spices that morning. I stood up and looked right into the eyes of Herman, who was peering at me through the hatch… CLANG…! I dropped the tray!

'Gott im Himmel!' Emmi came rushing over, her face red with the morning's cooking. *'Wass machst Du, Denise?'* (For heaven's sake, what are you doing?) She bent to scrape up an apple that had rolled under her spotless, sensible white lace-ups.

'Es tut mir leid, Emmi,' (I'm sorry) I replied, as I tried to retrieve the precious apples, which had taken on a life of their own. Thank goodness the floor was as spotless as Emmi's shoes, as there'd be no time to make another dessert. I risked a glance at the hatch; Herman was watching the proceedings with interest. I couldn't have planned it better – he smiled. From now on, Herman was mine.

Our first date was a trip to Munich, or München, as he insisted I pronounce it, and because he lived there, we went often…museums, art galleries, churches, theatre, the ballet and classical concerts.

'I want to take you to the opera,' Herman said one day as he took my hand in his own with its neat, manicured fingernails, while we sat in the *Zur Post*, a restaurant in Bayrischzell, one balmy August evening. Were his nails the result of Tannerhof treatments, I wondered, or was he normally so fastidious? I stared at them, wondering if they might give me a clue as to his character. We had just polished off a delicious supper of mixed cheeses (some of them quite daringly full fat), potato salad as only the Germans can make it, and fresh green salad, all served with a platter of different textured and coloured breads. Our plates were breadboards, with a painted apple in one corner.

'In fact, more than one,' he added, vying for my attention, which was transfixed on my breadboard. 'The Ring Cycle is coming to München. You have never seen it, *ja?*'

No. And I never want to. Loved opera – loathed Wagner. I was never sure if it was the Hitler association (Hitler being one of his biggest fans) or whether it was simply too heavy for my untrained ear. I might have managed one, but definitely not the whole bloody cycle; it went on for days. *Days?* That meant I could be with Herman several evenings in a row. It wouldn't be difficult to pretend I adored Wagner – and at the same time, accelerate the romance. Regular dating with a real boyfriend. I hesitated. No, not even for Herman was I prepared to stomach Wagner.

'I don't like Wagner,' I said – quite bravely, I thought.

'You don't like *Wagner?*' I noticed his voice had become a little shrill. 'You cannot be serious. *Everyone* loves Wagner!'

'Not me.'

'But you say you love classical music.'

'I do.'

'But you cannot possibly love classical music if you don't love Wagner.'

It was our first argument. Herman was behaving like a typical chauvinist, and a German one at that. His beloved Wagner was not appreciated by this philistine Englishwoman, and I was terrified this would be such a deep blow for him that he would forget all the other things we had in common. So I chose to overlook it, and changed the subject. Soon he was laughing and chatting as though the little incident had never taken place. But it wasn't just the matter of Herman being disappointed by my not liking Wagner – it was the barely-concealed scornful expression that marred Herman's pleasant features. As though my taste in music was inferior to his. And maybe it was.

Well, love is blind, as they say, and although I wasn't in love – not yet, anyway – I didn't want to louse up such a promising relationship over some dead composer. Not when I felt I'd hit the jackpot.

There was just too much at stake. A well-heeled man of whom I was growing fonder by the minute and with whom I had loads of interests in common. He made his living as a successful lawyer, and owned a couple of substantial buildings in Munich. Best of all, he was looking for a wife! Well, he didn't actually say so, but I could tell in the little things he said, such as how he didn't really care to live on his own, and although he could cook, he couldn't be bothered after a day at the office, especially when there was only him. A girl knows about this sort of thing.

I knew things were serious when Herman took me to meet his mother – a little old lady with an eagle eye, who looked me over and proceeded to fire questions in near-perfect English as though she were on target practice. When I told her my mother was half-German, that she had a German father from the First World War, although she never knew him, Frau Bedelmaier nodded to her son. Things were going well.

Except one thing – one very important thing. Making love. During love-making, I was privy to the view of Herman's sweating face – hot beads would roll from his forehead down his nose, dropping like lemmings to the safety-net of my face. I couldn't forgive the way his thinning hair gradually resembled pieces of wet string, self-adhesively clinging to his perspiring crown – just like one of those awful styles you see on some bald men who grow a few strands of hair incredibly long and sweep them across the tops of their heads, erroneously believing they are fooling us women. While Herman was panting – his eyes closed – I would watch this metamorphosis with a detached horror. Worse was to follow. Immediately after he peaked (I'm making him sound like a whisked egg white), he would let out a high-pitched giggle, roll off and say, 'How vas zat for you, *meine Liebling*?'

'Well, the earth didn't move,' I was tempted to reply, but he might have been puzzled, as I doubted Germans would have the same metaphor. So I'd just smile and murmur, '*Wunderbar*, as always, Herman.'

It wasn't just Wagner who had come to town. Vidal Sassoon had recently opened in Munich. I was thrilled, and decided a decent haircut was essential to remind me that I had a life outside the sanatorium, and that I was, in spite of my lowly status in the kitchen, a woman. And I didn't want Herman to think I had nothing and was after his money – even though it would have been pretty close to the truth. I had *some* pride. For a month I'd saved my pocket-money to pay for this treat, and had persuaded Mieke to come with me and get hers cut too. She was a rich glossy brunette with a nondescript cut, so what better than to let Vidal get his hands on both of us in one go!

Herman arranged to meet us for lunch – good, as we'd never be able to afford to eat as well.

We didn't see Vidal at all that morning, but it didn't matter a scrap, as we had two luscious young men, both with tight bums and wearing cowboy boots and long layered hair. I suppose they must have been gay, though we didn't use that word in those days, except when you were feeling happy, but Mieke and I had had too sheltered a background to recognise one. They seemed to take the greatest pleasure in sweeping our hair up over the backs of their hands, letting it cascade to our shoulders again, and sighing, '*Schön, schön!*'

Neither of us had been used to all this attention. Long fingers caressed our cheeks as they indicated how far they were prepared to go (with the length, that is) and Mieke and I, who were sitting next to one another, made eye contact in the communal mirror, and weakly nodded. Snip, snip. They twirled us around on our chair wheels, winked at us in the mirror, and re-snipped. These boys were experts. An hour later we emerged, flushed with excitement and the heat of the drier; one dark, the other blonde, but with identical, highly-fashionable bobs. We loved our new look. So did Herman.

'*Wunderschön,*' he smiled as he proffered both arms. 'Two lovely ladies.' (A bit different from the kitchen-maid and the cleaner.) 'Everyone in ze restaurant will ask, 'How did he get two such beautiful ladies? One, perhaps – but *two*!' ' Charmingly directing his attention to both of us as we marched along the wide Munich streets, Mieke and I on high heels we weren't used to, he finally stopped outside an expensive fish restaurant I had read about in one of the glossy magazines that a guest had tossed to one side only yesterday when she had been called in for her massage. A handsome waiter opened the door, and with a courtly bow, gestured us in.

Wagner… the earth remaining static… what did it all matter, when I'd got the most delicious plate of nosh in front of me?

CHAPTER 12
PROMOTION!

THE NEWS BUZZED like an irritating fly at a picnic. It flew round the kitchen workers, into the laundry, next door to the cleaning staff, over to the therapists' rooms, and finally outside to alight on one of the gardeners.

Irene (pronounced Eraynah), who had sole charge of the *Rohkost* Room (a room where all the raw food and juices were prepared), had run off with Herr Schmidt, one of the maintenance men. Apparently, she had given no warning, and her little salad room stood forlornly without its mistress. I had made a habit of popping in to have a chat with her most days, which wasn't easy – me with my very halting German, and her coming from Romania. But somehow we managed to communicate. She prepared everything – müesli, salads, vegetable and fruit juices. I used to watch her, fascinated, while she worked, deftly filling what seemed like hundreds of individual glass plates ready for the waitresses to collect.

'*Ach, so,* Denise. You are to be promoted,' Frau von Mengershausen informed me the same day Irene absconded. 'You will go to *Rohkost Zimmer* and prepare ze salads for lunch and dinner. Tomorrow you will prepare breakfast.'

I was delighted with this news as although Emmi no longer watched my every movement like a greedy cat squints at the comings and goings on a bird table, I knew the kitchen crew often looked over my shoulder, even at a distance. Emmi didn't usually pounce, but she was always ready… just in case. Just in case I didn't chop the parsley finely enough. Just in case I took a tea-break… how lazy! Just in case…

It would be fun to be on my own, choosing the recipés and basking in the compliments from podgy guests whose new calorie intake would not even satisfy a cockroach (not that one would dare to put its head round *this* kitchen door). I jerked out of this little reverie when it hit me that I would be making salads for over sixty guests, not to mention the staff, with no likelihood of a practice run.

'Will someone show me what to do, Frau Mengershausen?'

She thought for a moment. 'I will ask Traudl to show you for ze first day.'

But Traudl, the friendly young waitress, was hardly the right person, I would have thought.

'And if I get really busy, can I ask for some extra help?'

Frau von Mengershausen looked puzzled. 'Irene did all on her own, always. We have no-one else.'

I refrained from reminding her that Irene had fifteen years' experience and could speak the language fluently, to boot. You didn't argue with Frau Mengershausen.

It was an intensive morning but Traudl was a darling. She switched on the grater, which stood on the floor like a moon-lander, humming with life. She threw in a bucket of carrots and several roughly-quartered cabbages, and seconds later mountains of sweet-smelling orange and pale-green shreds emerged. Traudl had already prepared the yoghurt dressing and within minutes she had forked together all the ingredients into a delicious coleslaw. I was impressed and relieved that the machine, which I'd been dreading, looked pretty straightforward.

I helped her make a couple more salads – a tomato and dill salad with a simple lemon and olive oil dressing, and a more exotic one involving artichokes. Then we laid out the plates, over a hundred (I had forgotten how many staff there were) on the scrubbed wood work surfaces that edged two of the walls. Traudl then quickly tore the leaves from what seemed like dozens of lettuces and tossed them in a bath-sized sink of water, swirled them around, then swept them up with both arms and laid them all out on huge cloths to soak up the water. So different from nowadays in England when all the salads are in bubble packs, ready-washed and ready-depleted of any nutrition they might have had, thanks to all the insect sprays and preservatives. We covered half of each plate with these frisky young leaves, and spooned on the three salads, tucking a tiny stainless steel jug of dressing in between.

Seconds later, Maria came to the door to make sure we were ready.

'*Alles gut,*' she nodded approvingly towards the waiting plates, and proceeded to take up several at a time, balanced along her capable arms, for our famished guests. I barely had a moment to imagine their first rapturous mouthful when Traudl announced:

'You must now learn ze müesli wiz ze Bircher method.' She explained that Dr Bircher had invented müesli over a hundred years ago and to eschew any commercial packets as they were completely against his health cures. Several different grains had to be soaked overnight... I began to lose my concentration at this point. We had not sat down for even five minutes, nor had we had so much as a sip of water. To add to the exhaustion was the small matter of translating most of Traudl's instructions from German into English, and my brain was screaming for a break.

'Could we sit for a few minutes and have a drink?' I asked tentatively.

'We will drink herb tea,' (not quite the same as a cup of coffee, but I didn't dare argue) 'and I will use ze time to write you ze müesli directions.'

Rosehip tea never tasted so good. I tried to spin the time out, but Traudl had written out the recipé in record time. She jumped up and stated, 'I only have three-quarters more hour. I show you what I can in ze time.'

So I learned how to make the müesli (Bircher was right – it bears no resemblance to the wood-shavings you get from a packet), fresh fruit and vegetable drinks and three more salads and their appropriate dressings in forty-five minutes flat.

'You are doing *gut*, Denise. I zink you are okay for zis evening. I go now. It is my free time.'

She noticed my panic-stricken face and patted my arm. 'Don't worry. You can do it. You are a normal.'

I think she meant 'a natural', but I wasn't feeling either normal or natural. My head was spinning, I was petrified to be left on my own, and dammit – I was hungry! And I wanted more than a few fancy lettuce leaves.

I stared after her straight slim young back as she left me in my little room, the weight of responsibility almost bringing me to my knees.

Most of my free afternoon was spent in a fitful siesta, where I drifted in and out of one nightmare after another. Skeletal people were holding out empty plates and demanding food that I had forgotten to prepare. In the end I gave up and got ready for the evening onslaught. It was a quarter to three.

I felt very pleased that I had sensibly allowed myself all this extra time. Calmly, in total control, I breezed through more fruits and vegetables, turning them into delectable dishes. Time now to prepare the dressing. Traudl had recommended that I make one of sour buttermilk. (I know it sounds revolting, but take it from me – it's delicious.) The recipé looked simple enough. That was until I glanced up at the stern school clock and was alarmed that I had used up far more time than planned on the salads. There was only five minutes before Maria would be collecting the plates, and she would not be at all amused to be kept waiting. It had taken me a long time to get on the good side of Maria, and then it was only because she discovered I loved Mozart, who was one of her favourite composers.

The huge blender whirled into action in sympathy as though it knew I was so behind. Seconds later, buttermilk, oil, lemon-juice and quark had happily conjoined to make a creamy liquid. I threw in a handful of finely-chopped parsley – thank goodness this was 'one I had prepared earlier' – and stopped, fascinated, to see such a beautiful minty-green colour, sprinkled with emerald-green snippets. Salt and pepper to taste. Not quite enough salt. I worked like a Trojan, washing my hands for the thousandth time – no time to dry them. Picked up the enormous packet of salt yet again, which by now looked very bedraggled with its soggy edges. Measured out another quarter teaspoon. Blender still running – oh, no! I watched in disbelief as a huge chunk of cardboard from the side of the salt packet fell into the machine as accurately as a professional diver, and immediately whizzed into a myriad specks. No time to make a fresh batch. Without daring to taste it, I poured the liquid, which had now thickened with its surprising new ingredient, into the waiting jugs. Right on cue, Maria came to collect the plates.

'*Gut Salat*,' she approved, giving me a wide smile that set off her gold-capped tooth. '*Sehr gut.*'

I nodded guiltily. Was there such a thing as cardboard poisoning? Would there be complaints of mysterious stomach pains – or worse, slow death? Especially amongst the feeble ones who had just come off their week of fasting. I braced myself.

Herman, who was back at Tannerhof for another three weeks of stress-busting (made worse since he began dating me, no doubt), was the first to appear at the kitchen hatch.

'Ze salads were *wunderbar*, Fräulein Barnes' – he never called me Denise when we were at Tannerhof and other staff were around – as though they didn't know what was going on – 'but ze dressing…' *Oh, no, here it comes…* '…zat vas…' And he kissed his fingertips.

'*Danke schön*, Dr Bedelmaier.' I didn't dare look him in the eye. He would have thought I was a complete idiot, and I wanted to shine where he was concerned.

At half-past seven, I and the rest of the kitchen workers finally sat down to *our* supper. Everyone was munching away, and generously pouring on the dressing. I watched the jug as though hypnotised as they passed it from one to the other… until it finally came round to me.

I shook my head. 'No dressing for me, *danke schön*.'

Chapter 13
Enter Barry

'Denise, do you know someone who is interested to work in ze garden?' Frau Mengershausen asked me one early-August day. 'John will finish in two weeks and we must have help for Herr Koch and Herr Kruger.'

John, who I mentioned when I first arrived at Tannerhof, was an intense American boy, thin and blemished as a carrot, who survived on vegetable juices and *all* raw food – except potatoes – and who told me this was the only diet that would keep his skin clear. I didn't like to point out that the raw regime wasn't working. He had a room next to mine in the *Gockel-Hütte,* and we occasionally spent an afternoon listening to his particular brand of music – not always to my taste, but he was determined to get me out of classical mode and into his Whiter Shade of Pale.

It only took me a few seconds to think of Barry Wakeling. Barry was a boy I'd met three years before, in a suburb of Atlanta, Georgia. He was at the time seventeen and I was twenty-five. He kind of hero-worshipped me (when he reads this book, he will vehemently deny this) and I treated him like the kid brother I never had. His family had emigrated from Ireland to the States when he and his sister were children. We'd met when I was doing a full-time secretarial course at the local technical college and had to earn my keep (I was living with my sister and her family at the time) by making the painful metamorphosis to a waitress in the evening. The restaurant called Grants was based on one of those awful cheap diners, tacked on, as an afterthought, to the side of a similarly cheap department store, which was piled high with Hong-Kong-made clothes and a breathless variety of useless trinkets. The vinyl-clad upholstery in the restaurant sported cigarette burns as prolific as measles, and the tables were overhung by dirty bulbs in fly-ridden lampshades, which produced a curious surreal effect. The whole place reminded me of American movies in the fifties.

Barry's title was Short Order Chef – even though he'd never had a cookery lesson in all his 17 years. On my first day, one of the waitresses introduced me to him saying, 'This is Berry.' (That's how she pronounced it in her Southern-Belle accent.) 'He's also from England.'

'Ireland, actually,' corrected Barry. I looked at his large-featured, smiling face on about the same level as mine; spotty, like mine, but his was the result of a daily dose of Grant's special fried chicken and chips, and coke (as in cola); front teeth crooked, also like mine, and a thatch of Brillo-pad hair – here, the similarity thankfully ended. I liked him immediately. 'Are you the new waitress?'

''Fraid so. I've never done it before. It's not *quite* the career I had in mind. But here I am, willing to have a go.'

I noticed the other waitresses looking a bit dubious as to my capabilities, but Barry said, 'I'll show you the ropes and you'll soon get the hang of it.'

'If I don't hang *myself* on the ropes in the meantime.'

He did, and I didn't, but in those three waitressing months, we had tremendous fun – usually at the expense of the customers and sometimes of our fellow workers.

'One freshly-caught trout,' I'd call to him, parodying the description from the menu, and seconds later I'd hear the satisfying ping of a triangular-shaped fish as it hit the metal griddle, 'and one slice of Momma's home-made apple pie with dairy-whipped cream.' I would wait patiently while Barry tore another cardboard box open to release the contents of what we privately renamed Beige Goo. A flash of one of Barry's professional knives, and a vulgar-sounding squirt of 'shaving cream' from an aerosol can completed another 'wholesome' meal for some unsuspecting customer.

'If Ah hadn' read it with mah own ahbolls, Ah'd sway-er this apple pah came from Miz Beddy Crocker,' a customer said to me quite challengingly one lunchtime.

'*What* a thing to say, Mr Tarleton.' I dared not look directly at him. 'You know the menu never lies.'

'Ah guess. And you're just too darned purdy to lah.'

My waitressing days were over the day I spurted milk from one of those horrid little tight pyramidal packets all over a man who *would* happen to be dressed in a business suit. I was mortified but it didn't save my job. Barry could only look on helplessly as I packed my things and left a pathetic little bundle of uniform on a seat behind the counter. But we'd kept in touch over the last two years.

He was also trying to earn his keep while studying for a degree in modern languages. Coming to Tannerhof would be a perfect opportunity to give him a few months' work experience and improve his German.

Frau Mengershausen thought he sounded nice and asked would I write to him.

'He must pay his fare and I will give him back half when he returns to America.'

So I wrote, and this was the reply:

Dear Denny,,

Receiving your letter today offering me a job in Bavaria on a health farm is one of the most exciting days of my life. Yes, I will definitely come and will let you know dates and travel arrangements as soon as I know. Will you be able to meet me in Munich or shall I make my own way to Bayrischzell?

See you soon.

Yours excitedly,

Barry

He flew into Munich one bright blue September morning, swept me into a bear embrace and said, 'You look great! Do you have today off?'

'No, I have to help them serve lunch, and I'm back on duty this afternoon. You'll be doing well if *you* get the day off.'

Barry looked worried. His brow wrinkled most unbecomingly at my next question – 'How's your German?' – as we trundled towards the exit for the *Bahnhof.*

'Poor,' he admitted.

'Well, make the most of speaking it,' I advised. 'The main thing is… don't be shy. Just speak, even if it's wrong.'

I was full of more advice on the Bayrischzell train, and, rather cruelly, I gave him a warning. 'You know I have a German boyfriend?'

Barry nodded.

'So please don't rely on being with me every minute of my spare time. I'll do *some* things with you, and you know I'm around. But don't hang onto me – you've got to stand on your own feet.'

Poor Barry. His face dropped. He was, after all, only nineteen, and had come a long way to a foreign country at my instigation, where I was the only person he knew. He'd only arrived five minutes ago and I was already abandoning him.

'What's he like?'

'You'll meet him. He's very nice. He's got a good sense of humour...for a German.'

Barry looked doubtful. 'What's his name?'

'Herman.'

'Herman the German?'

We both burst out laughing.

'Tell me about the people I'll be working with,' Barry said, wiping his eyes.

'You'll mostly be under the assistant gardener, Herr Koch,' I said, daring him.

'Herr Koch! How exactly do you spell his name?'

'K-o-c-h, but it doesn't matter so long as you don't pronounce it 'cock' in front of *me*.'

'You'd think he'd change his name.'

'Why? It only means 'cook' in German. You really *do* need to get down to your studies.'

'And here's the man himself,' I said a few minutes later as we were once again met by Herr Koch, red-faced and unsmiling, as usual, as he swung the luggage into his van.

But Barry was undaunted. He couldn't wait to have his first German conversation.

'*Guten Morgan. Wie geht's?*'

'*Gruss Gott*,' was the short reply.

'We're very religious round here,' I said with a sombre expression, which set Barry off again.

'You *need* to be religious,' Barry said, gripping the back of Herr Koch's seat, as HK drove in his manic way up the hill, taking bends as recklessly as a toddler vrooming his toy car. Thank goodness it was only a short ride.

'It's not much, but it's home,' I said, pointing. 'There's Tannerhof. But don't get *too* excited. We don't live in the main house – your room is next to mine in the shack down below.'

It didn't take long for Barry to become a hit with the kitchen staff. I almost felt jealous as I watched Emmi pile his plate with extra millet rissoles. It had taken me months to get a smile from her, and suddenly – there she was – flushed and beaming as she pushed his overflowing plate through the hatch. But for his first few days he was just another *Gastarbeiter* like the rest of us, and no more specially treated. In fact, his first day in the kitchen garden was a fiasco.

'You will start by weeding – like so,' Herr Koch demonstrated by plucking bits of greenery from a row of beans. 'You will start there,' indicating with a jerk of his gingery head. These directions were, of course, all in German, and this is Barry's rough translation.

After a back-breaking two hours, he meekly inquired, in halting German, whether he might stop for breakfast. Herr Koch nodded his permission and Barry tottered up the steps into the main house where we all – guests and staff – ate our meals. I was just coming out of the *Rohkost* Room where I had prepared the müesli, and caught him looking down at his bowl like Oliver Twist.

'It's perfectly adequate for a grown man who's about to be put to hard labour,' I told him.

'Will there be bacon and eggs to follow?'

'You're joking. We get boiled eggs on a Sunday for a treat…and *real* tea.'

'As opposed to *what*?' Barry looked seriously worried.

'This,' I said, and presented him with a cup of clear red liquid with a slice of lemon floating on top, accompanied by three or four vanilla pods.

'What's *this*?' Barry's face was beginning to lose its sparkle.

'*Hagebutte*. Or rosehip, to you.'

'*Rosehip*?' Barry screeched. 'I'll take coffee instead.'

'We don't serve real coffee.'

'So what is it if it's not real?'

'Dandelion.'

This was too much. Barry had obviously not paid any visits to health shops lately. I felt a bit sorry for him but could only say, 'When in Rome, and all that. Have another helping of müesli – that should keep you going. And don't forget, you can have all the bread you want.'

I watched his stocky figure disappear into the dining room. I didn't see him again until 4 o'clock that day.

There was a loud thump on my door as I was quietly sitting at my desk trying to memorise a few choice phrases to be parroted to the kitchen staff that evening. It wasn't easy. A sentence such as 'No, I did not notice where you hid the key to the fridge today' does not trip lightly off the tongue in German. Nor is it easily found in a phrase book. *'Nein, ich habe kein Kenntnis wo Sie seine Schlüssel zum Kaltzimmer verstecken hat'*, or words to that effect. It was those darned verbs. Waiting to trip you up at the ends of sentences. I often forgot what the subject or question was by the time they got to the verb.

I put down my pen and opened the door. A heap of shaking, moaning sub-human flesh fell into the room, heaved itself onto my bed, face down, and for a minute it didn't speak. Then a muffled sob. 'I've *never* been so tired in my whole life!'

After he had slightly recovered on a cup of soothing camomile tea, Barry told me how every bone and muscle in his body was screaming, and if he never gardened again, it would be too soon.

'What's put you off?' I asked him in an innocent tone.

'I've weeded, I've wheelbarrowed, I've weeded again, I've dug, I've re-weeded… and then I did something *awful*.'

'Oh, no, what?'

'Herr Koch just now asked me to weed a strawberry patch and I pulled out all the strawberry plants!'

'By mistake?'

'*Course* it was by mistake. You don't think I would do it on *purpose*?' He sat up and looked woefully at me. And then we clung to one another.

99

'Weren't you just a teeny bit suspicious that the 'weeds' were growing in neat rows?'

'I just thought that was how weeds grow in Germany.'

'*Mein Gott*,' I said. 'Was he angry?'

'*Angry?*' Barry's voice cracked. 'He turned as red as one of his beetroots. I thought he was going to have an apoplexy. I couldn't understand exactly what he was saying, but it sounded like verbal abuse to me. And I think I recognised the word 'moron' a couple of times.'

'Well, you're supposed to know about gardening,' I said, feeling for Herr Koch. After all, he had Herr Kruger, the head gardener, to answer to.

'*Moi!*' chortled my little friend, pointing to himself with an earth-encrusted finger. 'I've never *ever* done any gardening before in my life!'

Chapter 14

Brenda Puts Her Foot In It

I wanted my mother to come to Tannerhof. She'd never been to Germany and I felt it was important that she should see where her father came from. I knew she would have an affinity with Germany, as she was as spotless and organised as any *Hausfrau*. Besides, she worried about me all the time, and I wanted her to see for herself how well I looked. I had put a few pounds on my skinny frame (those were the days), my spots had practically cleared up with the sqeaky-clean air and all the fresh food, and I had a very becoming light-golden tan. Yes, it was time for Mum to see these improvements in her daughter.

Mum was a very nervous traveller, being agoraphobic, and although she swore she had been prepared to travel on her own, one of her younger sisters, Brenda, rang and asked if she could go with her.

'What could I say?' Mum said later, but I knew she was relieved not to have to face the journey on her own. Fond though the sisters were of one another, there was always an element of jealousy on Mum's side. This was partly because she disapproved of Carole and me paying Brenda too much attention. Mum thought it took away our feelings for her, which was, of course, all part of her insecurity. But Carole and I were fond of Brenda as she'd lived with us for five years in London when we were small and we had always kept in touch.

The last thing I wanted was a family row at Tannerhof, but not knowing any of my misgivings, they arranged to come in September to coincide with my week's holiday, when the weather would still be warm and sunny.

The trouble with Brenda was that she was married to John. He was an alcoholic and had made her life pretty miserable over the years. Bad enough to have to put up with his boozing, but he was also overbearing and possessive and made a good job of influencing her thoughts and opinions. It was a great pity as he was intelligent and witty, and could be quite charming if he put his mind to it, which was becoming increasingly rare. Brenda always longed for a temporary escape but he never let her out of his sight, so I was amazed when Mum wrote that Brenda had actually booked her ticket.

Brenda is twelve years younger than my mother, and is very much like Liz Taylor in looks and figure, so she has always been in the limelight. She has never been short of money (except when she and John were first married, but then, wasn't everyone?) and John allowed her to spend it on herself, so her wardrobe was, and still is, expensive and prolific. My mother was just as pretty in a fair way, with her lovely bone structure and forget-me-not blue eyes, but Brenda was always known as the beauty of the family.

I think Brenda imagined that Tannerhof would be the German equivalent of our Champneys, and I decided not to shatter her illusions. She would find out soon enough that she would not be able to top up on beauty treatments.

Barry and I met them at Munich airport. I took Barry as I knew he'd be jolly useful with all Brenda's luggage. But we weren't prepared for how much. They were only staying a week, and Mum had one normal-sized case. Brenda looked as though she was about to embark on a world cruise. Her trolley was stacked with cases, special beauty case, hand luggage – it might have been Liz herself arriving. To my relief, they were both smiling – maybe I had worried for nothing.

'How did you manage to escape from John?' I asked Brenda when we were on the train to Bayrischzell.

'I think he thought I couldn't get up to much if I was with my sister.'

It seemed too easy.

Tannerhof was full, so I had booked them into a delightful *Gasthof*, just outside the grounds, and run by a very nice lady called Frau Harm. But they were to have their main meals in our guest dining room, courtesy of Frau Mengershausen.

Mum and Brenda settled in, fussed over by Frau Harm, and as they were eating breakfast – their first home-made müesli, which Barry and I had brought from Tannerhof to Frau Harm's – we planned the next day.

'We'll just walk to the village and potter around the shops,' I said, knowing that the word 'shops' would meet with both their approval.

'I'll walk down with you,' said Barry.

I was as proud as if *I* had created the blue sky that beautiful sunshiny morning. I wanted to show where I lived in its very best light, and Mum and Brenda were suitably charmed. They both looked lovely in their summer clothes – Mum in a brown linen skirt that showed off her slim shapely legs (she normally covered them up in trousers, Hepburn style), with a cream shirt and silk scarf, and Brenda in a fabulous turquoise and white spotted sundress with a deep-cut square neckline and full skirt. Definitely designer.

Turquoise strappy sandals completed her outfit, and I didn't like to tell her that they were unsuitable for walking to the village. She wouldn't have taken any notice anyway – fashion, to Brenda, always won over comfort.

Brenda bought several souvenirs, which were not the usual tat you find abroad. The Germans adhere to good-quality materials and craftsmen who are highly skilled. She picked up a cowbell, a finely-embroidered tablecloth and napkins, some Moselle glasses – the ones with the bright green stems – and some wool to knit a sweater.

'We'll stop at Café Stumpp,' I said. 'It's my favourite café.' There were certainly plenty of cafés to choose from in such a small village, and they had all been packed throughout the tourist season. Most of the tourists had now gone home, and it was more authentic to be with the Bavarians who actually lived in Bayrischzell.

'Bang goes my diet,' said Brenda wistfully, as she scoured the cake menu.

'I'll warn you,' I said, 'the portions of cake are *huge* in Germany. You only have to look at the women to see how fattening they are, especially with all the cream.'

'Well, we're on holiday,' said Brenda. 'And I know Barry will have one.'

'What, a whole cake to myself?' Barry said, sarcastically. 'Denny usually makes me split one with her.'

'Only because I'm trying to watch the calories. For both of us.'

Mum was incredibly proud (and rightly so) when I asked for the various cakes and coffee in my well-rehearsed German. And even more impressed when everything was accurately brought to us by a smiling, aproned and plaited-haired waitress.

Feeling guilty, but with a contented feeling of cake, we walked back to the clinic – Brenda and Barry in front, chatting away, and Mum and I a few steps behind. Brenda and Barry got to the main road first, ready to cross, when an oblivious German driver swept by, spraying an enormous cow-pat from beneath his wheels. Brenda looked exactly like a patient who had had a mud-bath at Tannerhof but had forgotten to first remove her clothes. Barry caught just as much but, at the sight of Brenda's look of horror and disgust, lost complete control of himself and collapsed onto the grassy verge, dissolving into hysterical spasms.

Brenda was *not* amused. Not only was her dress ruined, but it was in her hair, on her eyelashes, and had delicately splashed her once-elegant sandals. But that was not the worst. The smell. It was as though you had gone into a ward where all the new-born babies were having their nappies changed at the same time. Brenda and Mum were both gagging by this time (Mum, I think, in sympathy, as she was splatter-free) and Brenda did not appreciate it when Barry chortled, 'It was so fresh, it was still steaming!'

Somehow, we made it home, and the two of them got cleaned up, with much tutting by Frau Harm. It was good to see Brenda looking her usual band-box self again, but she'd had enough excitement for the day, and decided to spend the afternoon reading on the verandah. She'd be safe there.

Barry and I often went to the *Heuboden* dancing, so that evening we persuaded Mum and Brenda to go with us. It wasn't really their scene, but I wanted them to experience Bavarian folk music.

'It's only a short walk down the hill,' I told them. 'Not even as far as the village.'

Everyone got dressed for the evening's entertainment, and the four of us set off.

We had only gone a few hundred yards when Brenda cried out, 'I don't believe it!'

She had stepped into a little heap of dog dirt in her spare pair of Gucci sandals.

'Back we all go,' I said, not daring to look at Barry.

'It's a sign of good luck,' said Barry. 'The trouble is — things happen in threes. Well, that'd be impossible as we know where to avoid it on the way back.'

Brenda appeared in yet another pair of sandals (I could under-stand now why she'd brought so many cases) and we made our way to the *Heuboden* for the second time.

Despite the day not having gone *quite* as we would have liked, we enjoyed the music evening. Mum and Brenda were fascinated by sturdy dirndl-clad women carrying beer in barrel-sized mugs, five or six of them in each muscular hand.

We watched as they dumped these pitchers on tables, and both men *and* women stretched out their arms to embrace them. Seconds after downing the contents, they would reach for another jug, already lined up.

Brenda was delighted when a pleasant-looking chap dressed in full Bavarian costume came over and stood in front of her. He was extraordinarily tall, with straight hair the colour of marmalade, and a solid physique.

'*Tanze?*'

Brenda was quick to translate that he was asking her to dance.

'I've never tried Bavarian dancing,' she answered, but he simply got hold of her hand, pulled her to her feet, and escorted her onto the dance floor. It wasn't long before we spotted Brenda, dark curly head thrown back, laughing, as she was twirled around in true native style to the Duo Bavaria's shouted instructions and folksy beat.

'Phew!' she said, dog dirt all forgotten, as the young man led her back to her seat. Her face was flushed, and her eyes sparkled. 'It's really good exercise.'

Mum gave her a look that said, *I don't think John would see it like that.*

We all walked home without further mishap but Brenda told Barry and me the next morning at breakfast the previous night's happenings.

She had to get out in the small hours for a wee (no en-suites in those days) and her bare foot stepped into something warm and soft on the landing.

'Oh, my God, I've trodden on a rat!' she screamed, bringing a white-faced Frau Harm from her bedroom, brandishing a walking stick.

'Whatever's the matter?' My mother had come into the fray. She stood like a ghost in the doorway.

'Oh, Molly, I've trodden on a rat!' By this time, Brenda was almost sobbing.

'No rat in *zis* house.' Frau Harm flicked on the light switch and they all backed against the wall looking down at the rat. The rat didn't move. How could it, when it was just an inert pile of puppy poo? Frau Harm's new addition to the family had made a mistake in his German mistress's immaculate home.

'Ah, you very naughty leetle *Hund*,' admonished Frau Harm. Hansie, the puppy, looked up at her adoringly. He had a long training in front of him before he could take his rightful position in a German residence. 'No rat,' Frau Harm repeated in a hurt voice, looking at Mum and Brenda. 'No rat in *zis* house.'

Barry and I were in hysterics by now and even Brenda had to join in. Mum just looked relieved it hadn't happened to her.

'I told you everything happens in threes,' was all Barry could manage.

CHAPTER 15
FAMILY FIASCO

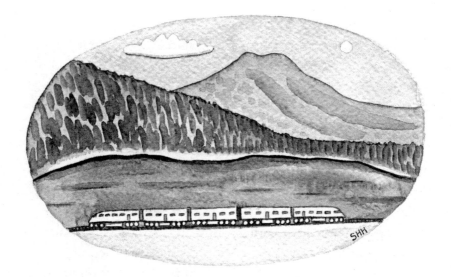

THE NEXT DAY, I decided to take Mum and Brenda on a scenic trip. We would get the early train and follow a route around the lakes, admiring the typical churches of the area, the wild flowers, and generally relax. Let the train take us.

It did. Right over the border into Yugoslavia, as it was known then. As we trundled happily along, the countryside started to lose its familiarity – I just didn't recognise anywhere. And yet I had been on this journey several times over the last months. My heart started to beat a little faster.

'*Fahrkarte, bitte,*' a ticket inspector called out, as he edged his way along the corridor. I handed him our tickets. Frowning, he looked at me and said something in a strong accent that I couldn't understand. The train pulled into a station, and he pointed to the sign. It was a foreign name, and I don't mean German.

'Oh, no!' I stuttered. Brenda and Mum gave me anxious looks. It was no good pretending. I turned to them. 'I think he's saying we're on the wrong train!' I didn't dare mention Yugoslavia. With luck, the sign would have meant no more to them than a German sign.

Mum looked worried, but I knew she trusted me to get us on the right track, so to speak.

'We'll get off here,' I said, grabbing our bags. Too late – the train had moved off, and was gathering speed.

'How long before we stop?' I asked the ticket inspector, who seemed to be enjoying this little drama. It probably made a change from the usual passengers who knew where they were, and more important, where they were going. A blank expression. He wasn't being awkward – it was probably the first time he had heard a demented Englishwoman speak. I tried again.

'*Wie lange zum nächste Halt?*' (How long is it to the next station?)

He looked at his watch. '*Zwei Stunden.*'

No, No, No, No, *No*! *Two hours*! I would have to put up with two hours of looking like an absolute twit in front of Brenda and Mum, when I had wanted to show off a little with my command of the language, and the area I lived in.

'Well, we might as well sit back and relax,' I told them. Then I decided I'd better come clean. 'We've gone over the Yugoslavian border, and it's non-stop until we get to the first town. And that won't be for two hours.'

I must say that in a situation like this, when it's beyond my control, I always accept what's happened, and go along with it, but my family was far too nervous, and not used to travelling without a man. Tension ran high when Brenda said, 'John would say this is another Barnes fiasco.' Mum might be alarmed, but she was not going to have me put in a bad light. So the two of them had a few words.

'Calm down, you two,' I told them. 'Look at that lovely view outside.' It was very beautiful, although we hadn't gone far enough for it to look much different from Bavaria. We were just skirting a huge lake, and wild flowers were scattered haphazardly over the meadows. It was an idyllic scene. Pity it wasn't echoed in the carriage.

Those two hours were the longest ever. If I had been on my own with a book, I would have made it into an adventure. And I would have definitely looked around the first town over the border when we finally arrived. But Brenda and Mum had other ideas. They wanted to get the next train straight back to Bayrischzell.

'We ought to see the town as long as we're here,' I said.

'We haven't got the right money,' my aunt pointed out.

'There are banks,' I said, but Mum and Brenda weren't having any of it.

I gave up. I approached a porter wearing a very smart uniform, although a button of his jacket was threatening to burst over his protruding stomach.

'*Können Sie mir helfen, bitte?*' I asked him. (Can you help me, please?) He cocked his head on one side in an enquiring manner, and I was encouraged to carry on. 'Bayrischzell?'

He pointed to the other side of the tracks. '*Drei Minuten.*'

'We've got to run,' I said. 'The next train leaves in three minutes.'

Somehow I got them both over the bridge and down the other side, and just as another porter was about to blow his whistle, I tore open the door and we piled in. This second porter sped along the platform and slammed our door. We were away. Two and a half hours later, I was never so pleased to see the sign BAYRISCHZELL.

You'd think we'd had enough excitement for one day. But that evening, as we were walking over to Frau Harm's so that Brenda and

Mum could change for dinner, a taxi drew up and a man staggered out. He had a familiar look, and we stared in amazement. It was John! He tossed a note to the driver, nodded to him to keep the change, banged the door shut, and almost ran into us.

'Surprised?' John taunted.

Brenda acted very annoyed, but I always thought she was secretly pleased that he had made such an effort on her behalf. Couldn't she see that he couldn't bear her to do *anything* without his being in control? Mum was livid – and rightly so. His presence put a dark cloud over their holiday.

'I asked the taxi driver if he'd been a Nazi,' John smirked in a loud voice, as he dumped his overnight bag in the hall, knocking the stand holding umbrellas and skis as he did so. 'He'd be about the right age. But no, he'd been a medic on a train – they always say that.'

'Sh-h-h-h!' I warned him, embarrassed that someone might appear who understood English, and even if they didn't, they would pick up the 'N' word. John grinned. Brenda was back to doormat mode and was silent.

'Right, what are the sleeping arrangements?'

'Brenda and I are sharing a room at Frau Harm's, just down the road,' said Mum.

'Well, *you* move out, Molly, and Brenda and I will have the room.'

'I am *not* moving out of my room,' Mum flashed. 'You can ask Frau Harm if she has another room. You weren't invited, so you can make your own arrangements. Brenda and I aren't going to have our holiday spoilt by *you*.'

Here we go.

'Where's the meat?' John demanded at supper. 'What's all this rabbit food? Come on, Brenda, we're not staying to eat this rubbish. We'll go into the village and have a steak in a proper restaurant.' He got hold of her arm and marched her off. Barry and I sat there stunned.

'It's because he can't get his drink,' Mum said. 'He couldn't care less about the food – he barely eats anything.'

'I can't believe Brenda just up and left.' Barry looked bemused.

'She daren't do anything else,' said my mother. 'I wish he'd clear off and go home, but he won't, not without Brenda.'

Barry was enjoying this. His family never quarrelled and he was fascinated.

Luckily, it didn't take John long to realise that herbal teas at Tannerhof would not be a satisfactory replacement for his alcohol levels, which constantly required topping up. He spent his few days, and the rest of Brenda's holiday, taking her to different restaurants in the village, and getting taxis to Munich, a distance of around fifty miles. Heaven knows what that must have cost. But at least it gave Mum and me the chance to enjoy our remaining time together.

I must say, I was quite thankful to say goodbye, even though I felt sorry for Mum, who had had the edge taken off her holiday by her insufferable brother-in-law. But most of all, I felt sorry for Brenda – she had to live with him.

When I asked John why he couldn't have let his wife have a holiday on her own for once, he said, 'I just did it to wind everyone up.'

CHAPTER 16
MIDNIGHT FEAST

BARRY'S MISSION IN life was to squeeze every drop of fun out of every day. It reminded me of the time I took my mother to Shrubland Hall, a health farm in Suffolk where you were given only raw food. (They still practise this regime.) At night, when we were getting ready for bed in our palatial suite, a young waitress would bring each of us a flask of hot water with lemon. After we'd sipped this detoxifying nectar, Mum would pick out the piece of lemon and suck out every scrap – pips and all.

'Mum,' I said, quite shocked when I saw her do this the first time. 'Whatever *are* you doing?'

'I'm still hungry,' she'd wailed through puckered cheeks.

I'm sure the guests in the Fasting Room at Tannerhof frequently felt like this.

But we were talking about fun, not hunger pains. The Tannerhof workers simply weren't used to disarming young men who charmed their way into their hardened hearts – once they'd forgiven him, that is, for pulling up all the strawberry plants. Emmi made sure all his favourite dishes appeared regularly on the menu. But it wouldn't be Barry if he didn't get into scrapes, like some over-sized schoolboy. It was just a matter of when.

He and Herr Koch began a relationship rather like Robert Louis Stevenson with his travelling donkey – Herr Koch being quite strict, and Barry braying whenever he was worked too hard. And like RLS, you could tell that Herr Koch was warming to his 'donkey' by the way he sometimes let him off a bit early, or allowed him a carrot break. However, Herr Kruger was a different matter. He may have had a bit more patience with Barry than Herr Koch, but he had great difficulty making himself understood. This manifested itself one miserable wet day on Barry's second week at the clinic.

Herr Kruger had a job for Barry to do. In Barry's words: 'Herr Kruger said, "My coat is on the back of the chair. Hang the coat up and weed under the chair." I thought it was a strange kind of order, but I was so proud I understood, so I did what he asked – or attempted to. I removed the coat, hung it up, and got down on my knees looking for non-existent weeds – hardly surprising, seeing as we were indoors! Then I noticed the rain was bucketing through two open windows and I thought... someone should shut those windows. Of course, that was exactly what Herr Kruger had asked me to do, though I still didn't realise it.' His crinkled eyes looked at me. 'Do you think I should give up the idea of a career as an interpreter?'

'I'm just glad the British didn't have to rely on you as an agent in the war,' I replied, getting up. 'Well, I've got to go and start supper as it's nearly 4.30 and I've got loads to do. Do you want to give me a hand? At least I'll bark orders in English.'

'What are you making?'

'Beetroot juice. Three salads – one I've never done, and a sour milk dressing.'

'Ugh!'

'And something with fruit,' I went on, ignoring him.

'Just like Grants,' Barry said, grinning, 'only hold the steak and fries.'

'We're using the cookery book Mum sent me,' I told him a few minutes later in the *Rohkost* Room, tossing him an apron, which he strung round his bulky waist. 'Wash your hands thoroughly before you start.'

'You sound like my mother.'

'I think we'll do tomatoes stuffed with kohlrabi and cream dressing,' I decided, flipping through the, by now, food-stained pages of the paperback. 'And then…let's see…a simple cucumber and dill salad with the sour milk dressing, and a green salad of spinach and lettuce and chives. That should do it. Then some melon for dessert.'

'Can I have a look?' Barry asked. He glanced at the cover. "Modern Vegetarian Cookery" by Walter and Jenny Fliess. Sounds German.'

'Well spotted.'

'Well, Jenny, I'd better get started then.'

'Okay, Walter, put the plates out. Around a hundred. And those little jugs for the dressing. And then wash and peel a dozen cucumbers, then…'

'Steady on, Jenny, one thing at a time.'

(Obviously, men couldn't multi-task in *those* days, either.)

It was great having an assistant to order about. The power. I wondered if that was how the kitchen staff felt when they ordered *me* around. Walter was now in his act, deftly washing lettuces, and throwing kohlrabi in the 'moonlander', as we had officially christened the grater.

'Keep the washing up down,' I instructed as I put the blender on to make the buttermilk and herb dressing.

'I can't see how you can get this done on your own,' Barry said, scraping the finely-shredded kohlrabi into a large mixing bowl. 'I think I'm better at this than gardening. Do you think they'd let me switch and be your assistant?' He paused and took a sip of water.

'Add some lemon juice right away,' I said, 'or it will start to go brown. No, I don't think they would, for a minute. Lovely though Frau Mengershausen is, she keeps a tight rein on the money side.'

'Well, it's not as if we get a proper salary,' Barry grumbled. 'Is it time yet for a break?'

'No chance.'

'I haven't even been to Munich since I came here,' Barry went on. 'I thought we'd be having a bit of culture now and again.'

'We will,' I promised. I was lucky – I had Herman to go culturing with every two or three weeks, but thought it best not to remind Barry, who had detested him on sight, and had told me in no uncertain terms that Herman was too old and too serious. 'And besides,' Barry had said, 'he ignores *me*.'

With Barry working with me, we finished everything a half an hour before I usually did.

'Can I take an extra plate back to my room?' Barry's voice was wistful as he looked at the small amount of left-overs.

'Aren't you getting enough to eat?'

'I get starving about 11 o'clock at night.'

'You need a midnight snack. Maybe we'll raid the fridge.'

Barry's eyes gleamed. 'Do you dare?'

'Do *we* dare?' I corrected. 'We'll meet tonight at 10.30 outside the kitchen door.'

'But they lock it.'

'Not the kitchen door, but they do the fridge. And they hide the key in a different place after every evening shift. I'll have to watch where they put it this evening.'

I know this is beginning to sound like a boarding school prank, and at 28 years of age I should have known better, but I'd missed these Enid Blyton jolities when I'd *begged* my parents to let me go to Wymondham College in Norfolk after passing the Scholarship. It was a mixed boarding school, which was probably the reason why they'd refused point-blank to let me go. Instead, I was forced to attend the same girls' grammar school as my sister in Norwich. Damn!

I had supper as usual that evening with my team, then cleared the table, helped tidy the kitchen, all the while keeping an eye on Anita, who was usually the one with the fridge key. I saw her open one of the spice drawers, which always reminded me of my eighteen months spent in a Dickension chemist's shop when I first left school. Mr Lincoln, the pharmacist, had a display of labelled drawers for the drugs he dispensed, except his were in an old oak cabinet, and these were shiny stainless steel. Anita, with a swift look round slipped the key inside the drawer. Second row from the top, third from the left, I memorised.

Barry and I, giggling and whispering, met as planned in the hall outside the kitchen door.

'Suppose someone sees us.' Barry said, nervously.

'They won't. They're all healthily in bed by 10 o'clock. And if they do, we won't be shot. The war's over.'

Barry looked unconvinced, but he only said, 'Lead on.'

We tiptoed into the kitchen, Barry stumbling down the step as he had never been in the kitchen before. It was out of bounds to anyone who didn't work in it.

'Sh-sh-shh!' I warned, taking the key from its hiding place. 'I think we'll have to put a light on – it's so dark in here.' I switched on a light over one of the worktops.

'I just don't want to be caught,' Barry said, his forehead creased in worry.

'Don't be daft. Come on, we're in. Oh, get a couple of trays.'

The walk-in fridge at Tannerhof is the size of a mini supermarket. Barry's eyes popped – he had never seen so much 'free' food. We grabbed cheeses, bread, quark, some left-over *rösti* potatoes, a bowl of strawberries, a couple of yoghurt desserts…

'Right, let's go,' I said.

'Oh, no!' From Barry. 'Someone's coming!'

There was no mistaking. And there was no escape.

'What *are* you doing?'

It was the tall figure of Frau Ooffey. If we had to be discovered, I'd rather it be by Ooffey than anyone else. She was Dutch and a masseuse with softened features under fine grey hair, pulled back in an unflattering bun, not unlike the style of my Victorian grandmother. Best of all, she was one of the few who spoke excellent English. She once told me that in Holland, as a child, you are taught four other languages – English, French, German, and usually Italian – as no-one ever learns Dutch. And if you think German is gutteral, then try speaking Dutch. She said that even the Dutch, when speaking their own language for a few hours, end up with a raw throat. One of the reasons she worked in Germany was that she saved loads of money on buckets of throat lozenges!

Barry, his face not a dissimilar colour to the two glasses of fresh tomato juice we'd poured ourselves, looked as though he were about to drop his tray.

'It's my fault, Ooffey,' I owned up, 'but we both get hungry at bedtime.'

Ooffey regained her composure first. She smiled. 'I won't say anything,' she said, 'but you must not do it again. Emmi will not be so kind as me. You can take some food to your room after supper. Then Emmi can see what you do. But first I speak to her.'

Dear Ooffey. She didn't have any children; I don't think she had ever married, but she treated us like the naughty children we were, without reporting us.

We trotted back to our rooms with our bounty and had the best midnight feast. Just like the ones I used to read about at Mallory Towers. (Enid Blyton *The Naughtiest Girl in the School*, in case you've forgotten.) Funny how dreams can come true in the oddest places at the oddest times. Funny how thoughts come to you as well.

'There's just one thing that's bothering me, Barry... What do you think *Ooffey* was doing up at this time of the night? Just a thought.'

CHAPTER 17
CULTURE VULTURES

EVENINGS WERE PRETTY quiet at Tannerhof. Dull, some people would describe them as. There wasn't much laid on for the guests at Tannerhof in the evenings, though we did have a Bavarian dancing class once a week where usually only one man would turn up and, needless to say, would be extremely popular. Although we were only in our twenties, we were so dead tired after a long physical day that we couldn't have coped with too much excitement. We had the *Heuboden* just a few minutes' walk from the sanatorium with the wonderful Duo Bavaria playing most nights: well we thought they were wonderful at the time – we probably wouldn't give them the time of day now, but in 1973 they seemed quite virile in their *Lederhosen* and certainly worth flirting with. But even *we* knew that to spend an evening at the *Heuboden,* though great fun, was hardly an evening of culture.

We would normally go on a Saturday night, which was a particular treat if we didn't have to work the next day. Remember, we foreigners were working six days a week, and only had one weekend off once a month, which didn't always correspond with each other's free weekends. And after our day at work we were on our knees and the last thing we wanted was to be twirled around by a hefty Bavarian. (*You* should be so lucky, I am thinking as I type this many years later on the last day of my fifties.)

Once a week, however, Maria, the head waitress, would see to it that we tasted a bit of the classical world, as opposed to our obsession with tasting food, and she would put a notice on the board in the reception hall to announce the composer she had chosen for that week.

Maria and I had already discussed our love of music and we particularly liked the piano, so it was no surprise to me to see 'Beethoven, *heute Abend*' scrawled in her large handwriting, when I came back from a healthy walk to the village one afternoon, not along after my arrival.

'*Wunderbar*,' I said to Maria as she was setting out the cups and plates for the evening meal. Her stern features softened into a wide smile.

'*Kommen Sie heute Abend*, Denise?' she inquired.

'*Ja*,' said I in my brilliant German. '*Ich liebe* Beethoven.'

'*Gut*,' said Maria as she bustled away to get the cutlery this time.

These musical evenings were very relaxing and I always treated them as a proper evening out. On this occasion I changed into a pair of black crepe trousers and a red V-necked sweater and arrived in the Fasting Room at about twenty past seven. All the tables had been cleared to one side and rows of chairs had been set out, concert style, for the musical soirée. Maria was choosing the record from a huge stack, and she pounced on Beethoven's Moonlight Sonata.

'*Meine Liebste*,' she said, her eyes dreamy. (My favourite.)

Some of the guests began to arrive, and I was pleased I had made an effort as they all looked very smart in their pleated skirts and silk shirts. I was the only female in trousers, I realised, but that sort of thing never bothers me. As far as I can remember, very few men ever appeared for the music night, and in fact there were very few male guests anyway in those days.

We all took our places, some of the women greeting one another even though they had just eaten supper together, and Maria started the record-player. Beethoven's silky notes poured over my tired brain and I closed my eyes and gave myself up to him. No-one cleared her throat or coughed. We could have been in a concert hall in Munich, we were so reverential. The music took me in dream-time back to my love affair with Don – the quiet romantic parts perfectly echoing our first magical falling in love, and the dramatic parts where things went wrong, and then the reconciliation at the end, exactly coinciding with the music.

I loved those evenings but Lorraine and Del and Mieke never came to Maria's concerts, although Barry did when he arrived in September, as he was a real classical buff. He had been a ballet dancer as a young teenager and I think had only given it up by the pressure of jeering peers. What a pity – I might have known a professional ballet dancer. He might have been the first male swan in Swan Lake, though rather a chubby swan.

Barry quickly realised that our pocket-money would never cover a grand Munich evening, even though we had planned to go only once a month. And even though we hardly spent a *Pfennig* during the month. When you'd been to all the souvenir shops in Bayrischzell and admired the variety of Bavarian crafts such as embroidered tablecloths, baskets, pottery and leather goods jostling alongside cow bells and little squirly signs carved in wood and painted blue (it's always blue) with either your name on it, or Küche (kitchen) or worse, WC, so you never get muddled as to whether you're going into your bedroom or to the loo, all you needed to spend any money on were a few stamps to remind your friends and relatives that you hadn't actually died, and would they bloody well hurry up and send you a letter so you felt a connexion of sorts with the outside world.

The only real expense we had was at the Café Stumpp and the Café Hubert, the best two cake and coffee places in the village – probably in the world. Every day one of the cafés would beckon us and we would succumb to hot chocolate with whipped cream piled as high as the depth of the mug (there was no low-fat in the seventies, and even if there had been, the hearty Bavarians would have ignored it) and a slice of *Kuchen* the size of a brick. I looked at Barry. He hadn't lost an ounce of weight owing to Emmi taking such a liking to him and feeding him up. And I was so obsessed with food I ate twice what I would have done at home, and the only reason I hadn't ballooned was that I was doing such heavy work and going on daily walks. Also, I erroneously believed that my twice-weekly saunas were sweating away any extra fat that I might have picked up in between each cake-eating session.

'We've got to limit the cafés to once a week,' I told Barry firmly. He looked alarmed.

'That's the only thing that keeps me going every day is the thought of our hot chocolate and cakes. I don't think you understand what hard work it is in the garden.'

'No more hard than the kitchen,' I retorted. 'But at the rate we're going we won't fit into a seat at a concert anyway. We've got to start saving. Trouble is, some of our money will be spent on train fares.'

Trust Barry – he came up with an ingenious idea.

'We get four extra Marks if we miss a meal,' he said. 'So if we stock up on food – except I absolutely refuse to do anymore midnight raids – we can probably save at least three meals a week – that's twelve a month, giving us an extra fifty Marks each.'

That would have equated to an extra £17 – enough to pay for the train fare and a cheap meal standing up at one of the eateries, a glass of wine, coffee, and the entrance to a couple of museums or art galleries. The month's wages would be blown in one go for an opera or the ballet in the evening. It was beginning to look possible.

No-one queried when Barry and I told the kitchen crew at odd times that we would not be eating a meal, and as planned, our meagre wages increased considerably by the end of the first month.

Munich – here we come!

We caught an early train the following Saturday, relishing the feeling of escaping from an institution, however pleasant and safe the environment. Barry was pleased we were on our own so I could give him undivided attention and enjoy his whacky sense of humour, and I was pleased to show off how well I knew Munich. Pride comes before a fall.

Barry wanted to head straight for Marienplatz, which is a lovely square and a good place to begin sightseeing. He was intrigued to learn that serious jousting went on here in medieval times and I glimpsed a far-away expression of knightliness hovering over his pimply face.

'You only want to gawp at the carillon,' I told him.

'What's that?'

'The mechanical figures at the Town Hall. It's probably the biggest tourist attraction in Munich. And that's not just with the foreigners – the Germans are just as keen.' I looked at my watch. 'We've just got time for a coffee, as it starts at eleven.'

Five minutes before time we joined an enormous crowd in front of the New Town Hall, called, in German, the *Neue Rathaus* even though building began as long ago as 1867. The carillon is housed in the tower and everyone was looking up at it expectantly the way the English do when they think they spot a rain-cloud or hear a twin-engine aeroplane swooping above them, but nothing would happen here until precisely 11 o'clock.

And on the dot machinery whirred and mechanical figures performed two dances simultaneously in their Gothic setting. The upper storey represents a tournament held in 1568 for the wedding of Duke William V and Renata of Lorraine, and the lower storey is what is known as the Coopers' Dance commemorating the end of a severe plague that had spread throughout the city in 1515. The figures are quite large; I'm not sure how big but I could see them without binoculars – unusual for me as I normally have the vision of an earthworm. The carillon plays four different Bavarian tunes to the dances and I have to admit, I find it all very fascinating, even now, when I've seen it dozens of times. Barry was suitably impressed.

We spent some thirty minutes in the Cathedral; we admired the Frauenkirche, or Church of our Lady, which I always think is the landmark of Munich (you know you're in Munich when you see those twin towers topped with their green onion domes) and we wandered through the Botanical Gardens wishing we had had the sense to have brought a sandwich so we could have had a free lunch in idyllic surroundings. Then we remembered we were going to the famous *Hofbräuhaus* for an unhealthy German lunch. You have to experience it to know you don't want to bother ever going again.

Smiling *Fräuleins* holding jugs of beer the size of water-butts, half a dozen in each hand, and forcing their bulky frames through the tightly-placed tables, not to mention the smoke, to deliver their wares to equally bulky, sausage-devouring Bavarians. Barry, of course, loved every hot stifling minute. He was riveted to the nearest folk band to us. It was not terribly good but he had no comparisons. There were several bands going at the same time, but no-one was listening as everyone was busy shouting to each another.

'Isn't this great?' Barry turned to me but his words danced with the smoke in the air.

'What?'

'Isn't it great!' he shouted.

'It's hardly the culture we've come for.' But Barry chose not to hear me.

I finally managed to drag him away from the cacophony and got him, unprotesting, into one of the museums (I forget which), but most of the afternoon we were captivated with the Residenz. This was originally the residence of the Wittelsbach family and the whole area contains several buildings from the fourteenth to nineteenth century, all belonging to the same family. The district is a riot of baroque, rococo and neo-classical, yet somehow it all lives happily together under the name of Renaissance art and architecture.

I think we saw the ballet at the theatre in the Residenz. It's called the Cuvilliés Theatre and it must have been recently refurbished, because we apparently went on the very first night it was re-opened to the public. But we got to it in rather a roundabout way. At first, we tried to show our tickets in a completely wrong building a block or so away. We took no notice of the doorman shaking his head and pushed through into a room that didn't look very theatre-like. It was more like a cinema, and in fact, someone was showing slides of what appeared to be an expedition in Iceland! Of course that set Barry off giggling as he grabbed my raincoat and got us out.

After one or two more false starts we finally got to the right place, and very grand it was too. Too grand for the likes of two foreign workers whose status was probably below that of a student. But unfazed we bought our tickets for the expensive stalls to the surprise of the ticket man. Not that we looked that bad but we didn't compare with the rest of the audience who were draped in furs and jewels – and that was just the men.

'I need to hand in my raincoat,' I said to Barry.

'Oh, here's the cloakroom.'

A woman, at least six feet tall and elegantly dressed in the black uniform of the theatre staff, looked in horror at my offering. Okay, my raincoat was black plastic, which had been all the rage in the sixties, but I didn't see why I should give it to Oxfam just because it was no longer *de rigueur*. And anyway, that didn't justify her taking it from me between thumb and forefinger and holding it away from her skinny body as though it were contaminated with nuclear fall-out. With a curl of her perfectly painted top lip, she hung it right at the end of the row of minks and sables.

'At least she'll find mine first after the ballet ends,' I said to Barry, who was trying to pretend he wasn't with me.

The interior of the theatre was dazzling. There were several tiers of boxes – oh, to be in one of those – with gold swags on a gold background defining the different levels. What looked like red velvet dressed the inside of the individual boxes, which in turn matched the red velvet seats we were sitting on in the stalls. A myriad chandeliers lit up this magnificent room as though it were a palace, and we would just say today: 'Wow!'

The programme was in four parts – two classical and two modern ballets. The first one was my favourite: La Dame aux Camelias, and Chopin's music played all the way through. I was in heaven, and glancing at Barry, I could tell he was totally absorbed. In the interval we had to keep in our seats as we couldn't afford a drink, but it didn't bother us. We couldn't run to a programme either but I do remember how much we enjoyed the modern sections (to my surprise) and after the finale came out of the theatre on a high.

'I bet we appreciated it more than anyone else,' Barry said. 'You can see they've all got pots of money and this is a normal evening to them.'

I had to agree. 'But I also bet they'd rather be them, and that they're willing to sacrifice the fact that they may not appreciate it as much as us. And they're thankful that none of them owns a black plastic raincoat.'

We got back to Tannerhof very late, and for once I was glad that I didn't live in the main house like Del and Lorraine and Mieke, as the door would have been firmly locked. Our *Gochel-Hütte*, on the other hand, was open to all.

'Do you want to come in for a few minutes?' I asked Barry. 'I'm really tired but you can talk to me while I get undressed.'

I felt quite safe saying this as my room was like the black-out when I pulled the heavy curtains across.

I began to get undressed in this pitch dark, all the while chatting to Barry when suddenly his voice broke in, rather apologetically:

'Denny, my eyes are starting to get used to the dark!'

CHAPTER 18
PRINCESS ANNE GETS MARRIED

THERE WAS GREAT excitement at Tannerhof. A hundred chairs were crammed into the Fasting Room where a television had been specially brought in for the occasion and placed on the shallow platform alongside the record-player that Maria lovingly dusted each day. It was the 14th November and Princess Anne was getting married to the dashing Mark Phillips, a lieutenant in the Army. I was surprised that the Germans were taking this much interest, but staff and guests alike were taking their seats well before the service started, which was 11 o'clock.

I was delighted as I'd resigned myself to the fact that being in Germany, and on duty, I wouldn't be able to see the wedding, and of course in those days, you couldn't ask anyone to record it. All we knew was that it was to be very special and that Princess Anne was to wear a beautiful dress, pre-hyping the later wedding of Prince Charles and Lady Diana Spencer.

'Denise,' said Frau Cygan that morning. 'You may go today early to see your royal wedding.'

So here I was, being ushered into a front seat, no less, by Frau Mengershausen, who was sporting a new navy-blue dirndl with crisp white apron. There was no sign of Del or Mieke or Barry, which seemed a shame considering it was our royal family.

'Come, Denise, you are English, so you must have a front seat.'

Everyone smiled and nodded at my hesitancy, and I thought how kind they were to give me the 'best' seat; I certainly needed it with my shortsighted eye, which did its utmost to compensate my other longsighted eye, as the TVs in those days were never more than fourteen inches across. Miracle of miracles, this was a colour job. Right before eleven, those of us at Tannerhof, both workers and patients who could get away for a half-hour or so, were seated, and after many affectionate greetings (though some of them had been together for several hours that morning), they fell silent in the darkened room, watching the gathering crowds. The day had been declared a national holiday in England, which brought even more people out on the streets. Then the TV cameras panned onto Westminster Abbey and we saw the family arriving, the women, including the Queen, beautifully hatted and jewelled.

When Anne finally appeared just late enough to keep everyone guessing, our little audience murmured appreciatively. Her dress really was gorgeous. It was off-white (or appeared to be on German television) and designed and embroidered in Tudor style, with choker neckline and long mediaeval-styled sleeves. Her hair was swept off her forehead in a queenly style and she wore a crown of pearls with a long white veil drawn mysteriously over her face. Lieutenant Phillips, not to be outdone, was in the full scarlet and blue uniform of his regiment, his new mum-in-law's Dragoon Guards. Princess Anne had chosen her nine-year-old cousin, Lady Sarah Armstrong-Jones, daughter of Princess Margaret, to be her bridesmaid, together with her youngest brother of the same age, Prince Edward, to be her pageboy, and they both behaved impeccably, which was a bit of a bore as I love it when something goes wrong at weddings.

I took a sneaky look round in the gloom, interested to note how everyone was taking it all in. Most of the patients had quite a good knowledge of English, but the lack of it didn't seem to impair the enjoyment of the staff who were following everything very closely.

After signing, the newly-weds walked down the aisle, the unveiled Anne glowing as she held onto her new husband's arm, may I say, quite possessively. I noticed her looking at him, but Mark had his eyes fixed in front, though he was smiling. If he was camera shy, he'd have to get over it pretty quickly. He wasn't going to be out of the limelight much from now on.

Hundreds of people had camped out in the Mall the previous evening, but although they must have spent the most miserable cold night, they laughed and waved and cheered as though they had just stepped out of their own houses when the horse-drawn carriage came in sight. I wanted to give the happy couple a cheer as well, but I thought it might be going a bit far. Imagine my surprise when later the two of them appeared on the balcony at Buckingham Palace and the Germans around me clapped. I had to admit, it did give me a nice feeling that they were sharing this special English moment. The British are so good at these kinds of spectacles.

I seem to remember that the ceremony went on for hours. In the end, I knew I had to leave so that I could help get lunch, but I don't think I missed much. It was a day to remember, a wedding no-one would have ever thought would end in divorce sixteen years later. Looking back, I suppose Anne's was one of the longer royal marriages!

CHAPTER 19
HERMAN PART 2

My romance with Herman was developing fast. Even Anita began to tease me when she saw me go red as he greeted me on his way for his daily walk. I still wasn't in love – in fact, I was waiting for it to happen. Waiting for the magic I'd had with Don. It eluded me, but somehow it didn't matter. I was quite content. I knew he wouldn't want to lose me, though we were no further than lovers. No questions, no answers, no commitments.

'Come to Munich when you can get away,' he said. 'Come for ze weekend.'

I only had one weekend free a month, but I soon got into the habit of spending them with Herman. Besides, it wasn't long before he had another three-week stint at Tannerhof. The summer flew by in a frenzy of work. Then a nip in the air. Goodness, it was already autumn. I hadn't heard from Don since my birthday, except a post-card, but that was probably because I'd told him I'd met someone else. Don had always shied away from any commitments, and I couldn't trust him where women were concerned, so I suppose at twenty-eight I felt it was time to settle down with someone who genuinely put me first. And I'd made that person Herman. It sounds so unemotional as I write this, but it didn't seem so at the time.

But with the first snowfall in November, I began to think when, oh, when, will he ask me to marry him?

Christmas was approaching fast and Herman took me to his house the week before, saying he had a surprise for me. I was ordered to stand in the hall until he called me in, and then… my first Christmas tree with lighted candles. Against the darkened windowpane, the flames looked like flickering stars. Herman laughed at my expression.

'I know you are not allowed in England,' he said, 'but if we Germans are told zat we cannot have real lit candles on our trees at Christmas, zere will be a revolution!'

How romantic. And hardly impaired by the present he made me unwrap, which turned out to be a large no-nonsense hard-backed German/English dictionary.

'So you can learn *gut* German,' he smiled, pressing it in my hands. When I'd finished kissing him for giving me such a lovely practical present (I wonder if he'd be gratified to learn that some thirty years later, I've had his present constantly by my side to remind me of certain German words I've needed whilst writing this book), we went out for supper and spent the weekend together at his house, as usual.

'I'll ring you in a few days,' Herman promised.

And he did. Two days before Christmas. Maria handed me the receiver in the hallway.

'I am having Christmas wiz *Mutti*,' he announced, 'and after I go skiing wiz my friends until New Year.' (No mention of any invitation for *me*.)

'Herman,' I said, very slowly and clearly, 'are you saying that you won't be spending Christmas or New Year with me? That you'll be spending it with your *mother*?'

'I have to tell you, Denise…' (I loved the way he pronounced my name) '…I am looking to get married. I sink you are ze one.'

Bloody hell, he's proposing to me!

'I sink you are ze one, but I am wrong.'

Wrong? What's he on about?

'We have to stop seeing us.'

What?

'You have been to my house many times now – and you stay…'

Yes, yes…

'And you never do any help.'

'What on earth do you mean?' I finally squeaked.

'You let me do all ze work – cooking, cleaning, make bed… everysing. I want a wife for zat.'

No time ever had Herman hinted he was displeased with our relationship. My grip on the phone tightened.

'But if you came to *my* house, I wouldn't expect *you* to start vacuuming. You'd be my guest.'

'I need a *Frau* to do zis work. And you will never be a good *Hausfrau*.'

Why was his accent starting to irritate me?

'Do you know, Herman, you're absolutely right. As always. I would *never* make a good *Hausfrau*… and do you know something… crazy though it might sound… I don't *want* to be one.'

'As you like,' Herman replied stiffly.

'Goodbye, Herman.' And I slammed the phone down.

Back in my room, I burst into tears, and sobbed for the next hour. All my plans down the pan, even though at the back of my mind I knew I had never been in love with Herman, and there were times when his German-ness got on my wick. It was a pride thing, plus the fact that I would never have had to worry about money, unlike with my first (American) husband, Lonnie, when we were so poor in Denver that we lived on chicken wings and livers and jam sandwiches for a year, until he was finally promoted by the US Air Force to Sergeant.

Still snivelling, I answered a knock at the door. It was Del. She looked askance at my swollen face. 'What on earth is up with you?'

'He wasn't right for you,' she said, when I had poured out my pathetic story. 'Much too old, and no sense of humour. You'd have been bored sick after a year, and worn out with all that Haus-frauing.' I had to smile. 'Come on, get your face washed, make up, posh frock – we're going out dancing.'

'I couldn't possibly.'

'See you in half an hour,' was Del's parting shot. When Del made a decision, you had to go along with her. I was ready just as she banged on the door.

'That's better,' she said approvingly.

The barn was packed. The Duo Bavaria were playing guitars and slapping their leather thighs, and shouting commands for some fancy footwork from the crowd who were already dancing. Del and I strolled towards the bar for a drink but I didn't get far. The most heart-stoppingly handsome man barred my way.

'I wish very much for you to dance with me.'

Without waiting for a reply, he took my arm and led me onto the dance floor. Christian was tall, muscularly built, and young, with thick hair, the colour of nutmeg, and Paul Newman eyes. He was a skiing instructor from Austria. We danced every dance for the rest of the evening, and I was amused to see Del whirling round, giving me a wink and a nod of her head in Christian's direction.

I was gratified to learn that he hated Wagner, and couldn't resist telling him Herman's opinion on the subject. He just laughed and said that was typical of a German. I was feeling better by the minute.

What fun the next day to have my own personal ski-instructor. Up until then, I had been a poor skier, but it's amazing how quickly I improved under Christian's direction. I won't go into detail – only tell you that his hair stayed fresh and crisp at all times!

Chapter 20
Mince-pies and Mayhem

December. I wasn't feeling very Christmassy even though I hadn't, as yet, been dumped by Herman. Barry had already told me he was going home in time for Christmas, but I thought I could persuade him to stay on.

'It will be so different from the States,' I tried to tempt him, as we sat in my room one afternoon drinking fennel tea, the sweet aniseedy smell reminding me of when I used to buy ten aniseed balls for a penny at the corner tuck-shop on the way home from school. Barry was as usual pulling a face, but he knew it was all there was on offer. 'Probably your only chance to experience a German Christmas.' Not that I had much idea what a German Christmas would be like.

'I really want to be with the family,' Barry said, running his hand through his thatch of hair, 'and I've already booked my ticket. Anyway, there's not a lot to garden at the moment.'

We looked out the window and I had to agree. The Snow Queen would have felt right at home.

As I waved him goodbye at Bayrischzell station, I had that same feeling of isolation I'd had when Carole left. Yes, I had Del and Mieke still, though Lorraine had already gone back to England and, of course, Gisela, but Barry was almost family. It made me think of Mum spending Christmas on her own, with both daughters living abroad. Luckily, she had the Honourable Stewarts to cook for (Mr Stewart being the cousin of Lord Callaghan) and they thought the world of her.

'You stay and enjoy Christmas in Germany,' Mum had written, so there was no need to feel guilty. Yet I had to admit I was suffering from plain old homesickness.

I didn't get upset for long – as usual, I am a bit of an 'out of sight, out of mind' person, and it was only a matter of hours before I was swept up in the preparations for Christmas at Tannerhof. A German-style Christmas is completely different from an English one. Traditions are upheld, religion is in the foreground, and good, but not over-indulgent food around the family table is much more important than loads of presents. The majority of Bavarians are devout Catholics and very serious about the meaning of Christmas so even though I've never been religious, I felt myself growing more divine by the day, enfolded in the reverential arms of Tannerhof.

We were open to guests over the whole holiday, including New Year. At first I was puzzled. Why would anyone want to enter into the strict regime of a health clinic at this time of year? But I suppose it stopped any temptation to binge, and a guest who was on her own (as most of them were) would be in like-minded company and made to feel part of the family.

Preparations began in the kitchen at the beginning of December. I watched Emmi roll out a lump of dough as big as a football onto a floury board, her hands in rhythmic motion, knuckles tight over the rolling pin, as though she was rocking a tetchy baby in a pram.

'*Was machst Du*, Emmi?' I asked. (What are you making?)

'*Stollen*,' Emmi replied with a rare smile, lighting up her fair blunt features.

I had never heard the word so Emmi explained that it was their traditional Christmas cake made with yeast, and raisins and almonds. The almonds are made into a soft, buttery marzipan filling, flavoured with one of my favourite spices, cardomom, a capsule that comes from a tropical plant of the ginger family, but is more subtle. This mixture is spread onto the dough and is rolled up, strudel style. You can, of course, buy *Stollen* in this country now, as you can *Pannetone*, the Italian Christmas cake, but there is nothing in the world that smells and tastes like home-made *Stollen*, or to be precise – Emmi's *Stollen*.

But… *but*… they didn't have mince pies. Had never heard of them when I discreetly enquired. I was determined to make some for our Christmas Eve gathering, and to do them from scratch. That meant home-made mincemeat. I got Mum to send me a suet-free recipé, which looked a bit boring when it came a few days later. No booze, and not a great variety of dried fruit. So I decided to create my own recipé. In the early days, Frau Cygan and Emmi would never have allowed me to start preparing anything without checking, but they were used to me by now and so long as there was nothing urgent to do, I had a certain amount of leeway. No-one even bothered to ask what I was up to – they were too busy with all the extra baking.

I mixed the dried fruit and the other ingredients together in a shining stainless steel bowl, but my secret ingredient was brandy, which I had sneaked from an obscure cupboard – amazed that they should even have any alcohol in the kitchen. Certainly, the guests were not allowed to bring wine onto the premises – I doubt whether it would have even crossed their minds. Again, this is so different from an English health farm, where if wine was not on the menu, the guests (usually the women) would smuggle it in, and the management would turn a commercial blind eye. I vaguely wondered if I'd get into trouble if they found out what I was pouring into my bowl, but what the heck…it *was* Christmas!

Every day, after lunch, when only long-suffering Suna was still around washing the pans next door, I would add some more brandy, and stir the gooey mixture. My mother always used to stir her mincemeat every day and make a wish but even though she was a marvellous cook, her mixture didn't smell quite so interesting as mine! Mine was beginning to smell delicious. And it wasn't just the spices.

That day, I cautiously lifted the lid and was nearly knocked backwards by the boozy blast. Without giving it the lucky stir, I clamped down the lid, and looked round guiltily, to see if anyone had caught a whiff. But Emmi was immersed in her *Stollen*, Anita was sniffing a saucepan of fresh-flowered camomile tea (before I came to Tannerhof, I used to make up this concoction to use as a final rinse when I shampooed my hair to bring out any blonde highlights lurking – I never realised people actually *drank* the stuff!), and Frau Cygan was tasting her celeriac and potato soup. And not in the way that I have seen in kitchens of English restaurants either, where the cook puts a wooden spoon in the saucepan, slurps a mouthful, and puts the same spoon back in the saucepan to stir it… ugh! No, at Tannerhof, and I suspect elsewhere in German kitchens, we used two spoons – one to dip into the pan, and that, in turn, was transferred to a smaller spoon that was used for tasting. Anyway, everyone was busy. I decided to let it all marinate for the next few days until Christmas Eve.

Frau Weilland and her team were busy in one of the dining rooms making beautiful table decorations. They seemed to be enjoying themselves in a Germanic way, Frau Weilland's rabbit teeth digging into her lower lip as she concentrated on the bits of greenery and pine cones, which weren't behaving *quite* as they ought. Only the odd word broke the silence. But if they'd been a group of English women, there would have been cups of tea, and maybe a sherry, as it *was* the run-up to Christmas, and lots of laughter and chatter and a brief touch of an arm to emphasise a joke. I have to admit, though, that the German ladies' efforts were far more professional and tasteful than you would normally see at home, unless you were in a very posh hotel, which Tannerhof never set out to be. But I couldn't help wondering if we Brits, being more relaxed, enjoyed life more.

The main house began to take on a very festive look with its holly and ivy swags, and even more candles sprinkled around than usual; big thick red ones tucked into bowls of greenery that had been plucked from fir trees graced the window cills of the dining rooms. As usual, this included our dining room. There were candles in the fireplace of the Fasting Room, and even in the treatment rooms. The atmosphere was contagious with everyone smiling and '*Gruss Diching*' each other all over the place.

'*Vorsicht!*' (Out of the way) puffed Herr Koch, almost knocking me over as he and Herr Kruger pushed through the main entrance, grappling with a fir tree as big as the offering Norway sends to Trafalgar Square every year.

I watched as they struggled up the slippery wooden staircase at the end of the hall; slippery because it was so highly polished, and the men's snowy boots made it even more dangerous. The tree was to have pride of place in the Fasting Room where it would take up the whole corner, the uppermost twigs brushing the ceiling.

'Who will decorate the tree, Maria?'

'The family von Mengershausen,' she beamed proudly, as though we were working for the family von Trapp and any moment we would be chorusing 'These are a few of my favourite things.'

'When do they do it?'

'*Weihnachtsabend*, Denise,' said Maria. (Christmas Eve.) 'We will all be together singing carols.'

No time to take a peep in the Fasting Room. I had mince-pies to make. First, the pastry. I was rather nervous. My mother's pastry was so mouth-watering. But then, she'd had years of practice.

I heard her voice saying, *Keep all the utensils cool, and roll out on marble, if possible. Don't handle the pastry too much and let it rest an hour or two in the fridge before rolling it out.*

Mum, you'd be proud of me, I thought, as I admired my flattened dough. I found a glass the right size to cut out the bottom of the pies, and a smaller one for the lids. Now for the filling. I gingerly lifted the top off my precious mincemeat. Mmmm. Wonderful. I thought I saw Emmi's nose twitch but she didn't glance my way. I must have put together over a hundred mince-pies, spooning in the rich concoction that was bursting with dried apricots, figs and nuts as well as the traditional currants, sultanas and peel. A brush of milk and egg-yolk, and into the hot oven they went.

Perfect. I carefully edged the trays out, one by one, and laid each pie on a rack so the air could circulate and the pastry wouldn't become soggy. When they were cool, I tucked a teaspoon of brandy butter under each pastry lid and sifted a little icing sugar over each one from the packet Mum had sent me. 'Killer-white' just wouldn't have been considered at Tannerhof.

One moment I was on my own, the next, Emmi, Anita and Frau Cygan had gathered round the table like preyful birds eyeing this crazy English girl.

'Special English Christmas pies,' I explained. '*Für heute Abend.*' (For this evening.) Oh, dear, they all looked very serious.

Then Frau Cygan said, 'So that is where the brandy went.'

I'm in trouble now.

'Did you think we didn't know, Denise?' Anita said, looking at me and grinning.

I smiled back, with relief. Anita was looking particularly well though she was putting on the pudding, as my aunt would have said. I suddenly realised that she was pregnant. Do I make a comment? What would become of her? Was the father going to marry her? Would she lose her job? A single mother in the seventies was still frowned upon. Anita saw my expression and grinned again, pointing to her stomach.

'It's okay, Denise,' she said. 'All is okay.'

And so it was. The father didn't marry her – in fact, I never heard him mentioned – but Anita was allowed to bring her baby into the kitchen where he lay in his cot, good as gold, while she carried on working exactly as before.

But I'm getting ahead of myself, so back to the Christmas preparations.

Supper was a fabulous affair. Traudl had told me that Christmas Eve was even more important than Christmas Day itself. We all sat at tables that had been dressed with beautifully embroidered cloths, lighted candles, and hand-made decorations –and were those actually *wine* glasses?

I can't remember a single dish we ate that night – but it was all scrumptious. I had decided to keep my pies until later in the evening when we gathered for the carol singing. After clearing away the kitchen, of course.

An hour after supper, Del and Mieke put their heads round the kitchen door.

'Need any help?'

'No, we've just finished, but I bet Suna hasn't.'

We trooped into the scullery. Sure enough, there she was – her back, as usual, hunched over the sink. Dear Suna, she was so pleased to see us. Minutes later, we were marching her out, and untying her apron for her as she ambled along the hall, and puffed up the stairs to the Fasting Room. The waitresses and I each took a tray of mince-pies ready to pass round to the guests and staff.

Normally, the Fasting Room was dead quiet. Guests who were consigned there had no energy for normal human activities such as movement and speech. Any stirring of life they might have had was conserved until their trays of vegetable juices and hedgerow teas were delivered a few times a day. But now, it was a-buzz. The room was straight off a Victorian Christmas card. In the corner, stretched to the ceiling, branches bent under the weight of a myriad lighted candles and waxy-red apples tied onto the fronds in between, was the most beautiful tree I had ever set eyes on. No other decoration. But that was all it needed.

Why do the English decorate their trees with such tat? Tinsel and cheap glass balls, and plastic fairies with horrid silver wings falling forward at unnatural angles. Not only did this tree look stunning, it wafted the freshest smell of pine, which made you feel you were outside with nature. But no-one was paying it the least bit of attention. They obviously took it all for granted. Everyone was chatting and smiling, but there were no shrieks of laughter. Frau Mengershausen, looking very Tyrolean in her dirndl, was standing by the door as the guests and staff came in, greeting us all. The female workers had followed her cue and were dressed in their Sunday dirndls – pity they hadn't put on a touch of make-up. It would have made all the difference in the glamour department.

Maria and Mena began to hand round my pies. I could hear various guests asking what they were, and I was amused to hear the waitresses explain that they were traditional in England at Christmas, and that Denis-e had made them only that morning. Little did they realise how long I'd been working on them! I saw an eyebrow raise here, and a thoughtful bite there – surely they couldn't *not* like them? A flash of surprise, another more lingering bite, then a wider-than-usual smile, and suddenly exclamations of, '*Köstlich*, Denise, *köstlich.*' The room hummed as second and even third pies were devoured. Someone laughed quite heartily, and another joined in. Gisela's eyes were dancing.

'I think your pies have crossed the barrier between the English and the Germans,' she laughed. Being half German and half Dutch, she could get away with those kinds of remarks.

After a half an hour or so, Frau Mengershausen, along with her entourage, began to position a few dozen straight-backed chairs around the fireplace in the semi-circle of a classical Greek theatre. I was pleased to see her guitar slumped against one of the chairs as that meant carol singing. I had tried to learn some carols in German over the last few days, and was quite proud of my progress, but it might be a different matter when I had to put the foreign words to music.

We began with '*O Tannenbaum*.' (Oh, fir tree – it doesn't have quite the same ring in English, does it?) I read an article recently about a traditional Bavarian Christmas, and the author said that this is often the first song a German child is taught, with Silent Night being close on its heels. Imagine that happening in England.

The singing was sensational. They sounded as though they had been practising for weeks, they were so harmonious. And '*Stille Nacht, Heilige Nacht*' (Silent Night, Holy Night) made an orgasmic shiver travel over my entire body and scalp.

'*Noch einmal*,' I pleaded. (One more time.) Frau Mengershausen looked up at me, and her still-pretty face broke into a smile. She began softly strumming, and the guests melded their voices with hers. You may have always thought (like me) that German is a harsh gutteral-sounding language, so nothing prepares you for such a pure and beautiful sound.

Too soon, the carol singing came to an end, and guests who, let's face it, were not used to the luxury of eating pastry at Tannerhof, as they had done in the pie sampling, trundled off to bed, tired but very happy. We helped to tidy up the room, which didn't need a lot of attention with such clean and tidy people.

By this time, it was getting on for eleven o'clock, and I heard Mena tell Maria that they should start getting ready to go to Midnight Mass. That sounded like a nice idea to we English girls, even though I don't think any of us were Catholic, but first I wanted them to come to my room to see my own *Tannenbaum*, which Herman had inspired me to put up. I made them stand outside my door, just as he had, until I had gone in and lit the candles, and then they were allowed to come in.

'It's lovely!' they cooed.

'Well, enjoy it,' I told them. 'You won't ever see anything like it in England.'

We quickly downed a dandelion coffee, and then bundled ourselves up in thick coats and scarves, ready for the walk down the hill to the village.

Bayrischzell church looked like a diminutive Ludvig II's castle under its mantle of snow as we crunched up the path to the main door. Inside, where rococo almost knocked you over, shining angels, lit by dozens of candles, greeted us; a crib, hand-made and about half life-size, took pride of place at the side of the altar, and expensively-dressed people, many swathed in furs (and that was just the men) were already streaming into the pews. Although we couldn't understand much of the sermon, it was all rather uplifting, and we managed to join in with one or two of the carols that we'd just 'rehearsed' at Tannerhof. Then, after the final tingly 'Silent Night', we stretched our cramped legs, and made our way through the crowds, calling out *Schöne Weihnachten,*' like we'd lived there all our lives.

It was half-past midnight. We were in a fuzzy Christmassy stupor from all the extra carbohydrates, the wine which we weren't used to, and the heady spiritual stuff of the Midnight Mass. Nothing prepared us for our arrival back at the ranch.

'Come in for a night-cap,' I urged. 'I pinched the last of the brandy specially for this occasion.'

I opened my door. Froze. Del was behind me.

'What's the matter?' she said. 'Oh, my God!'

A flame was just caressing the edge of one of the curtains. Even as we stood – gaping – it flared in a whoooosh.

'WATER!' I screamed. 'Someone get some water!'

As there was no sink in my room, Del rushed out to the communal washbasin and flew back with a bowl. She leaned over to fling the water over the fire, and at the same time a lock of her long blonde hair swung across the burning red heating element that I had carelessly placed across the top of my electric travel jug – much too near the curtains – and had stupidly left switched on. A second later... a horrible singeing smell. Del shrieked and we all rushed over to inspect the damage.

'Am I bald?' she demanded.

'Only a small patch,' I assured her. 'There's quite a lot of hair still left. But at least you put the fire out. That's the main thing.'

'No it bloody isn't.' Poor Del was in a bit of shock. She was very proud of her hair. Or rather, she had been.

'Can you imagine what would have happened if we hadn't come back when we *did*?' Mieke was always pessimistic.

'Well, we did,' I replied irritably, knowing that I was responsible for Del's hair going up in smoke, never mind the potential extinction of the sanatorium.

'Even if you had not left the kettle on, Denise, the *Gochel-Hütte* could still catch fire,' said Gisela, pointing to my Christmas tree. Oh, no! I'd forgotten to put out the bloody candles! They were still burning merrily right down in their holders.

Well... I think it's time they passed a law in Germany to stop the dangerous custom of allowing real lighted candles on Christmas trees.

CHAPTER 21
SILVESTER

Silvester

SILVESTER – ISN'T THAT a lovely name for New Year? Germans make quite a fuss of New Year and in 1974 it was no different. Preparations began immediately after the Christmas celebrations, such as more fancy cooking, decorations without looking Christmassy, and a relaxed party atmosphere.

But I decided I wanted my own party as none of we English girls had ever given one.

'I'll do the main part of the food,' I told the others, 'if you could between you do the bread and crackers, and cheese and nuts – that sort of thing. We'll get the men to bring the drinks.' I felt we knew enough men to make it a proper party.

Del invited Dave, an American whom she'd met at the *Heuboden* of all places, and was pretty seriously involved with, and Gisela, of course, invited Parvis. Mieke didn't really know anyone that well so didn't bring anyone. And me... well, Don seemed to be back on the scene after Herman's departure, so I rang him to ask if he would like to come, and was pleased that he said he would be delighted. Good. That meant he hadn't already made any New Year plans with someone else.

I thought we should have a theme for the party, and eventually settled on a Russian evening. Whether I felt like a change after ten months in Germany, I don't remember, but Russia it was. And borscht soup was going on the menu as the *pièce de résistance*. Thirty-two years later, writing this, I can clearly see myself making that soup. What a lot of trouble it was peeling hundreds of beetroots, not to mention making mushroom stock and potato-peel stock. Even now, I can't believe I made stock out of potato peelings. How Russian can one get? And when I'd finished, my hands looked as though I had slit a goat's throat single-handedly. It made not the slightest bit of difference when I scrubbed them, but I couldn't spend any more time on them as there was still loads to do. It was already gone seven and they'd all be here in less than two hours, and I hadn't even had my shower, washed my hair and done all the other things that a woman has to do before her man turns up.

The soup was great... though not the events that followed.

At nine o'clock friends began to arrive with their offerings, all looking very glamorous to welcome in the New Year. It wasn't often we foreign workers got the chance to wear our best evening togs and it was difficult to recognise ourselves out of our overalls.

I was in my usual nervous state with the anticipation of Don coming to my party, and wanting everything to go perfectly. As usual, I hadn't seen him for several months as he'd been quite put out when I'd told him I was dating someone else. And even more galling was that Herman was cultured and had pots of money. That really needled him. I know it sounds as though I treated Don badly but I had a lot of past to forgive and this went only a zillionth of an ounce towards balancing the scales from an episode in Altanta two years before. We had planned a six-month Grand European Tour and were due to set sail from New York to Southampton on the S.S.France – a fabulous traditional old liner that no longer does the Atlantic crossing in such style, but instead was bought up by the Norwegians many years ago, and is probably a *Smörgåsbord* restaurant by now.

Five days prior to embarking, I almost called the whole thing off, not caring that we already had our tickets. A week before we were due to leave, Don said he felt we shouldn't see one another until the day we travelled – that it would be more romantic. I must say, I was surprised, but like an idiot, went along with his suggestion. The following afternoon I needed to ask him where we were going to meet at Atlanta airport, and made the phone call from my desk just before packing up for the day.

'Allo.'

I stared at the receiver in disbelief. A woman? A woman's voice. What the hell was going on? I realised instantly that it was Dalva, a Brazilian woman whom Don had told me about when we'd first met, explaining she was a kind of guru, as she was about 15 years older than him, and extremely cultured and wise. Don admitted he had always been fascinated by her though he assured me there was no need for me to be jealous. Why do men always say that? He said that at the beginning they had had a sexual relationship, but for the last year or two it was just philosophical (!) and no longer physical. And that although he always kept in touch with her, he had told her he'd fallen in love with me, so he hadn't seen her and didn't intend to, since we met. What a lie.

I felt sick and shocked when I heard her voice and without hesitating, I decided to go and find out what Dalva was doing in Don's flat. Mumbling to Haskin, my boss, that I had a headache, I left the office. I don't know how I drove, what with tears pouring down my face, but somehow I got there without causing an accident.

Don's car wasn't in the drive, so I waited a hundred yards or so away. I didn't have long. Twenty minutes later his open top Renault drew up and he got out and went round the other side like the good southern gentleman he was to open the door for Dalva. I gave them time to get indoors, and then I walked up the drive and knocked on the door. Don opened it.

'Denise! What…?'

'Here's your ticket,' I handed it to him. 'I haven't made up my mind whether to go now or not, but even if I do, I don't want to see you around.'

He looked thunderstruck though he quickly recovered and pulled me indoors, attempting to kiss me as though I was just coming to see him on a normal visit. I turned my face away. It was the first time I had ever snubbed him. He pretended not to notice and took me into the sitting room where Dalva was just removing her orange chiffon headscarf to reveal shining raven hair elegantly swept back in a chignon.

'It's Denise,' Don said. 'She's upset and doesn't want to go with me on Saturday.'

Upset! I think I was a little more than upset.

Dalva at once took control of the situation. 'Denise. Don's told me all about you.'

By this time I was in a terrible state, with my weeping eyes, but Dalva simply held out a slim-fingered hand, which shone with jewels.

'I'm so pleased to meet you.'

I couldn't in all honesty bring myself to say the same. Instead, I studied her face. Dark mysterious eyes under thick black lashes, an aquiline nose, and lips not full, but generously wide and smiling at me. Yes, I could see why Don was intrigued. And I didn't doubt for one moment that they were continuing their relationship. Don could never resist a woman, especially one so exotic as Dalva.

'I think you should leave Denise and me on our own, Don,' she said.

'Fine,' Don's voice was heavy with gratitude and he immediately left.

Dalva explained their relationship amazingly in the same way Don had. She said she was passing through Georgia and wanted to take the opportunity to see Don (naturally!). He had told her our plans, of which she entirely approved.

I bit back the words: I don't give a damn if you don't.

But it was when Dalva said, 'Denise, it's you he loves. He never stops talking about you. You must believe it,' that I knew she had won me over. She continued, 'And you must follow your plans. Don talks of Europe with you and he is so happy.'

After a half hour or so, Don came back, looking relieved and pleased that his two women were having a reasonable conversation, and that Dalva's eyes were still intact. Between them, they persuaded me that I should go with Don to England as arranged. I am not sure to this day whether that was a wise decision, but I do know that I couldn't help liking Dalva – she was such a genuinely warm person – and I was very sorry to hear, years ago, that she had gone into hospital at the age of sixty-two for a minor operation and had died on the operating table.

So now you know why Don had to have the rough treatment from me sometimes.

Back to the New Year's party. A knock at the door, and there he stood, outside my funny little wooden room at Tannerhof, a Robert Redford look-a-like, smiling that lop-sided smile, and holding out a beautiful bouquet of roses and a bottle of champagne. Everything was going to be all right.

The party went, as they say, with a swing. Parvis was late, but that was nothing new although I hated to see Gisela anxiously watching the door the moment anyone came in. But when I thought she'd more or less given up hope, he arrived at an hour to midnight, rather flushed, so I suspected he'd already been partying: Gisela immediately sparkled and whether she questioned him or not, I don't know, but they appeared to be getting on rather better than usual.

Del and Dave were obviously hopelessly in love – well, I could see Del was anyway, and hoped Dave felt the same. She'd had a rough time in the past – we'd had some chats and she'd told me things in her life that had gone horribly wrong, and were desperately sad. She deserved some happiness. Unfortunately, it was not to be, but that night, no-one knew what lay in store for her. Thank goodness, none of us do.

Several German friends we'd made at the *Heuboden* (Bayrischzell is too sleepy a little village to break through into any real friendships and the young ones have long gone to Munich to 'get a life') came to the party but I can't remember their names any more. I suppose we were about twenty in total, which was a lot when you think of that many squashed into one modest bedroom. We put the food out on tables in the hall, which thankfully was larger.

Mieke was looking a bit bereft of a partner so I introduced her to Don as she'd only heard about him from me – and that was not usually very complimentary. I thought they would get on okay as Mieke, although very serious, was a clever girl and as we now know of Don with regard to Dalva, he admired and was even a bit in awe of clever women.

Don came over to me after a few minutes and said Mieke was tough going as she was quite shy and didn't seem used to talking to men. That suited me as I wanted his attention all to myself, which he pretty much gave me until five minutes before midnight when we were all asking each other who had the most accurate watch. Mine was always at least twenty minutes fast as I was terrified of over-sleeping when I had to be at work at such a god-awful hour. Gisela's, we decided, was the most accurate as she had to be very careful not to run late with her appointments or it would put out the guests' timetables for the rest of the day. I looked round for Don. Nowhere in sight. 'What a daft time to pick to go to the loo,' I said to no-one in particular, and went outside into the freezing cold air with no coat to look for him.

There he was, snuggled in Mieke's arms, having a pre-New-Year's kiss.

'When you've quite finished,' I said in a voice to match the temperature.

Don had obviously had one too many glasses of champagne and, true to his character, could not resist a green-eyed woman, or a woman with any other coloured eyes for that matter, and Mieke… well, I don't really know what she was thinking, but I suppose she also couldn't resist his charm. I was livid with both of them, but especially with Don, who I felt had ruined what I'd imagined was going to be a special evening.

Don insisted afterwards that Mieke had thrown herself at him.

'It would have been bad manners not to have responded,' he had the nerve to say.

Can you believe the bloke? '*Yes, I can*,' I hear every single woman reading this book saying, or at any rate nodding. But as usual, Don stopped me from acting like a viper and swept me into a magical, tender, full-of-love kiss, which inflamed on the stroke of midnight. *Silvester*… It *is* a lovely name.

Chapter 22
Fasching and Farewell

It was time to start thinking about the future. Like where was I going to be in a month's time? I'd been working at Tannerhof almost a year and I couldn't exist much longer on pocket-money. Besides, Frau Mengershausen had more or less stipulated a year when she had first offered me the job, so I needed to know what I was going to do. I definitely wanted to stay in Germany and find some interesting work, preferably in Munich, but I knew my German wasn't good enough. Take me out of the kitchen and I would flounder.

I asked Frau Mengershausen if she had any ideas. She suggested that I enrol in the *Goethe Institut*, an excellent school where foreigners from any country could learn good German. She meant '*Hoch Deutsch*', 'High German', rather than the Bavarian dialect with its strong accent that is strangely inflected but which I was used to, and indeed, was all I knew. I thought this was a sensible suggestion until I sent away for the brochure and saw the price. There was only enough money in my savings to pay for three months, but I thought that as I had *some* grounding, I would accelerate the process.

The nearest *Goethe Institut* to Bayrischzell was at Kochel-am-See, which was about an hour or so away by bus. I wasted no more time. The new quarter term started at the beginning of March and I would be there. I filled out the application forms, wrote the cheque and waited to hear. But until then, we had *Fasching* to look forward to.

Fasching, the carnival season, comes around every February. It's a time for Germans to really unbutton their *Lederhosen*, if they happen to be Bavarian, and go wild before the serious business of fasting for Lent. Not that many of the Tannerhof guests would notice a lot of difference whether they were fasting for Lent or just on their normal Tannerhof fast.

Fasching can be traced back to ancient Roman festivals where the idea was to wear hideous masks to scare away the evil spirits so as to allow spring to come scampering in – and hot on its heels, an abundance of crops. Also, Saturn, the Roman god of Peace and Plenty, gave everyone the opportunity to be equal, whatever class they happened to be – masters even waited on their slaves. Men dressed as women, and women as men. I wonder if those ancient women who dressed up as men for the carnival ever felt that suddenly the world was opening before them, or they behaved differently – freer and bolder. The *Fasching* Germans in the seventies kept pretty much to the tradition of depicting sinful man as a fool – hence the 'Ship of Fools' – and they portrayed him in an assortment of crazy costumes such as a little tight cap with donkey ears.

Having nothing like this in England, I was fascinated. I'd always wanted to be in Venice in February for their pageant, and apparently *Fasching* did have a Venetian influence, so I was interested to see what people would do in Germany. Maybe *Fasching* was not quite so spectacular and the canals were missing, but it was a lot of fun all the same. It had come at a perfect time so far as I was concerned. The magic of Christmas and the jollity of New Year was over; Barry, Del, Lorraine and Mieke had all left, so I wallowed in another bout of homesickness. Luckily, I still had Gisela, and I'd seen Don since the New Year's party, but my Tannerhof friends were rapidly thinning out.

I knew if I could be beamed over to England and see Mum, and beam on to Georgia to see Carole and her family I would be fine and it wouldn't be long before I'd want to return to Germany. Although Mum missed me, she was happy to know that I was enjoying myself and had made some friends. There was nothing else to entice me home. England is just as grim in February but without the clean snow (snow is always clean in Germany) and without the carnival.

One of my Bavarian dancing partners, Klaus, asked if I had a costume ready for *Fasching*. This was the first I'd heard about it so he tried to explain.

'You must wear a mask, and zen we have laughing.' (Why do Germans always tell you to laugh at the time they consider appropriate? When I hear a German say something like that, I want to laugh at the wrong time, just to see the reaction. You simply cannot laugh to order.) 'I zink zey have a party at Tannerhof, but we could go later and meet some friends for a drink.'

'Sounds fun,' I responded. Maybe with a few young people around me I could laugh to order after all. 'What will you wear?'

'Ah, zat is a secret.' I thought he was going out of his way to be mysterious, but I later learned that you never discussed your costume and mask with anyone. Whether it was bad luck or you just didn't want anyone else to copy you, I never found out.

Yes, Tannerhof did enter into the spirit of *Fasching*. The older women especially became quite animated when they discussed the carnival, and I panicked wondering what I could wear. I hadn't brought anything with me that could possibly do for a fancy dress outfit but there was always my last resort. Whenever I have to go somewhere in costume (and we're talking about in England) and can't come up with an original idea – it happens frequently – I put together a tart's outfit.

No matter how ugly the masks were, I recognised all the Tannerhof staff even before they spoke. Did they stifle a Teutonic giggle? If they did, it was muffled behind their so-called disguises. My first thought was that none of them had chosen very glamorous costumes and masks, except Suna. She had lost some weight and had become a curvaceous Hawaiian woman in a grass skirt with a garland of flowers adorning her neck. Her eye make-up that night was particularly stunning and enhanced her beautiful brown eastern eyes. I noticed what a seductive mouth she had – long and very uptilted at each corner; her glossy fuchsia-pink lipstick showed it off to perfection. In contrast, Herr Koch was a donkey and Herr Kruger a goat, and there was the usual array of witches with noses to make Pinocchio blush.

I knew my outfit wasn't exactly sophisticated or even flattering, but it would have to suffice. Very short bright-red skirt (I rolled one of my old skirts over and over at the waist), thick white sweater that came down almost as far as my skirt, white knee-length boots, cheap earrings culminating in dice that had come from a Christmas cracker, though not a German one, I hasten to add, and which jangled every time I moved (which was quite a lot really), lashings of make-up including lipstick to match my skirt, and a cigarette holder with false cigarette! (Where on earth did I pick up one of those?) I looked exactly like I set out to look – a real Tart. I don't think Tannerhof was quite ready for me! And I'm jolly certain Herman wouldn't have been. He would have been horrified at my outfit as he was so conservative. Perhaps it was just as well he had decided I wasn't wife material. I swiftly ate my supper, enjoying the slightly worried glances from my co-workers (I think they were puzzled as to whether I was in costume or not, and didn't want to make a comment in case it turned out to be one of my regular going-out-in-the-evening get-ups) then I nipped back to my room, waiting for Klaus to collect me.

I laughed aloud. He had come as a very plump Viking, complete with horns. I don't think his outfit was meant to be funny as he looked rather hurt.

'Very manly,' I managed. His hurt changed to disbelief as he took in my outfit for the first time. Maybe I'd gone too far in this well-behaved country.

'Very original,' was all he could come up with. Well, what did I expect? He could hardly say, 'Very feminine', could he? I was ushered out of the *Gochel-Hütte*.

To this day, I don't think his friends appreciated that I was in costume. I really believe they thought Klaus had picked up this English bird, and that was how we normally dressed. I got into my part, swinging myself onto a bar-stool in the *Zur Post*, so my skirt rode right up my thighs, and Klaus and his mates politely looked away. That would never happen in Italy. Or England.

But as the night wore on, and everyone got a few more beers under their belts, the noise level rose, and the waiters began moving tables to make a dance-floor. Klaus whisked me off my pedestal (!) onto the floor and whirled me around and around to the thumpety-thump of the Bavarian band. Goodness me. The Germans were really letting rip!

The following Sunday I unenthusiastically packed, ready to catch the bus the next morning to Kochel-am-See. It felt strange to be leaving. Tannerhof had been my way of life for what seemed much longer than a year, and I knew the experience had changed me. Physically, I looked much better than I ever had before (and since!). My skin, which had looked as rough as a pair of *Lederhosen* when I first arrived, now glowed with youth and health, and I was definitely fitter. Also, I felt that for the first time in my life I belonged.

As I flattened my cheap bits of clothing into my suitcase, I had a moment of panic. Living at Tannerhof was safe. I'd been looked after, was well fed, there were doctors if you were ill (even if it meant taking drops of blue medicine), and so long as you pretty much obeyed the rules and made a real effort with the language, you were accepted. My thoughts were interrupted by a sharp tap at the door. It was Gisela.

'I've come to say goodbye, Denise,' she said, 'as I go early tomorrow to see Parvis. Promise you write.'

I was amazed to see her lovely eyes fill with tears. She'd been a good friend and I swallowed hard, remembering all the laughs we'd had, the dances we'd been to, the lovely massages she'd given me when I'd had a particularly hard day in the kitchen. I hugged her.

'I promise,' I said, meaning, really meaning, to keep my promise. But we lost touch.

Dear Gisela. I often wonder if you ever went through with it. How horrid of Parvis to encourage you to have what would be a major operation and not love you just as you were. But Gisela wasn't always so dear. I found out later that she had made off with Herman the German, but to be fair, I had left Germany by then. And Herman had left me so I suppose she thought he was up for grabs. Well, good luck to her.

It was time for my next adventure at the *Goethe Institut* in Kochel.

'I'll be back as a guest one day,' I told the staff as they waved me goodbye. They just smiled.

PART II

MARCH 1996

Chapter 23
Tannerhof Revisited

I HAD MADE a promise that one day I would return as a guest. They just smiled.

Twenty-three years rolled by. I got hooked up with a couple of exotic boyfriends – well, an Italian, and an Indian – with Don, the American, still making an occasional appearance, so I guess you could loosely class them as exotic. I'd worked at the United Nations in Geneva as secretary to Madame Kyriakopoulos, a French lady married to a Greek, in the Narcotics Department, and I'd been a chauffeuse (we always used the feminine noun in those ancient days of the seventies) to a Swiss multi-millionaire in Zurich. I'd fallen in love with Edward, an Englishman, and married him; changed jobs several dozen times, and finally became an apprentice estate agent (that last one being at my sister's persuasion). After six years, working for others, I had opened my own estate agency and built up a chain of four branches, completed an Honours Degree through the Open University, and decided to live on my own, although Edward and I live very near to one another and remain close friends. And through all of this, at the back of my mind, I knew one day I'd return to Tannerhof.

Then within weeks of going through her second divorce, Carole told me that she had been diagnosed with breast cancer. How can everything be fun, or even just okay, one minute, and turned upside down the next? I was terribly worried.

'You're going to be fine.' I hoped my voice sounded reassuring even though I was quaking inside. 'Look at Mum. She had breast cancer twenty years ago and she's fitter than us. She's always doing her yoga and exercises.'

Carole agreed with all my platitudes, but deep down, we were both scared. Mum had had a mastectomy and I couldn't bear that to happen to Carole. But all went according to her doctor's plan, and she had her operation, which, thank goodness, was 'only' a lumpectomy, and radiotherapy. We were looking forward to seeing her get well again, but a month went by and even with Mum's delicious home-made soups and tempting dishes, she still hadn't regained her appetite. I was worried that she would start losing weight. She'd pick at everything, just like she used to do, Mum said, when she was three years old. Unlike me, who always ate everything on the spoon that I was given. Worse – her old sparkle had all but gone.

'You need a break,' I said one grey evening in early March. 'Fresh air, fresh food, plenty of exercise… I know just the place.'

'Oh, no, not Tannerhof,' she said immediately.

'It's perfect. Just the place to pull you round. Besides – we'll have a laugh. Do us both good. I know *I* need a holiday.' I was on my knees, having opened my fourth estate agency office in Tunbridge Wells on New Year's Day.

'Well, I'm *definitely* not going on the train like we did twenty years ago,' she said.

'Twenty-three,' I corrected. 'I always told them I'd go back as a guest one day, but I didn't think it would be quite this long. The good thing is, it will get me started on my book. You know I've always said I'd write about my year at Tannerhof. This'll be a recce for me, but to do it properly, we *have* to go by train – just like the first time. I was planning to go on my own, so you'll be company and help me remember all the detail.'

Mentioning the proposed book was a good move. Carole had always encouraged me to write it.

'I suppose, if I'm helping you,' she said, 'at least I'll feel I'm doing something. But I'm not going on the train.'

We went by train…

A delightful young man, all smiles, met us at Bayrischzell station, and together with an elderly lady who was also a guest, drove us up the hill to Tannerhof. Carole and I grinned at one another. I knew exactly what she was thinking… the first time we'd arrived, twenty-three years ago almost to the day, Herr Koch had raced round the bends, terrifying us. We had been seriously worried about where on earth we were going. Today, we could relax.

My heart was beating like mad as though I were meeting an old flame (I suppose I was in a way) when I glimpsed Tannerhof again. It's amazing how you can become so attached to a house, like Manderley in *Rebecca*. Except Mrs de Winter's was a fascination mixed with horror. Tannerhof, to me, represented a kind of second family, second home. It's been here all these years, I thought. Welcoming, inspiring, and healing. Staff and guests coming and going, yet I don't suppose much has changed. I have. Twenty-three years of anyone's life would be bound to throw up good and bad, wonderful and terrible, and *my* life was no exception. But Tannerhof remained constant. It was as if the last twenty-three years had suddenly compressed, and it seemed as familiar as though I were here only a month ago.

As soon as we opened the front door, Carole said, 'Oh, it smells just the same.'

The delicious smell of wood, apples and cinnamon. We were back. No sign of Frau Mengershausen. I knew she was still alive and indeed, still in charge, as I'd spoken to her on the phone when I'd first had the idea of going back with Carole. Still no formal reception area either, I was pleased to see. I was steeling myself to note any changes, as I didn't see how they could improve a winning formula. A young housekeeper came to welcome us. So Frau Weilland has gone. But her smile was just as sincere as she said in English:

'Frau Barnes and her sister?'

To our nods of assent, she said, 'I am Annie. Your rooms are ready. I will put flowers in zere soon. Come wiz me, please.'

We followed her up two flights of stairs, and I saw that everything was exactly the same. The same Bavarian-painted wardrobes and doors on the first oak-floored landing, and the rag rugs that Carole so admired, the Fasting Room, though no-one was inside, but it was not quite lunch-time. We were shown rooms 17 and 18 where Del and Lorraine used to live. That felt a bit odd, yet it was comforting and brought me near to Del, in particular. We had remained close friends long after Tannerhof days, and kept in touch through all the years she was married to Dave, her American, when they lived in Delaware (very appropriate, I used to think). She had two children; a boy called Kylan (named after her Bavarian who was so exuberant in his dancing and had smashed her head against the beam) and a little girl called Julie.

There was a sad ending to this idyllic-sounding story. When the children were only seven and five, she brought them back to England to see her mother, who was dying. A week after the funeral she arranged her booking to return to the States, when Dave rang her the day before take-off and announced that he had fallen madly in love with a girl of nineteen. He must have been about forty. He told her it was pointless to come home, and that she should stay in England with the children.

A heartbroken Del went back to the States anyway, leaving the children with her sister, to try to save her marriage. She had told me only a couple of weeks previously that her marriage just got better and better each year and that they were still crazy about each other. A week later she was back in England and had moved to Newcastle, where she had friends. Two years later, at forty-two, she was dead from leukaemia. Dave did at least come to England for the funeral, but it was mainly for the purpose of collecting his children to take them back to the States. I couldn't bring myself to speak to him. And for the children, their mother must be a distant memory. I'd love to see them again and tell them some funny stories about her and bring her alive for them.

Dear Del – I still miss her and her sense of fun and adventure. She would have been intrigued to know that Carole and I were back at Tannerhof, though she never understood why I loved it so much.

Our rooms were charming. No en-suite, though there was a wash-basin and a comfortable bed; a painted wardrobe stood against one wall, and a table and chair by the window, with an easy chair on the other side. Carole and I both opened our doors to our private balcony at exactly the same time.

'Is your room okay?'

'Perfect,' she said. 'Oh, look at that view!'

There was the Wendelstein, my favourite mountain, peering over the tops of its younger and smaller companions – a snow-capped, ragged but dominant outline, berating me: 'It's about time you came back.'

'Something smells good,' Carole sniffed the air. 'What's the time?'

'Time for lunch. Let's go.'

She did a quick lipstick without a mirror – I don't know how she does that – and we trolled downstairs. And noticed the first change. A salad bar where you could help yourself.

'That would have made my life easier,' I said to Carole, 'instead of having to set out hundreds of plates and fill hundreds of teeny jugs…'

'With your famous cardboard dressing.'

A dirndled-waitress led us to our table in the corner. I'd only eaten in one of the guest dining rooms during the first five days when Carole was with me in 1973 so being a real guest was strange and I was determined to make the most of it. Several elderly guests, mostly women, were chatting quietly as they were tucking into their food. We sat on a padded corner seat and took our napkins out of their paper envelopes, with the handwritten 'Frau D Barnes' and 'Frau C Barnes' so they didn't have to launder them every time. When you needed a fresh napkin you left it out of the paper envelope; that was the sign for the waitress to give you a new one.

I looked around. Most of the furniture such as the heavy oak dressers and sideboards were the same, but had they changed the tables and chairs to a lighter wood? I couldn't be sure. All I knew was that the atmosphere was just as I remembered with diners looking relaxed and happy in the gentle daytime candlelight.

We munched our way through some delicious salads generously topped by sprouting alfalfa seeds and pinenuts, and then the waitress brought us our hot meal. I can't remember it in detail, but I know that we polished it off, and she brought us a smaller second helping, and laughed when I said in my best German:

'That would never have happened twenty-three years ago.'

All the staff knew I had worked in the kitchen, and that I was back with my sister who was getting over her operation, and they seemed especially kind, although I noticed they were lovely to all the guests.

Just as we were finishing the fruity yoghurt dessert, Frau Mengershausen came in. Hugs and kisses all round. She looked marvellous; obviously much more lined, but she could not have been far off eighty, and was still attractive and still spoke excellent English.

'I will show you ze changes since you were here, Denise.'

Oh, so there *are* some changes then. She showed us round the kitchen. My *Rohkost* Room had been taken over by the kitchen staff as apparently the rules are that as a kitchen worker in a commercial enterprise, you are now not allowed to eat in the same kitchen. How ridiculous. For what reason? Frau Mengershausen said there were so many rules and regulations from the hygiene people that they now have to conform to, they have had to undergo a lot of expensive alterations. Frau Mengershausen's tone meant 'and most of them needless' as nowhere could have been more hygienic than Tannerhof.

I saw Suna's ghost in the scullery. She would have loved those great big modern shiny sinks that had been installed over the last few years. And there was a man doing the washing up. How sensible. I had been looking forward to seeing Emmi and Anita, as I knew they were both still working in the kitchen, but it was Anita's day off and Emmi only worked once a week to give the main cook the day off. I was surprised to learn that she had got married to someone who looked after the greenhouses.

'Emmi will be in tomorrow,' Frau Mengershausen told me, 'and Anita will be on duty also. Now I must leave you, but I invite you both to come for tea tomorrow afternoon and we can tell ourselves all ze news.'

It was going to seem funny seeing Emmi and Anita again in totally different circumstances. I didn't dare ask about Frau Cygan – she couldn't still be alive.

We decided we should get some air and walk down to the village. The air almost knocked us back, it was so fresh and clean after Tunbridge Wells. Even though there was snow as far as our eyes could see, the sun cheerfully shone and had some real warmth to it, so we didn't feel at all cold. I drove Carole mad calling out, 'Oh, I remember this,' and 'I remember that,' and 'Do you remember that's where we got kitted out with our ski stuff?' Even Carole greeted the

Café Stumpp with a cry of delight, no doubt remembering all the mouth-watering cakes we'd devoured in those first five heady days. Nothing appeared to have altered. Same gift shops, post office up the far end of the village, *Apotheke*, (chemist), bank, church hadn't moved and was still the centrepiece of Bayrischzell…it was all there. We stopped for tea at the *Deutsches Gasthaus*, sitting outside in the sun (imagine doing that in March in England – you'd freeze) and an enormous waitress forced (!) us in a very twinkly, sales-practised way to try the house speciality, *Käse Strudel* with sauce.

'We'll be good from now on,' I said, not being able to resist. 'But this is our first day after a long journey.'

'*Zwei Mal?*' asked our waitress. (For two?)

'*Ja, bitte.*'

'*Sehr gut,*' she replied.

It was a light-as-air sweet quark and raisin strudel with homemade wine-flavoured frothy custard. I can taste it now as I type these words. Never have I tasted any pudding that good. We scraped our plates. Yummy!

'I wish we had a movie camera,' I said to Carole, watching several people, some of them quite elderly, walking and jogging and toting skis. 'It's another world. I wonder why it's taken me so long to come back. And I wouldn't be here now if it hadn't been for you.' I looked at her. I don't know if I was imagining it, but she looked better. And her appetite had certainly made an appearance at lunch. I knew Tannerhof would work its magic.

When we got back from our walk, Annie, the housekeeper took us on a tour over all the new building works that had been going on when I left in 1974. The new building joined the old Tannerhof so you didn't have to get rained or snowed on to get to the fabulous swimming pool and the adjoining showers and changing rooms. Carole is not a keen swimmer, but her main reason is a dislike of being cold. The water was bath temperature when I dipped my hand in. Great. I was determined to get her in.

The sauna was still in the same building but there was one major difference. Although they still segregated the men and the women in the day, in the evenings the notice clearly stated it was mixed! Not for this English gal, it ain't.

We both crashed onto our beds for a late afternoon nap, and didn't wake up until we heard the supper bell. More salads and a variety of cheeses. It's a good thing we're used to eating lots of raw food or we might have found it a bit labour-intensive with all that chewing.

We had an early night in spite of the nap.

'I'm going to try to finish your hat,' Carole said. She had started knitting me another Bavarian hat on the train journey; it had been like *déjà vu* watching her, but I don't think she did more than a couple of rows that evening: I had my book, as usual, but found myself nodding over it and doing that horrible sickly jerk when your brain wants to close down for sleep. It had been quite a day.

Chapter 24
The Floating Man

I COULDN'T PERSUADE Carole to come with me for a 7 am *Wasser Gymnastik,* which is, as the name suggests, exercises in the swimming pool. Eight of us turned up in varying swimsuits hugging varying figures; five women and three men, and a fourth man who was the instructor. The pool was huge, but only 4' 6' deep throughout, which is excellent as I have a phobia about the deep end. Our instructor was a masseur and a big chap who surprisingly got into the water with us. In English spas the instructor stands nice and dry on the edge of the pool, barking orders, if he's a male, and waving his arms and legs in a vague imitation of what he wants us to do under the pressure of water.

I didn't feel all the exercises were as controlled as some English health spas I'd been to, but maybe it was because I misinterpreted some of the things you were supposed to do. Still, I was getting along fine until our instructor told us to take a partner.

The other four women immediately turned to one another, arms outstretched as though they were reaching for lovers, and two of the three men turned reluctantly towards each other, realising that there was no chance of a mixed partnership. Our instructor asked the third man if he would swim across to him so that he could help demonstrate the next exercise. The Third Man (as I was beginning to call him) obediently swam over. He was a hefty chap so a good match for the instructor. At this point I was bobbing about in the water, which was just on the edge of cool, perfectly happy on my own, fascinated to see what the next exercise would be. It was to be one of trust. You had to stand with your back to the other person and he had to push you gently forward and you had to let yourself fall back onto his hands, which would push you forward again.

After the demonstration, it suddenly dawned on The Third Man that I was the odd one out – and a woman, at that. It dawned on me a split second later when I saw him breaking into a grin as he swam towards me. He signalled that I would be the one to be pushed. Why is it always the man who takes over? Doesn't matter whether they are German, British or Chinese; I'm sure it's the same the world over. Why was it not at that point that I said, '*Nein,* I will push *you.*'

Meekly, I got into position, The Third Man behind me, too close for my comfort, but then, I was a nervous inexperienced swimmer, so I wouldn't have liked to think that he might be standing a long way away from me. He couldn't win either way. I was terrified even to *hear* this exercise described, let alone actually do it – falling backwards in water was one of my favourite nightmares – so I turned to face him and tried to let him know in frightened German that I simply could not do this exercise. He sounded concerned.

'*Haben Sie Angst?*' (Are you frightened?)

Yes, I had bloody *Angst* and said, '*Viel Angst.*' What an understatement.

'*Nein, nein,*' and he turned me so I had my back facing him and proceeded to push me forward. In the end I thought, What the hell, if I start drowning, someone's bound to notice…and rescue me. So I let myself go – back and forth, back and forth. It *almost* felt pleasant, but not quite. Presumably that meant that I *almost* trusted him, but not quite. Then we changed over and it was my turn to push him. Unlike me, he lapped it up (the attention, not the pool).

For the next exercise our instructor got hold of my Third Man, laid him horizontally on the water and got both arms under various parts of his body and walked him all around the pool to everyone's admiration, except mine. I wanted to laugh. Until he said, 'Now it is your turn', or German words to that effect. The Third Man swam back to me for the second time: I couldn't believe that I was supposed to float this great hulking German, but he immediately got himself into position for me to float him. I shook my head but he nodded his quite vigorously (his head, that is) and I was forced to carry out the exercise. Actually, because he was overweight, he floated quite nicely, but I did bump him into another man who was floating his partner, but only the once, and I was sure the bruise that erupted on his head would not be long-term. I felt such a fool walking this beafy specimen around the pool and I thought, If Carole comes in and sees this spectacle, we shall both scream and I'll drop him.

Then it was my turn to be floated. I didn't relish an intimate exercise like this, and besides, it was not one that my phobia could cope with, but I was forced to succumb. He put his right hand underneath my neck and shoulders while his left hand gently cupped one of my buttocks. He could easily have placed his hand around the tops of my legs, but once again I thought, What the heck. I'll never see him again. At first I was very tense and he told me to relax. Relax? I tried to let one or two muscles go limp but my buttock remained rigid. The instructor said that if we could *completely* let ourselves go, and give ourselves up to our partners and to the water, it would be a very pleasant sensation, but I never quite reached that peak of ecstasy.

'You should have been there,' I said to Carole over our dandelion coffee break. She was eating a chocolate biscuit the size of a satellite dish and almost choked on one of the hazelnuts as I told her my story. I don't know how she sneaked it in, let alone how she had the nerve to sit at a Tannerhof table and plough through it.

'You're not really a health farm person, are you?'

'Not really,' she said, offering me a chunk. I must say, it was scrummy.

Chapter 25
The Revelation of Saint Hubert

The Wendelstein looked very beautiful the next morning when I opened the French windows onto the balcony that Carole and I shared and stepped out. It rose above all the other mountains, and what with the bright blue sky behind it and the sun pouring over it, I decided we had the two best rooms for the view, and made a note that when I came again, I would request Room 17.

Carole's plimsoles were laid out on top of thick snow that had collected onto the balcony the night before, but there was no other sign of her yet.

Pooh! What on earth's that horrible smell? I thought. Like burning rubber. I must tell someone about it before breakfast.

There was a great change in the breakfast routine. Instead of the müesli being put out in individual bowls at each place setting, there was a buffet outside the kitchen door. The müesli was disappointing; it was sloppy and not at all how I used to make it. Also, it only represented a small part of the meal, whereas in 1973 it was the main part of the breakfast. Everyone ate it unless they were on a fast. This morning, there was a big platter of fresh fruit and several cheeses, but only two kinds of breads, when I was used to seeing a half a dozen. I hoped the standards weren't slipping. Carole said it all looked good to her and to stop comparing.

After breakfast I put my head through the hatch and there were Emmi and Anita looking genuinely pleased to see me. Feeling very strange, I went into the kitchen and gave them both a big hug. How can that length of time fall away when you see people again? They looked exactly the same, just with years of extra lines, so I expect that's how I appeared to them. Emmi wore her neat little white cap, as usual, as she whisked a bowl of eggs, and Anita, going grey at the sides, was busy chopping spring onions.

'*Und Ihre Sohn?*' I asked Anita. (And your son?)

'*Er ist drei und zwanzig.*' (He is twenty-three.)

'*Er war ein Kindlein wann ich habe ihn letzt gesehen.*' (He was a baby when I last saw him.)

Anita's brown eyes crinkled as she laughed, and mimed how tall he was now. Seemed like he was about seven feet.

They were surprised when I handed Emmi a jar of Mum's homemade marmalade, and Anita one of Mum's cakes. I tried to tell them that someone had cooked for *them* for a change.

I asked Emmi if she would make my favourite raisin pudding with wine sauce, but she shook her head, and explained that she wasn't the head cook any longer so didn't have any influence over the menus. She had more or less retired, and just came in when the main cook was off-duty.

I asked Anita if the *Heuboden* was still going, as I thought it would be fun for Carole and me to have an evening or two there.

'*Nein,*' she said. '*Es ist geschlossen.*' (It is closed.)

'*Warum?*' (Why?)

She explained that the owner had had an accident in the mountains one winter's night, about five years ago, and had frozen to death. He'd been discovered half buried in the snow the following morning. No-one had bought the *Heuboden* so it had remained closed. How awful.

Carole and I were bowled over with tiredness after lunch, so we took a nap, then walked to the village. We were admiring some murals on the outside of one of the houses, when the owner came out and spoke to us in English, and described their meanings. After a chat when I told him I was an estate agent and Carole was an interior designer, he said:

'Would you like to see inside?'

Try to stop us!

It was a typical Bavarian house at the posh end of the scale, built of spruce. There were several religious items such as a crucifix, statues and paintings, and some soulful-looking deer faces bolted to one of the living room walls. Why do people who live in mountain regions decorate their rooms with the heads of animals? And often deer. They're not exactly ferocious animals so you couldn't count them as trophies, I wouldn't have thought.

One of the outside house paintings, the owner told us, was of Saint Hubert.

'Saint Hubert had a vision one day when he was out hunting ze deer,' the owner explained now we were indoors. 'He saw ze cross of Jesus between ze antlers' (I don't suppose Saint Hubert was a saint at this point), 'and he realised zat maybe when you look at a live animal, you don't have ze right to kill it.' (Good gracious, what a revelation!) 'Of course, one must still make hunting and shooting' (must one?) 'but at least we don't do it as a joke or a sport or a hobby – we do it because it is necessary, and we have given it some serious thought.'

'I expect the animal feels a whole lot better knowing that it's being killed with serious thought,' I told him, but he chose to ignore my sarcasm.

At this awkward moment his wife and daughter came in and he introduced us; we were soon all nodding and smiling and shaking hands, the family speaking in rapid German, which I couldn't follow. He translated for us that we couldn't go upstairs because his wife was busy moving things. Later, Carole and I wondered what on earth she could be moving, that we weren't allowed to see.

It was time to thank our host (are you a host if you haven't offered your guests anything to drink?) and make our way back to Tannerhof for that cup of tea we were dying for.

Upstairs, I went into Carole's room to ask her something and was nearly knocked back with the same smell I'd smelt on our balcony.

'Whatever is it?' I said, pulling a face. 'It's awful.'

'It's my plimsoles,' she said. 'I've had them outside to air all day, and as soon as I brought them in, they've immediately stunk the place up.'

'How much did you pay for them?'

'£1.99.'

'No wonder. Horrible objects. I hope the stink doesn't waft into *my* room as well.'

The next morning I bumped into my Floating Man and we both gave each other a little knowing smile. He was actually very nice and didn't look quite so plump with his clothes on. I pointed him out to Carole

'You didn't have to tell me, Den. I knew at once who he was.'

After breakfast we came back to our rooms to find the cleaning staff had already been in. Carole looked into my room.

'Oh, Den, was your door opened as well?'

When I said it was, she said, 'Oh, thank goodness. I thought the cleaning lady had left my door open to get rid of the terrible stink of those rubber shoes and I was so embarrassed.'

'Where are the shoes now?'

'I put them out on the balcony again.'

I looked outside. To my horror I saw a little old man, bundled up like a mummy, completely outstretched on *our* sun-bed, with his face, the only part uncovered, turned towards the sun. You could never imagine an Englishman taking a sun bath in the winter with snow all around, but he looked totally relaxed. I looked again. He was too still. Carole's plimsoles were neatly placed just inches away.

'Carole,' I whispered. 'Come here.'

'I didn't know we were sharing the balcony with anyone, but he does look peaceful,' she said, peering through the French windows.

'He's either sound asleep,' I said, 'or he's been poisoned with the stink of your plimsoles. And I'm not going out there to find out!'

Chapter 26
Slip-Sliding

The massages at Tannerhof are so much better than the wimpy ones at home. Following my Floating Man experience, I floated over to the therapy rooms where I had booked a massage, although it was only back and feet. But what a winning combination. Actually, I had put up with a painful shoulder, neck and head for several weeks, and decided that Jurgen, the very same instructor who had taken our swimming pool gymnastics, was just the man to ease away those aching muscles.

He was waiting for me, already dressed in his whites. Now at an English health spa, the masseur would tell you to undress, lie on your back or stomach, and hand you a bath sheet to cover yourself. At this point, they would leave the room so you could carry this out in private. Not Jurgen, nor probably any other German masseur.

'Please to take off all ze clothes.'

'All?'

'All,' he said firmly.

Not only did he stay in the room while I undressed, he didn't even turn his back to me. It felt very weird undressing in front of a strange man who wasn't saying a word, but I bet was thinking: *I love my job.* He must have a hard time trying not to pinch himself in front of all his clients at his good fortune in choosing such a vocation.

'Take a deep breath from here,' and he pointed to his stomach. This was difficult to do as he'd ordered me to lie on my stomach. He pressed a spot on my shoulder and told me to keep breathing deeply and to relax. Aaaaaaaaaagh! How can you relax when there's this spear impaling your skull? He kept pressing with his thumb with no let-up, and by then, he'd pressed through an excruciating pain barrier to a place where there was only numbness. He pressed several more painful spots and I started to perspire. Sometimes I wanted to scream with agony, but mostly I managed to contain myself and merely let out a sob. He took absolutely no notice.

'Please to lie on ze back.'

Breasts were now on full view. What could he be thinking?

'Do you like a blanket?'

I nodded, pretending I was cold. The blanket fell over my breasts and I relaxed a squidgen.

The foot massage was wonderful even though he managed to find all the painful points. He kept up a running conversation, asking me how long I was staying; have I read Goethe – you know, the usual sort of questions one is asked whilst having a massage. Then he said: 'It starts to snow.'

It seemed quite romantic lying on a massage bed with a hunky German manipulating my feet and telling me it was snowing outside, and I decided so far as I was concerned this could go on forever. But after another five minutes he splashed a kind of camphor lotion on my back and feet that now tingled like the rest of my body.

Time to get dressed. I felt terrific, until I slipped on the bare floor with my oily feet.

'Don't rush,' he said, as he watched me desperately try to get my bra on as quickly as I could. Any woman knows that when you're in a hurry, putting a bra on at top speed is all but impossible. First of all, you have to swing it in front of you to hook it up (regardless of how the M & S ladies admonish you and tell you that you are supposed to lean forward and drop your breasts into each cup, whilst at the same time grabbing the two ends behind your back and hooking them onto the appropriate eyes), but with my method, and I suspect most other women's, I had to swivel it round, hoist the straps over my shoulders and hope that each breast was more or less in the place it's supposed to be.

'Don't rush,' Jurgen repeated. 'There is no stress in my room.'

Not much.

He said I should go back to my room to rest, but I couldn't take his advice as Carole and I were due at Frau Mengershausen's in a half an hour.

Frau Mengershausen lived halfway up the side of a mountain. We knew we should have taken walking-sticks when we struggled in the snow and ice to get there, but we arrived safely and Frau Mengershausen gave us a cosy welcome. She had set the table with candles and best tea-set, and the picture window looked like an actual hanging picture of the snow scene outside. We spent a pleasant two hours catching up on all the news over the last twenty-three years. She has certainly been an adventurous lady, back-packing and youth-hostelling her way all over Europe.

It was time to leave.

'I will pack you some *Stollen*,' Frau Mengershausen said. 'I know it is Denise's favourite.'

'Thank you for the delicious tea,' we said, giving her a kiss. 'We'll see you later this evening. Are you going to bring your guitar?'

'Yes,' she smiled. 'And we will all sing folk songs.'

'Isn't she kind?' I said to Carole, keeping the *Stollen* firmly in my grip as we started the descent. The snow made that satisfying crunch under every step, but we didn't realise there was packed ice underneath. I'd only gone a few steps when I lost my balance and tried to slide over to the bank where the snow was piled up; didn't make it, and instead fell heavily on my side, legs in the air.

'Are you all right, Den?'

'No, I'm not. I feel sick.'

Floundering, I managed to pull myself up; Carole couldn't help me as she was having difficulty keeping her own balance while she seemed to be looking for something.

'Carole, I've lost my *Stollen*.'

She told me it had flown up in the air, come out of its plastic wrap and landed in a snow drift.

'I'll have to try to rescue it,' she said, 'as Frau Mengershausen will be coming down this path later on, and if she sees the two pieces of *Stollen* flung into the snow, she'll think we didn't really care for it, particularly as she'd told us Emmi didn't make it.'

That made us laugh, and I nearly fell over again. I limped along, the pain now burning down my right-hand side from chest to knee, just as I had been feeling lovely and supple with all that swimming and floating and massage. Well, I knew I'd fall down at least once on this winter holiday, so perhaps it was over and done with. It reminded me of another time I'd fallen at Tannerhof – in 1973. That time had been potentially serious.

I had been all dressed up ready to go to the *Heuboden* one summer evening. I had come out of the front door, stood on the top step for effect, thinking I looked particularly fetching that evening, tripped on the second step and went head-first down the whole flight, to the horror of Del and Lorraine and Mieke who were waiting for me at the bottom. They couldn't break my fall as they were standing in the wrong position, but instead of smashing my head to pieces on the concrete drive, my head landed in a life-saving border of flowers. Talk about pride coming before a fall.

My friends had had to cart me up the hill to Frau Mengershausen who had got her doctor husband to examine me and prescribe some anti-pain ointment and aspirin. I remember she gave me a sugary cup of proper tea, (so it's not just the British that use that antidote) and once I was over the fright, I had managed to limp to the *Heuboden*, and even twirled through a couple of dances.

Back to this evening. Frau Mengershausen put us to shame. She had changed into a lovely dark blue and white dirndl and looked as fresh as if she had just stepped out of the pages of 'Heidi'. She had come down her side of the mountain carrying her guitar with no mishaps. She smiled at us as she settled in a chair in the Fasting Room and started to strum. I looked round at the guests. There were about a dozen, plus one or two waitresses, and as usual, only one man. They had all changed after dinner but not into anything sequinned. Most of the ladies were older and were wearing silk blouses and pleated skirts. It seems like a kind of uniform when a lady of means gets to a certain age. As I write this I realise they were probably not much older than I am now, but the Germans have never been wildly fashion-conscious. You didn't need a chunky sweater as the fire was roaring and all the radiators were full on. I was never cold in the actual house when I worked there, particularly as I had the warmest job by being in the kitchen, though I often shivered in the *Gochel-Hütte* as the heating was so spasmodic.

Frau Mengershausen had a pretty voice and she was determined that we were going to learn each song correctly. Some of them were in rounds, which at home usually sets Carole and me giggling. But here, everyone was serious. Carole got hold of the pronunciation very quickly (to my chagrin – I wanted to be the only one who could speak German, but Carole has always had a good ear. Maybe it was her French school she went to when she was only four years old). Frau Mengershausen gave a potted history of the origins of each song before we were allowed to start singing, which everyone nodded to, and then we attempted to sing the song once through. When Frau Mengershausen realised we hadn't got it right (none of us, not just Carole and me), she would make us substitute the words; but instead of an English la-la-la-ing, she made us non-non-non, twice over, until she was satisfied that we were ready to sing the actual words. The next time we got it right.

We talked to several of the guests afterwards. Some of the women had been to Tannerhof every year, sometimes two, three and even four times a year, for over 30 years, which of course meant that I had more than likely cooked for them. It was a pleasant evening in nice company, but when Carole and I talked about it later, we said how different it would have been if an English group had got together: we would have been laughing and giggling and throwing in comments, and having a jolly time; on the other hand, we would never have got to grips with any of the songs the way we did that evening in Bavaria.

Frau Mengershausen never mentioned the *Stollen,* and I could only hope that in the morning the early birds would gorge themselves and leave no incriminating trace.

Chapter 27
Heinz

'That chap at the next table has been dying to speak to us,' Carole said under her breath one lunchtime. She was feeling particularly replete after a catastrophe in the kitchen: we'd munched through a mountain of salad; freshly-grated raw beetroot (none of the vinegary cooked stuff you always get in England) and celariac and apple, together with masses of greenery, but we waited for ages for the main meal.

'I think they've forgotten us,' Carole said.

'No, the waitress smiled at us when she went by, so she knows.'

However, a few minutes later our waitress appeared, very flustered, and said there was a problem in the kitchen and she was really sorry but we would have to wait a bit longer.

'*Macht nichts*,' I reassured her. (It doesn't matter.) After all, we hadn't got a bus to catch or any other appointment. When the meal came it wasn't one of their usual kinds of dishes; they had put together something quickly – cheesy potatoes – but the vegetables were crisp and fresh and we were perfectly happy. The waitress, to make up for our wait and lack of a normal vegetarian dish, brought us an extra dessert, a banana quark. I couldn't manage my second one, but Carole did. I was delighted that she was back on her food. Good old Tannerhof.

Back to the chap at the next table, who usually sat on his own. He was a new guest who we wouldn't have met had we not been forced to stay an extra three days because my leg had been too painful to travel on the day we were supposed to have gone home. He was in his early forties, very dark hair, and stockily built, and although not fat, I imagined he was here to lose some weight. We had never got beyond '*Guten Morgan*' or '*Mahlzeit*' at mealtimes.

'Go on, Den, catch his eye. He keeps looking over at us.'

Why does she always make *me* do the initial opening? *She's* the official single one as I've never bothered to get a divorce.

I asked him in German if this was his first time at Tannerhof.

'Oh, no,' he answered in English, looking delighted to be chatted up by two (old) birds. 'Zis is my ten times. I have to lose.'

'How much have you lost?' Carole asked.

'Six kilos,' and he pulled out the waistband of his trousers for us to admire the gap.

'That's about twelve pounds.'

'Fourteen,' was his immediate reply. His English might not have been brilliant but he was rapid with his conversion rate.

At supper, now we'd broken the ice, we were able to continue the conversation.

'Do you know anywhere where we can listen to some Bavarian music?' This was Carole.

He could only suggest a typically Bavarian café in Fischbachau, a small town about ten miles away, which was not what either of us had in mind.

'Munich?' he said.

'Oh, no, that's much too far.'

'Not train,' he said, brightening. 'I have ze car.'

'But it's an hour-and-a-half away.'

'Not my car – only three-quarters hour.'

Carole gave me a kick under the table. For once I couldn't read whether this was to warn me not to take it any further, or to stop me hesitating because she would like to go.

'That would be lovely,' she said.

He glanced at his watch tucked in amongst the dark curling hairs on his wrist. 'I see you *funfzehn Minuten*,' he said.

Promptly, fifteen minutes later the three of us gathered in the hall, and in no time were whizzing along the main road to Munich in his expensive-smelling car.

As we were flying along, Carole, who had insisted on sitting in the back, and had apparently found out his name, said:

'Where do you come from, Heinz?'

'Mainz,' he unknowingly rhymed to perfection.

I heard Carole give a snort, and I sat as rigid as I could to stop myself from bursting into a fit of giggles. I suppose it had more flair than 'Ron from Bonn.'

He was a fast smooth driver and it was fifty minutes later (oh, dear, he was out by five minutes) that we parked and had a long freezing-cold walk. Poor Carole was not dressed very warmly; she only had a wrap as she thought we were going to be dropped off right outside the *Hofbräuhaus*, the world-famous beer hall, which is where Carole wanted to go, as she never went there twenty-three years before. It was like a sight-seeing tour; snow-covered Munich looking romantic at night in a sedate, lady-like way. It wasn't at all busy as we walked along pedestrian-only roads admiring the windows of expensive department stores and boutiques. But that all changed as soon as we set foot in the *Hofbräuhaus*.

What an ear-splitting noise. It's raucous; it's raw; and it's rowdy. Everyone was in various stages of inebriation and we couldn't hear each other speak what with the shouting and singing and beer-swilling. Big-chested waitresses cleaved their way through the smoke that masked fifty per cent of the customers, and several small bands were playing at the same time in various corners of this baronial hall, the size of the interior of a railway station. Carole had never seen anything like it in her life, and it was fun watching her expression.

Heinz didn't feel it was the right place for two women (how little he knew us) so he led us through the main restaurant, across a pretty courtyard, and up a flight of stairs where there were a couple of other dining rooms, still part of the *Hofbräuhaus*, but not quite the pandemonium. To my disappointment Heinz stuck to the first floor. I'd recently read that on the second floor was the banqueting hall where Hitler launched the Nazi manifesto in 1920, and was curious to see it.

There were long tables full of half-sozzled Bavarians, most of them giving Carole and me curious glances, but we found a table to ourselves and Heinz ordered our drinks – I was pleased to see that he only had an apple-juice, as Carole and I are paranoid about people drinking and driving, and the *Hofbräuhaus* customers didn't look as though they would be capable of steering a wheelbarrow. A couple of chaps dressed in *Lederhosen*, one playing the accordion and the other a wind instrument, sang several songs that some of the men in the room joined in with. Then an extremely short girl, dressed in a dirndl, with stick-out teeth complete with gap, took the microphone. She had so much sparkle and had the most marvellous yodelling voice that we really enjoyed it. After she'd finished, another two chaps came in to do Bavarian dancing. They set up a bench and started to dance over and across it in a very acrobatic manner, until one of them fell off. He glared at the other and they both put their fists up.

I thought, Oh, no, I can't believe this is going to turn nasty, and looked round to see where the door was. The audience started to laugh, and I realised it was all an act. Then a couple more male singers came on and I said to Carole:

'I'm going to request the Kufstein song. That'll get the whole room going. Just watch.'

'Please don't, Den,' she said, as always embarrassed by me, but I ignored her and went up to one of the chaps in the band and told him I was English.

'It doesn't matter,' he said, quick as a flash. 'I'm Bavarian.'

He grinned when I asked him to play the Kufstein song, and nodded. Just a quick explanation – Kufstein is a small Bavarian town, and the chorus is an easy yodel for the layman (like me) with a 'Cuckoo' at the end of each yodel. It's great fun to sing, and Del used to love it. It always made her laugh.

True to my words, everyone began singing the chorus and linking arms and swaying in time to the music. Poor Carole didn't share my enthusiasm. She crouched lower and lower in her seat as my 'Cuckoo' got louder and louder; there were lots of verses, and few words that I could remember from twenty-three years before, but that didn't stop my ebullience one bit. The customers loved it, and clapped more on that song than any of the others.

One of the singers, a plump cheerful lad, with a long black hood-like hairstyle, had his eye on Carole.

'Is he wearing a wig?' I asked her.

Carole, who used to be a hairdresser and always claims that she can spot a wig a mile away, peered over:

'No, it's all his own. But I wish he'd focus his singing on someone else.'

On that happy note it was time to leave, seeing as we had no business being in a smoky beer-swilling environment late at night. We were supposed to be de-toxing at a health clinic, after all.

I wanted to pay for our drinks – I tried very hard but Heinz insisted.

'Let him pay,' Carole hissed, as Heinz got up to settle the bill. 'He wants to be the man taking care of us, so let him. Anyway, he's loaded.'

'How do you know?'

'Because he drives a brand-new Merc, and his suede coat is so long it's swishing the floor like a bride's train,' she replied. Of course that started us off giggling. She said that when she looked out of the window when we came into Munich, almost every car was a Mercedes or a BMW.

My side still hurt the next day but at least we'd had a great evening. Heinz didn't turn up for breakfast – maybe the Terrible Twins (as Carole and I sometimes call ourselves) were too much for one German to handle. Carole said, 'Maybe Heinz isn't so loaded after all. Maybe the Merc is a company car and he's *hired* his suede coat,' which set us off again, wondering if it was true. Poor old Heinz.

We bumped into him in Bayrischzell later in the morning, as we were doing some last-minute gift shopping. We'd just stopped to admire a wedding, which was accompanied by a Bayerischer band. The bride wore a beautiful heavy cream dress, but someone in the crowd told us this was not traditional: a traditional dress would be a dirndl. I was so glad this bride was going against tradition. All the guests looked very smart and too sophisticated for Bayrischzell, so they'd probably come from some way away.

Heinz drew up in the (company?) Merc and gave us a lift back to Tannerhof where we had a typical German lunch rather than a Tannerhof one. Granted the sausages were vegetarian, but there was a pile of *sauerkraut* and potato salad that lay heavily in the stomach. While we were eating, Heinz suggested we go to Kufstein, which is where the song I had requested came from.

It was a scenic ride and when we arrived, we walked up the hill to the castle, where we were treated to an astounding view over the town and River Inn. Unfortunately, everywhere was closed. The museum was closed, the shops were closed, the restaurants were closed. We did find a café where they served a wonderful *Strudel* with vanilla sauce, so I was very happy. Heinz couldn't have any as he was on a low-calorie diet, but he said he didn't mind a bit watching us. I couldn't have done.

We ended the day with a jolly evening at the Hotel *Zur Post* in Bayrischzell.

'So you go tomorrow,' said Heinz, sounding sorry.

'Yes, but we've stayed a few days longer because of Denise's accident. We're flying back instead of going by train, as Den wouldn't be able to cope with her luggage. If we'd gone home on the day we planned, we wouldn't have met you. Which would have been a pity. So it's all worked out well.'

Heinz looked pleased and gave us his business card in case we were ever in his neck of the woods. I don't suppose we shall be, but one never knows.

'Expect he's married anyway,' said Carole.

CHAPTER 28
FLYING HOME

WE DIDN'T GO skiing, we didn't go up the Wendelstein, we didn't go on any long mountain hikes, as the pain in my leg was still quite nasty, and we were both grateful we had that as our excuse, but we managed to go shopping in Munich, take tea and *Apflestrudel* at Emmi and Karl's apartment, enjoy a Bavarian evening at one of the cafés in Bayrischzell, practise Yoga, learn some more Bavarian folk dances, sing folk songs, pick up Heinz from Mainz, had lots of laughs, and generally let Tannerhof work its magic. Carole looked great. The kitchen staff had given her generous portions, knowing her problem, and I don't remember her ever leaving a morsel. The appetite was back!

Because of my leg, we'd gained a few extra days, (and pounds) but now it was time to pack ready for the airport in the morning.

It had been a fabulous holiday. I felt proud as though I had personally wrought the change to put Carole back on her feet, and I had to admit – it was great being a guest and watching everyone rush around to make our visit so comfortable and happy. But because I had once been one of the team, I could appreciate how hard they worked and how tired they would feel at the end of another long day. And deep down, I had a little twinge of envy that they were staying, and I was going. I vowed not to leave it so long the next time – bloody hell, another twenty-three years and I would be... No, I wouldn't think about it.

We had our last walk down to the village and our last coffee at Café Stumpp. We'd met Emmi and Karl who were going to church, and now I was sitting in my room, which had a bare and lonely look. Tannerhof cleaners, and I suspect this applies to all good German cleaners, do not merely clean a room – they demolish it and start again. The French windows onto the balcony were open, the door to the landing was wide open, the rug was outside ready to be beaten, the little bedside cabinet had been moved over to the sink and had been washed down; the inside of the chest, which I'd never even used, had its doors flung open and the interior scrubbed out. Everything is done so thoroughly it puts English cleaners to shame.

I was feeling guilty because on my bedside table there was a linen cloth – not embroidered, thank goodness – and when I did my nails last night the weeniest drop of nail varnish, which happened to be bright red, landed on it. The cleaning lady had run some cold water in the wash basin and was soaking what she believed to be blood out of the cloth. She was going to be surprised when she found it hadn't come out. I wondered if she would think: *No wonder the English won the war – their blood is stronger than ours!*

PART III

JUNE 2005

Chapter 29
Back Again

I GO TO Germany by train as usual, but this time it's very different from that first trip in 1973 as Eurostar is now in operation and it's just a hop and a skip from London to Paris. Also, I don't have my long-suffering travelling companion with me, my sister Carole, but I needed to do this trip on my own, and finish another chunk of this book.

A little tip regarding Eurostar – pay the extra for First Class. It's not that much more, and they often do deals where you return, still First Class, but without having to pay any extra. The upgrade is worth every penny. First of all, if you're early, as I am, you are admitted into a posh lounge at Waterloo, which is all very civilised with a free bar and nice little tit-bits. There is a television but you can't hear it as the sound is so low it's just a faint murmur a long way off. That suits me. There are all the current newspapers and glossy magazines to while away the time and waiters coming to whisk your plates and glasses away and ask if you'd like anything more.

Once you're boarded, you notice there are fewer people in the carriage – I have a little table all to myself as no-one comes to sit opposite – and even when people use their mobiles, they are more subdued. Then the stewards, they call them, as though they're on aeroplanes, come round after a half an hour or so and ask what you would like to drink. I am travelling at 4.30 in the afternoon, so normally I would say 'a cup of tea.' But when free Champagne is on the menu, it's hard to say no, so I don't. The stewardess pours me a glass but only fills the glass two-thirds, so she promises to come round later to top it up. By this time, I've practically finished it, so she pours me another full glass, at the same time giving me a little bag of up-market nuts, presumably to help soak up some of the alcohol. An hour later the stewards come round wheeling their trolleys with the dinner; again, free with First Class. I wonder what sort of train food this will be and then remember I haven't ordered vegetarian. Surprise, surprise. Unlike in planes, when you have forgotten and ask the stewards, and they always say, 'I'm sorry, you have to order it when you're buying your ticket', on Eurostar the smiling stewardess says, 'No problem at all.' And I have to say, it was quite delicious: a quorn and mushroom and noodle dish, cheese and biscuits and French chocolate tart to follow, together with a quarter bottle of red wine, were just the right medicine for my migraine. So believe me, and go First Class.

I have another three-hour wait in Paris, and although the taxi queue for La Gare de l'Est is the longest I have ever seen in my life – so long that they have built those bars like a maze on the actual *pavement*, that when I get there, I still have over two hours to kill. All I can do is drag my case, which feels as heavy as a tank, to the nearest café. The reason it's so heavy, by the way, is not because of taking too many clothes, but rather, too many books along with my laptop, which I managed to lay inside the suitcase, on top of all my clothes, with the help of the case's secret extension mechanism.

Who said Parisians are rude? I've actually never been treated rudely in Paris. I think it is a matter of attitude. If you're charming to them (and I can lay it on really thick), they can't help but be charming back. At least, that's my theory. I feel awful only asking for an Orangina, but I'm not a bit hungry after my train supper. The friendly young waiter doesn't seem to mind at all, and moves my case for me so I am comfortable, and I make one bottle last for an hour and a half, sitting outside on this mild sunny evening, people-watching. I leave him a tip as big as the cost of the orange drink because he was so nice to me and I want him to think well of the English. He gives me an appreciative smile and a cheery 'Bon soir.'

At last I am on the platform ready to board the Munich train, which has just come in. I have ordered a couchette all to myself, and wander, or rather drag, up the platform looking for my carriage. Found it! A tall blond man in his thirties who is evidently a porter going by his crisp uniform – says, 'Guten Abend' and immediately I feel at home, even though I haven't left Paris. It's only that I am so much more familiar with German than French. I have to ask him if he can help me with my suitcase, which he does very politely and seriously, and moments later I am in my little sleeping wagon, as they call them in Germany. I can't believe it normally holds three people, but I have described these tight quarters in the second chapter when I went to Tannerhof with my sister, so won't go through it again. I've just forgotten how tiny they are, and also you would think that thirty-two years on they would be a bit more generous in size, as these trains are modern. I'm so happy to have it all to myself.

A little rotund porter squeezes along the corridor stopping at each cabin to explain to bemused travellers the workings of their wagon. He has such a strong Bavarian accent that I can barely understand him, but he shows me how to get water out of the doll's wash-basin (I tell him there is no water, but of course, being a German train,

there is – it's only that I'm not bright enough to find the mechanism).
Now I can't work the blind; it is fully down, and I want to look out
of the window as we pull away, so he shows me how to operate it.
Simple when you know how. There is no soap so he tells me to take
some from the shower room at the end of the carriage. Finally, do
I want tea or coffee in the morning, so I say, '*Kaffe, bitte*,' as that's
always a safer bet when abroad. The porter disappears and just at that
moment, the train starts to move. It's always a bit of an anti-climax
as one moment groups of people are chatting on the platform and
the next, some of them have broken away and hauled themselves
up the train steps to begin their journey. I rush to the window I
can now see out of, and feel smug and sorry for all the people left
behind on the platform.

Into PJs, remove make-up, clean teeth using special mug of water
that has a cling film top and a picture of a set of teeth so you know
what it's for, and what it isn't for, i.e. to drink; don't forget night
cream; yes, better take a half a sleeping tablet as I know I won't
sleep a wink unless I do; read book for a bit although it's bloody
uncomfortable with a pillow that is about as puffed up as one of
Carole's quilted place-mats she's always making, and with the swaying
of the train, now in a rhythm of its own, and the assistance of the
half a sleeping pill, I lull off. Even though I awake several times, and
look out of the window to see where we are and what's happening
– usually nothing much unless we have stopped at some station – by
5 am I feel I've slept. And best of all, my headache has gone.

I'd better get to the shower before someone else does, so down the
corridor to the shower room. I've been beaten, but not by someone
who's already had a shower, as the shower curtain and tiles are dry.
But every sample bottle of shower bath essence has been swiped, and
the evening before, when our little porter told me to take one as I
had no soap, there were dozens on the shelf. How mean. And how
mean that every towel has been taken or used. Luckily, I have my
face towel with me and to my delight, the shower works well.

As there's nowhere to stand, I get back into bed and watch the world, or rather Germany, roll by. I ring my bell at six, hoping it isn't too early for the porter to bring me coffee, and wishing he was going to bring me a proper breakfast as I am starving. Well, at least I have two emergency müesli bars. Two minutes later he knocks at my door and hands me a *tray* with *food* on it! I really enjoy my breakfast of a crispy roll, a very passable croissant, herby cream cheese and butter, and apricot jam, even though the coffee is black and only warm. After I've worked through my tray of goodies, I take my rubbish and go in search of the porter.

'Is it possible to have another coffee?' I ask him in German.

'*Natürlich*,' he answers, and pours me another, hot and with milk this time, and an orange juice and refuses to charge me. I ask him if he's been able to have a sleep. He is very surprised. It's been a long time since anyone has asked after his well-being.

We pull into Munich. Final stop. It has been a great ride and now I have to see whether the train for Bayrischzell is on the same platform as it used to be. I try to help a Frenchman who is going to see his sister who lives in Tegernsee, which is not that far from Bayerischzell, and thoroughly confuse both him and myself as I have primed my brain for German and am now having to speak in the most terrible French to this poor man. After what seems like hours of misunderstandings and arm-wavings, I realise we both need the same train, but I have to be in the first two carriages as they do some unhinging along the way. I am quite pleased I've worked it out for the Frenchman, although he still looks worried and when I leave him to find my front carriages, he's asking more people if he's on the right train. Obviously, I'm not to be trusted with my helpful information.

No need to describe the scenery as you've got it all at the beginning of the book. Just imagine everything the same as that journey, but without the snow.

As I open the train door onto Bayrischzell station, who should be getting *on* but Emmi. 'Emmi!' I screech, but of course she doesn't recognise me until I explain who I am, and then I give her a kiss and a hug, which she probably isn't expecting, or wanting, not being a very kissy person, and she tries to untangle herself as her train is about to leave, and me being so excited to see her, I'm not aware that she's just about to miss it.

It's funny that she's the first person I see.

No taxi at the station. So I phone Tannerhof but it is an answer-phone. All it keeps saying is '*Leider…*' (Unfortunately…) and the rest of the words are swallowed up by an accordion playing Bavarian music. So I don't know whether anyone will be back in five minutes or five hours. There is no way I can heave my suitcase up that hill to Tannerhof. I must be looking very worried, as a pleasant-looking man of about my age (quite young really) on a bicycle stops and asks:

'*Kann ich Ihnen helfen*?' (Can I help you?)

I tell him I am going to Tannerhof but there are no taxis. He tells me to wait two minutes and he will get his car and take me there. Of course I wouldn't dream of getting into a car driven by some strange man in England, but Bavaria is different. I always feel perfectly safe here. The man-on-the-bike, now in a large maroon car, pulls up, jumps out and heaves my cases into the boot, and in I get. We chat and I tell him I used to work at Tannerhof a long time ago and he says he remembers me, that I have been in his café. The Café Hubert.

'Are you the owner?'

'*Ja*, I am Herr Hubert.'

By now we're speaking in English, quite excitedly, and I recognise him too, but I realise that's mostly because I came with my husband, Edward, to Bayrischzell for two days last year on the way to a cycling holiday in nearby Lengries. We had tea at the Café Hubert with two super women who were also staying at Tannerhof. I remember Herr Hubert spent a long time explaining all the different and Pavlovian-inducing cakes. Now he is just driving up the lane to Tannerhof when a post-office van parked on a drive on our left (and Herr Hubert is, remember, driving a left-handed car) without any warning at all, backs down its drive, heading straight for us, and plummets into Herr Hubert's left-hand front wing. It's all happened so suddenly but Herr Hubert calmly brakes and jumps out. He appears to be most affable with the postman, whereas in England I'm sure that would have produced at least a modicum of road-rage, and after a couple of minutes gets back in and we continue up the drive.

'How awful,' I say. 'You're trying to do me a favour and in return you've had your car smashed. I feel so guilty.'

'It's not your fault,' from the gentlemanly Herr Hubert. 'Don't worry at all.'

I promise him I will come and see him for a coffee but so far I haven't been, as my light diet here at Tannerhof to detox from all those convenience foods and scones and coffee I have at home, certainly does not include such an assortment of cakes. He helps me right to the door with my cases, and tells me to have an enjoyable stay, and drives off in his battered old car, which was very nice and quite new really just ten minutes ago.

I know I'm back – there's the smell of apples and cinnamon and pine. I'm typing this on my laptop from my room, number 7, in the old house. It's on the first floor and although it doesn't face the Wendelstein, when I look up for inspiration (which is most of the time) I have a fabulous view of mountains all around me, pale emerald-green grass slopes interspersed with darker green firs and other trees, the names of which I am not quite sure of, and a little group of cows in the far distance looking like they've been plucked from a toy farmyard, except these have bells that jingle every time the cows move their heads. After the first few moments I always feel sorry for the cow, wondering if it ever feels it will go completely crazy if it hears itself jingle one more time. I shall miss all this when I get home. Tunbridge Wells has a distinct lack of mountains and cow bells.

I have an en-suite wet room, which I can't believe really works without my toiletry stuff looking like it's been pulled out of the

Titanic every time I have a shower, but of course it all works perfectly. After all, we are in Germany. My balcony is so private I can sunbathe nude if I want (I don't) but I like the idea that I can. I see they have demolished the little sunbathing shelter, which my body and I spent many a happy afternoon in. But this is heaven.

I unpack and go downstairs in perfect time for lunch. One of the young slim waitresses, who looks charming in her dirndl, long dark hair tied back, reminds me her name is Daniella (she was here last year) and she shows me my seat. Two women are already seated, both roughly my age, one of them with the most improbable red hair. Red, who is as delicate and small as an undeveloped twelve-year-old, introduces herself as Monika. The other woman, Brigitte, is taller than me, with long, fine blondish-grey hair, and I find out later that she is a psychiatric doctor who drinks too much and has come to Tannerhof to get off the booze. They both speak quite good English, Monika's vocabulary being superior, but Brigitte's flow easier to follow. Monika is so desperate to choose the right word that she hesitates after nearly every painful word in case she makes a mistake. She tells me she is a teacher so I expect that has something to do with it.

My napkin is already in its envelope with Frau Barnes written on it; it is a great relief that I'm in the system. Lunch is delicious but then, so is every meal that follows. Goodness, it's only 2 o'clock but I feel those tired waves floating through and over my head. I'll just slip my trousers off and lie on top of the bed and…

CHAPTER 30
SURPRISE GUESTS

THE FIRST THING I want to do is find out about the hundred year exhibition. This month is Tannerhof's centenary so I'm here for the celebrations, not to mention it will incorporate a 'big' birthday for me, which would be too depressing to spend at home. I take up the offer from the Housekeeper, Gretl, to make a tour of the house in the company of two Spanish ladies, as Tannerhof has been so extended and amalgamated with other areas that I easily get lost. As we go down one of the long corridors that joins the Old Tann with the New Tann and swimming pool, I notice there are black and white photographs, beautifully mounted and hung all the way along. I remark on them and Gretl says they form the exhibition. I ask where the rest of the exhibition is, but it seems these photographs, many though there are, is it. I'm disappointed even though

I don't quite know what I was expecting. I'll spend some time later looking at them more closely.

I run into Frau Mengershausen junior, although she is now senior, her dear mother having died a few years ago, and she gives me a hug and a kiss. We have a chat and I ask her about the exhibition. I'm amazed that the celebrations themselves are taking place only on one day – Saturday week – so thank goodness my two weeks' holiday covers that day. I thought it would be going on all month. I ask her who is coming and she tells me that Emmi and Anita will be there so I am very pleased. I ask about Gisela.

'*Schwester* Gisela?' she asks, and I say, yes, as I expect she must have been promoted to Sister by now.

'Yes, she is coming for a few days also,' says Frau Mengershausen, and that is great news for me.

It's time for supper. Who should I see but a diminutive lady who is a naturopathic doctor and author of health books, who Edward and I met last year when we were en-route on the cycling holiday, generously helping herself to some salads. At eighty-six, so she told me she was last year, she is dressed in clingy black jersey-knit trousers tucked into walking boots, topped with several layers of smock and thick grey Tyrolean jacket, even though it's boiling outside. This is what happened when I first met her. I was chatting to her outside the main house in English, which she was fluent in, and she asked me my name. I said Denise, and she said, 'I'm Vera.'

At that point, Edward came along and I introduced her, saying, 'Vera, this is my husband, Edward.'

'Allo, Edward,' she said.

'Allo, Vera,' he replied, and of course he and I almost fell over laughing, although poor Aloe Vera didn't get the joke. Edward said it was an opportunity that may not even come once in one's lifetime. He'll be delighted to know that I've seen her again, and was able to greet her accordingly. Sometimes opportunities come twice.

After supper on this busy first day back at Tannerhof, I go for a walk and pass Frau Harm's house, aptly named *Haus Harm*. An ancient little lady is outside talking to her terrier. I ask her if she is Frau Harm and she confirms it. I tell her who I am and that my mother and aunt stayed with her thirty-two years ago when they came to see me for a week while I was working at Tannerhof. (I decide not to mention John.) She remembers them, and that I used to bring the müesli over for them every morning. I tell her my mother died last Christmas, but my aunt is fine and would be pleased to be remembered to her. I mustn't forget to tell Brenda I have seen Frau Harm. Can't believe she is still going – Frau Harm, I mean, not Brenda.

Fabulous sleep and another surprise at breakfast. A lady in her early seventies, I would think, comes into the dining room with her husband. We chat and she asks me if it is my first time at Tannerhof. I tell her I used to work in the kitchen thirty-two years ago. She's astonished as she tells me she did also. I say, 'But not in the kitchen,' and she says, 'Well, it was the *Rohkost* Room.'

With disbelief I say, '*Nicht* Irene?'

'*Doch, ich bin* Irene.' (Yes, I am Irene.) Irene – I can't believe it! I haven't set eyes on her for all these years. And I have to say, I can now see it really is her. And she says in German, although she's actually Romanian:

'The English girl. I remember you took over from me in the Salad Room.'

'Yes,' I reply, 'when you suddenly ran off to get married.' Her husband grins at this point. 'I only had half a day's training from Traudl, the waitress, and that was it – I was on my own.'

She explains that this is only her third time back as a guest in the thirty-two years. And she and her husband have only come for three days. I tell her it is *my* third time back also, and we can't believe we have hit it at the same time. It isn't even that she is here for the hundred year festival – she didn't know about it when she booked and she goes home the day before. Irene… I never dreamed I would ever see her again.

I really get stuck into the book this morning and after lunch another snooze. I don't want to get into a siesta habit, and waste valuable time when I should be writing. But I am overcome again.

After I come to, I decide to go for a sauna. Apparently, it is the oldest sauna in the country, and was built in 1936, which doesn't sound that old really. Brigitte is already there, and I pass a pleasant ten minutes in the oven-like atmosphere, until I worry that I am now on my own (Brigitte has gone) and I will faint and be found in the morning as a pile of ashes. So I jump up too quickly and actually do feel a bit dizzy and have to have a lie down in the recovery room after my shower. Pity there's no-one around to pander to my every whim but the building is deserted. No, I can hear someone. Maybe Brigitte's back to see if I'm ready. But it's a heavier footstep. Oh, God, I'm not going to be murdered in the so-called recovery room, am I? I prop myself up, my towel not doing the best cover-up job, and my heart thumps an uneasy beat as nervous sweat replaces the sauna sweat of a few moments ago. A dark shadow falls across the doorway.

'*Es tut mir leid.*' (Excuse me.) A man swiftly backs out. I recognise him as one of the maintenance men and reproach myself for having such ridiculous thoughts.

Supper is a huge buffet. They do it every Saturday. The salad table seems to stretch from one end of the hall to the other, and the selection includes Greek salad, stuffed vine leaves, whole lemons stuffed with tuna, *raita* (cucumber in yoghurt), roasted vegetables, separately-roasted onions to die for, roast potatoes (no, not the English way in meat fat but with rosemary), dozens of cheeses and breads, and a tropical fresh fruit salad. It's all wonderful. I may start a light diet soon, but not just yet.

After supper I talk to a middle-aged couple who are sitting on the seat on the balcony outside the front door. The guests often gather here because the sun is still bright and warm. They introduce themselves as Volker and Jutti Heil. Their surname slightly worries me, but they are so nice. He speaks almost perfect English and she understands every word but won't speak it, although occasionally she forgets herself and says a few words, and then laughs and reverts to German. But Herr Heil tells me she used to read novels in English and that is why she understands everything. They have a great sense of humour and we all get on famously. I make it a habit to have an evening talk with them and find that we can discuss anything – politics, art, music, Germany today, education, even the war.

Frau Heil was very upset to see that there is a black and white photograph of Hitler actually smiling out of one of the exhibition pictures. He had been to Bayrischzell during the war and she thinks it in very bad taste of Tannerhof to use his title of Reichs-Chancellor under his photograph.

'He should be labelled *criminal!*' she fumes.

However, on this point I disagree with Frau Heil. It's history and there's nothing we can do or say that will change it. I think Tannerhof was right to show him – much better than to rewrite history as some of the schools in Germany have been doing until recently.

This reminds me of a book I read a few months ago called *Eva's Cousin* by Sibylle Knauss. Although it's in the form of a novel, it's based on Eva Braun's cousin, Gertraud, who spent time in Berchtesgaden in 1945, in Hitler's mountain retreat to keep Eva company. The book is based on Gertraud's memories where she was completely under the spell of the *Führer* and all he stood for, until much later in life when she learned of the atrocities. But towards the end of the novel, Gertraud tells how she goes to Bayrischzell which is not far from Berchtesgaden, several years after the war and books herself into one of the mountain cabins belonging to the nearby sanatorium. She doesn't specifically call it Tannerhof, but her description of the house and its close proximity to the village can be none other. I wondered if the cabin could be the same one that my sister stayed in during those first five days when we came thirty-two years ago. Also, if the von Mengershausens realised who she was. All very spine-tingling.

I see Irene again. She keeps saying how young I look. I *like* Irene. She says my top is sexy, but I say there's no fanciable man around so it's not doing much good. She laughs. I remember she was a bit of a character. She always wore a headband and thirty-two years later she still does. It's good that some things never change.

Herr Heil is just telling me this evening about his time in England after the war when Dr Schröeder comes along and asks if it will be possible for me to have my medical examination right away. As it's a Sunday, I'm surprised and disappointed that I wasn't going to have Frau Mengershausen as I know she speaks such good English, and I think perhaps it might be difficult if my medical is conducted in German.

Anyway, I go along with Dr Schröeder, a tiny woman who tells me she is seventy.

She asks why I've come to Tannerhof. I tell her I am stressed out, with my mother dying days before Christmas and just having sold my business, which has been going on for nine months and I was beginning to wonder if it was ever going to happen. It did, just two weeks before I came to Tannerhof. Dr Schröeder keeps nodding, and she tells me I am very tired and that I should do as little or as much as I like of the exercises, so long as I have plenty of rest and sleep. I promise her. I don't need to be told twice that I don't have to exercise if I don't want to.

She speaks enough English to get me through the medical and I am really pleased I will have her as my doctor throughout my stay as she is so kind and thorough. I have to say, a lot more thorough than some doctors I've had in England, and I tell her so. She says I can go on a light diet but not the intensive one, and I tell her it's my birthday on Wednesday, so can I start it Thursday. She agrees.

It would be brilliant to lose a few pounds, particularly round the stomach region.

When I have to go for a blood test the following Tuesday with no breakfast (just the thought of it makes me feel faint) Dr Schröeder extracts it with no fuss and I feel no pain or dizziness. She is the best person I've ever had to take blood. Thank goodness my blood pressure is very good (her words), as are my lungs, heart, etc. I won't go into any more detail as I don't think you'd be interested.

By the way, I haven't mentioned the weather, but it's glorious. Every day beautiful and sunny, even at 5.30 am. The sun washes over the mountains at quite a pace as the morning progresses. It must get to about thirty degrees most days, and I am making the most of it by settling on a sun-lounger near some trees so I can move under them when it gets too hot. I have my sun-tan lotion, sun-hat, sun-glasses, bottle of water, and my latest book. Bliss!

Annoying that they are having the same fabulous weather in England. I'm one of those horrible people who when I'm away, want to be the only one enjoying nice weather, and want to think of the miserable blighters at home.

My third day and I have a raging headache. The pain is worse than my usual migraines. This always happens to me at a health spa when I'm not drinking any teas and coffees. It's the caffeine-withdrawal symptom. It doesn't seem fair to have such a bad head when I've had no wine or chocolate. I walk to the village, which is a mistake as I really feel awful.

Brigitte and Monika go back home but both of them are returning to Tannerhof for a few days before I leave, which is nice. Today I have three sisters at my table, somewhere in their late sixties, early seventies. They are lovely. We speak in German all the time, which is not easy for me, having been spoilt with Brigitte and Monika, but I know it's what's needed else I'll never improve.

Herr Heil tells me this evening that his father was taken a prisoner of war after the Second World War by the Americans to Fort Worth,

Texas. I never knew this happened. What a culture shock those German POWs would have had. Munich to Fort Worth – it makes the head reel. But at least they would have had plenty to eat.

Talking of reeling heads – am having another bad head day. This is on a par with a bad *hair* day. Have decided that I must have some regular English tea instead of all the fennel, rose-hip, green tea, linden blossom, peppermint, ginger and vanilla… the list goes on as to what I've been drinking at Tannerhof. So I walk to the village again and find a café, the Königslinde, where they have Darjeeling and Assam on the menu – that's English enough for me. The owner who has a small earing, unusual in Bayrischzell, serves it to me beautifully. Lovely teapot, but with teabag in the saucer – I wonder why they do this. I often forget and think I'm leaving the tea to stew and when I feel it's ready to pour, it comes out clear water, which is too weak even for me. I have to send him back to change the milk as it's hot; also on the tray is a macaroon the size of a Euro. I manage to make it last for three bites; I am so thrilled to have something sweet that I give myself the excuse that it will help my headache.

To sit in one of the café's basket chairs in the sun, on a bright red and very comfortable cushion, with my book, and watch Bayrishzell go by…it really doesn't take much to please me.

CHAPTER 31

DÉJÀ VU

I've PUT MY name down on a list this morning to work in the kitchen tonight!

Apparently, every alternate Monday twelve guests can cook a meal in the kitchen under the auspices of the head chef, Frau Renate Julia Winklmüller, together with her kitchen crew. In 1973 no guest would ever be allowed in the kitchen, and rarely any other member of staff, so this is a giant leap for Tannerhof. Imagine…the last time I was cooking in the kitchen was thirty-two years ago! I feel funny just thinking about it. Can't wait to get started.

I have a lighter supper than usual, and as it only consists of salads and soup, it's pretty light anyway, but I've been told by one of the guests who cooked a fortnight ago, and loved it, that you eat the meal afterwards, so I want to leave enough room for a second innings.

We meet at 7 pm in the old Fasting Room to go over the recipés we'll be making. Frau Winklmüller has allowed two extra guests to cook, so we are thirteen women and one token man, all looking appropriately enthusiastic, and *all* with a copy of the cookery book Frau Winklmüller has written especially for Tannerhof: *'Die Vitalstoff-Diet'* (The Healthy Diet). I'm at a disadvantage without one, so I ask her if I can rush upstairs and buy one from the shop. The shop has been created from a first-floor bedroom, next door to Del and Lorraine's old room, and is a modern concept as it has only been in operation since January this year. I leap up the stairs two at a time only to find the shop open but no-one there. I grab a copy off the shelf making a mental note to pay for it tomorrow, and join the others.

Frau Winklmüller is charming, and her animated expression shows she is passionate about food. I would say she is in her mid forties, curvy figure, with reddish-dark hair in a casual layered bob. She has just called the register to make sure we're all present and correct, and as I am sitting next to her I see that she has already put a tick by my name.

'Verstehen Sie, Frau Barnes?' she turns to me frequently to make sure I understand, but as most of the German I know is to do with cooking, I can follow her without too much difficulty. What I don't know, I'll have to make up – just like the old days. We put our hands up to indicate which part of the dinner we would like to prepare, and will work in teams of twos and threes. I choose what I think will be easy to deal with as I more or less gave up cooking ten years ago and am very conscious that the others are probably far more experienced than me. It was funny – one day, I just got fed-up with the whole rigmarole of cooking and resorted to M&S delights. Except that I never enjoy them as much as the packet says I will. And when I saw a programme recently on TV about supermarket convenience food, those swimming-pool sized vats of sauces and soups put me right off, let alone all the salt and sugar they use, and

the e numbers. I'm hoping Tannerhof will inspire me to start cooking again when I'm home.

I've teamed up with a very nice lady called Ruth who sports a short grey bob with a fringe, which reminds me of Joanna Lumley's hairstyle when she used to play Purdey in The Avengers. Everyone in those days had their hair cut in the Purdey style, including me, but Ruth has clung on to hers, which somehow suits her. She has the kindest eyes and smile, and I find out that she was a missionary in Japan for several years where she spoke English. Her voice is soft and gentle, and even when we speak in German, I notice that her accent has no gutteral sound. We have chosen an avocado dish that looks like a lumpy dip in the photograph in Frau Winklmüller's book, but it requires no actual cooking, which suits me.

Into the kitchen. What an eerie feeling. My brain fast tracks, but it's got thirty-two years to run through before it finds my 1973 year at Tannerhof. It's a glimpse of your life flashing before you, but thankfully I'm not in any danger of drowning. I take a couple of moments to look around. The other participants are also looking around, but with normal curiosity. I feel dazed, like I'm in a time warp. Most of the others have no idea that this Englishwoman amongst them worked in this very kitchen so long ago. I stand transfixed trying to work it all out, while the rest of the group queue up at the sink to wash their hands, as instructed.

Yes, there has been some modernisation to the worktops and cupboards, and the kitchen table that used to stand in the corner and where we had our meals has gone, but the central island, although more up to date, is reminiscent of the old one with its gleaming stainless steel top and dozens of burners. The only difference is that this one has a useful little sink incorporated and a slop drain beneath, which sounds revolting, but is spotless and completely odour-free, and is a brilliant way of getting rid of surplus liquids fast.

The assistant cooks give us all a throw-away white polythene apron. Sensible. But I can't believe this next bit. Frau Winklmüller and her staff are handing out *wine glasses* to all of us and asking if we'd like red or white! This can't be. As you know, there was no alcohol in the kitchen in 1973 except the bottle of brandy I nicked for my mince-meat that Christmas. And the guests would not have been allowed to have brought in a bottle of wine even if they'd had the urge. I think in those days, you totally accepted that sparkling health didn't include having a drink. It makes me want to kiss the food scientist, or whoever it was who proved that one or two units of wine a day, particularly red, is beneficial for its anti-oxidant properties. In fact, I think it was a man (surprise surprise) who proved it was more beneficial to have a moderate intake of wine than to be teetotal. So now, here we are all these years later; we haven't even begun cooking, and we're kicking off with a healthy glass of wine. Fantastic.

A few sips put us in a jolly mood as at my instigation we toast one another on the way to our various work stations.

All the ingredients are laid out for us, spices and mustard already measured in little bowls, just like they are on the telly. Ruth asks me if I will chop the onion as it makes her eyes water, and she has had trouble during the day with watery eyes – probably from too much sun, I tell her. Just as I start peeling the outside skin, a young girl, who is one of the assistant cooks, comes over.

'Do you know how to chop an onion?' she asks me in German.

I look at her. She regards me very seriously. I try to keep a straight face.

'I think so,' I reply.

I take up a large knife (*Always use a bigger knife than you think you need*,' I can hear Anita say), hold the onion firmly on the board, and cleanly cut in half. Then put one half flat side on the board, and thinly slice it downwards, then slice it about three times horizontally, then slice downwards through the whole section again, so that the small chopped pieces fall neatly away onto the scrubbed board.

'*Ja*, I see you know how to chop an onion,' says the young cook, looking surprised.

'And do you know where I learned to chop an onion?' I ask her. She waits politely. 'Right here in this kitchen, thirty-two years ago.' Disbelief crosses her face.

'*Wirklich?*' (Really?)

'*Wirklich,*' I nod, and casually pick up my glass of wine, toast her, take a gulp and we all laugh. Passed *that* test.

Ruth and I work well together and when we finish adding the rest of the ingredients and forking them together, another cook comes to inspect and to taste.

'A little more seasoning, I think,' is her opinion.

'I would say more lemon juice,' I answer.

'Add both,' she says.

Yummy. Just perfect. We have already retained the avocado shells that have been soaking in a bowl of lemon water so they don't go brown, and now we scoop the mixture into each avocado half. We decorate them with half an olive and a sprinkling of parsley, but this cook adds half a cherry tomato to each one – for colour, she says. Privately, I think it looks like the nipple on a prosthesis, but she is pleased she has put the finishing touches to our dish.

I've heard some laughter from the others. Controlled, subdued laughter, but laughter nevertheless. Ruth and I walk round the kitchen and have a look to see how the others are getting on. It's beginning to smell wonderful. There is a rich-red, tomato soup with a mozzarella garnish and croutons; fresh salmon is laid out on a bed of leeks and asparagus, and the only chap cook (I never find out his name) is painstakingly whisking a yoghurt-based hollandaise sauce in a stainless steel bowl over a saucepan of boiling water. His eyes gleam as he thinks he sees his sauce finally pulling together after having whisked it the whole time Ruth and I have been making our avocado dip, but it's not there yet.

'Needs a chunk of cardboard to thicken it up,' I say, in English. Luckily, he doesn't understand the joke.

'Can you stir this for a few minutes?' he asks, in German, his smooth face pink and dripping from the steam that rises like a smouldering volcano from all the saucepans around him on the peninsula. I think he's the only one who hasn't had a chance to look at what the others are doing, so I unhook his fingers, which are welded to his whisk, and he scampers off like a puppy who has been attached to his lead all day.

The sauce thickens beautifully, but I can't see myself having his patience to stir for such a long time when I'm at home. The kitchen is buzzing. A very elderly, very tall, very thin lady dips cooked new potatoes in their skins into a concoction of oil and parsley and then shakes them into a serving dish, and another twosome (women, not potatoes) are making a delicate rhubarb sweet. Most impressive of all are two girls working next to Ruth and me. They are in the throes of rolling balls from a wonderful-looking chocolate concoction into truffles. A dusting of coconut and icing sugar completes the confection and the girls are carefully setting them out on doily-covered plates. Mmmmm.

'*Probier doch mal*,' says one of the girls, holding out a plate. (Try one.) Ruth and I each take one. It melts into a delicious dark-centred bitter-sweet dream, caressing our cavities and our hips. I go straight to heaven.

'We would *never* have had anything made with chocolate in 1973,' I tell the two girls. 'It would have been considered most unhealthy.' The girls look sorry for me. I bet they are thinking how regimental – and dull – it must have been.

'What else has changed?' asks Ruth, as she begins to stack our dirty dishes.

'For one thing, we weren't so artistic with the presentation as they are now. We'd get the food dished up on the plates as quickly as possible so it didn't get cold; I'd be standing by with a clean damp cloth to wipe up any stray blobs of sauce or gravy, then I'd sprinkle parsley, which I'd chopped only that morning over the whole dinner, and that was it.' Of course, no-one would have appreciated the blood, sweat and tears that had gone into all that *Petersilie* chopping by yours truly. It's only the end result that people notice.

'Are the menus the same?'

'Not really, but the flavours are similar, probably because of the fresh herbs. And we never had buffets at breakfast or in the evening like they do now. Everything was decided for the guests. Supper would be three salads with a simple hot dish of potatoes and quark, or an egg dish, or sometimes a hot pudding. And everyone was given a bowl of müesli at breakfast with no other choice unless you were on a special diet. But I like the buffets.'

'I do too,' Ruth smiles. 'It's all so healthy and everyone's so friendly. It's my first time here, but I'll certainly come again.'

We've finished. Two of the kitchen crew are clearing away the dirty dishes and sorting them in the dishwashers in the scullery next door where poor old Suna used to do her mountains of washing up mostly by hand. Wouldn't she have loved all these modern dishwashers? They don't know how spoilt they are today at Tannerhof. But I'm glad things are easier. And, of course, we guest cooks are also being spoilt having everything cleared up for us.

'It used to take us a good hour to scrub the kitchen from top to bottom every day,' I told Ruth, 'and that was with all of us working at top speed.'

Now we are ushered into the next-door staff dining room, which I used to go in on my day off, and where I first met Del. Again, it's a weird feeling going back such a long time. As usual, the two large tables are beautifully laid, just as they are laid for the guests, with small posies of fresh flowers and lighted candles in the centre. But tonight there are more wine glasses! And here comes Frau Winklmüller with a bottle of white. Yes, please.

The 'real' cooks serve us small portions, beautifully presented. Then they intermingle with us, which is lovely and would never happen in an English spa where there is a much stronger sense of not trespassing on guests' territory and becoming too familiar. I prefer the German way. There's such a happy atmosphere and I raise my glass to us all and toast.

'Bottoms up,' I say, wondering if anyone has ever heard that expression.

'Bottoms up,' they repeat, whether by imitation or knowledge, I couldn't say.

We clink with everyone, which makes them laugh. All this toasting sets the other table off toasting one another. If you can just break the ice, Germans *do* get into the atmosphere and love it; it's just that they always start any social gathering in a more formal way. I won't allow it. We lean over and toast as many as we can on that table. I'm delighted to see that we still have a waitress refilling our glasses. I raise mine after every course, and we clap the individual teams who made that particular dish.

I'm getting squiffy, which amuses the Germans no end. They're much more controlled. It's not that I'm a drinker – it's that I can't hold my drink. Even a mixture of wine and sparkling fruit water where the alcohol is no more than 5%, goes straight to my head after a few sips. I've always been a cheap date.

My German also amuses them. I speak more German now that I'm tipsy and words come to me that I've not uttered for decades. Sometimes, it's the wrong word and they correct me ever so politely.

Frau Winklmüller sits at our table. She speaks quite good English when pressed, but at the moment the conversation is all in German. I hear her mention Schwester Gisela to one of the other cooks.

'Sister Gisela is my friend.' I lean forward excitedly. 'Frau Mengershausen says she's coming to the festival.'

Frau Winklmüller looks surprised that I know her, but confirms that Schwester Gisela is indeed coming to Tannerhof's centenary this Saturday.

'We both worked here in 1973,' I say. 'I'm so looking forward to seeing her again. I just hope she'll recognise me.' Positive she will, but wanting to sound modest.

'I sink she does.' But Frau Winklmüller looks at me doubtfully. I expect she's thinking thirty-two years is a bloody long time, and she doesn't even know that before the festival I'll have yet another birthday to add. I'd better be more generous with my Super Restorative Nightwear this evening – doesn't it sound like an uplifting nightdress? – but it's my new nightcream, promising to fight those wrinkles, even as I sleep. You'll recognise me straight away, Gisela, I think, as I drop off. No question of it.

CHAPTER 32
BIRTHDAY WOMAN

I AM SIXTY! This is the first time I have admitted it and it may be the last. One of the main reasons why I am here is that I wouldn't have to celebrate this major birthday amongst family and friends in Tunbridge Wells. I just couldn't bear the idea. Especially as I sold my estate agency business two weeks before I came to Tannerhof. It had grown to eight offices and forty-five staff and I always said that I would sell before reaching this milestone but I only just scraped in. And I didn't want friends to inquire, 'What are you going to do now that you've retired?' Well, a) I don't intend to retire and b) I don't even want to hear that 'R' word directed to me. And anyway, I'm now a writer. That should keep me pretty occupied. The other depressing fact is that I am now eligible to claim a pension. That can't be true. So you can see why I am here. I need time on my own to take this all in. As most of the guests are older than me, it's an encouraging start.

My birthday begins by taking a urine sample first thing in the morning. Pretty original, eh? But the worry is, what do they mean by 'first thing in the morning?' Is it when I need a wee at a quarter-to-five? I decide it is, and grab the little plastic cup sealed with foil that was put out by my napkin at supper the night before. I had been sitting with the three charming sisters.

'*Was ist dass?*' I asked, holding up the cup. (What is that?) They tried to explain but I still couldn't understand. Finally, the sister on my left with the boyish haircut said, 'Pee-pee.'

'I might have known,' I told them, and they all looked relieved (no pun intended) when they realised I had got the message. Fancy leaving it at my dinner place, like a decoration. But when you think about it – why not?

So here I am, having remembered to remove the foil, struggling to aim my 'pee-pee' mid-flow into the cup. I put it discreetly into a brown paper bag ready to take it over to the doctors' reception desk at a more friendly hour. I needn't have bothered. Several women are carrying their filled paper cups over to the clinic without the paper bag. I do admire their lack of coyness in these medical matters. I place my 'disguised' sample next to their naked ones.

Next thing is that I have to take a weekly tablet to prevent the onset of osteoporosis. You have to take it with a glass of water first thing in the morning and not lie down or have any food or drink for a half an hour. If that doesn't make you feel old, I don't know what does. But I broke my wrist a year ago and had to go to the A&E department in the Kent & Sussex hospital, and my sister, who had come with me for moral support, said that I should definitely have an osteoporosis test. As I do regular exercise with my personal trainer twice a week, I pooh-poohed the idea, telling her that she was always so negative, and privately thinking it was probably Carole herself who ought to be tested as she didn't do any formal exercise, though she would argue that she gardens and walks a lot more than I do.

The elderly, but still flirty, (the only men who flirt with me nowadays are always elderly) Australian doctor at the A&E said he didn't think I had osteoporosis by the look of the X-ray, but it was always a sensible thing to find out via a scan. The very mention of the word 'scan' fills me with fear, but anyway, I went. To my amazement, I was just on the border of the first signs of having it, and when my sister was eventually tested, she was bloody well all right! Hence, calcium tablets and this weekly preventative, whatever that's got in it... loads of chemicals, I expect.

I'm not homesick but am glad I've brought a couple of birthday cards and a present from Edward looking suspiciously like a book. Great! I am devouring the four books I've brought at an alarming rate so am pleased I have a fresh one to read. I had put out a desperate call to my sister the other day asking for a particular book I wanted her to send me.

'It's in the left-hand book-case,' I told her. 'A paperback called *The Towers of Trebizond.*' I bought it last year and hadn't had time to read it. She promised to post it right away.

Just before I started out on this journey, Edward was unhooking my laptop for me and asked if I had packed enough books. Immediately, I panicked and took down a thick paperback from the top shelf.

'I think I'll take this one as an extra. I've had it ages and never read it.' It was called *Ladies of the Grand Tour*, and was about women travellers in the eighteenth century.

'I don't believe it,' said Edward. 'You might as well open your present now. It's rather heavy to take with you.'

I opened the brown paper and was astonished to see the hardback version of *Ladies of the Grand Tour.* 'But you were the one who gave me this five years ago.' It was unusual for Edward to forget these things. 'What a coincidence.'

'Luckily I've got another present for you,' and he handed me the second wrapped book.

I am sitting in my room at Tannerhof, on my birthday, opening this right now. I'm astounded. It's only an illustrated hardback of *The Towers of Trebizond*. What are the chances of something like that happening twice? Particularly as neither book is new. I must get on the phone to Carole to request another title.

I open the two cards. One from Edward and a funny one from my friend Jilly. So that's it, I think, as I prop both cards up on the shelf over my bed. Bit of a let-down. Then I remind myself that this was precisely the reason why I came away.

I open my balcony doors, step out and survey that marvellous scene which I can't think I will ever tire of. Sky's blue, the sun's come out for me, and it already feels warm so I have a quick shower and get dressed, taking more care than usual – after all, this is a special day – and go downstairs.

It's such a lovely day that I take my breakfast out onto the terrace and join four other guests who, like me, are passionate about eating outside. Such a treat not having to make the müesli, which I do most mornings at home, although it is only a matter of minutes to prepare. I spoon out a generous amount of fresh quark for the topping. Today's müesli is bursting with raspberries, strawberries, and a few fat blueberries. Delicious.

My companions are chatting to one another and I lazily follow their conversation, all the while interpreting it into English. I remember when I was working here and madly studying German, that I began to think in the language, and even *dream* in it. That was weird. They discover that it's my birthday today and all shake hands with me, saying: '*Gratuliere.*'

I go in search of my friends, Volker and Jutti Heil. They eat in a different dining room and usually come down later. But they're both there, smiling and standing up as I walk in. They also shake hands with me, and then Herr Heil looks at his wife, counts '*Ein, zwei, drei,*' and they chorus the German version of our Happy Birthday. After the first few words:

'*Viel Glück und viel Segen…*' the whole dining room stands up and joins in. (See page 62 to remind you of the rest of the song.) Their enthusiasm is as touching as their singing. Everyone is smiling and then they all come up and shake hands and congratulate me.

Gretl, our cheerful bedirndled housekeeper, who I later find out is Emmi's much younger sister, comes in carrying a tray bearing a candle, a full-blown coral-coloured rose, and a bottle of champagne that bears a Tannerhof label. How super. I decide I *do* like fuss, after all.

'We'll open it tonight after supper,' I promise the Heils, 'and we can sip Champagne on the porch and catch the last of the evening sun.'

They think it an excellent idea. I tell them I must have a photo of the tray so I get my camera and we take pictures out on the terrace; they take several of me at this strange new age of sixty. I try to hold my stomach in as tightly as I can without swooning, and Herr Heil does his best with a strange non-digital camera in brilliant sunlight, so hope they turn out.

Must run… off to a massage. This is the life!

Pop back to my room to change, and there to greet me is a stunning bouquet of red roses. Don. After all these years he rarely fails to send me roses on my birthday, no matter where I am. But this is a complete surprise. I bury my nose in their velvety depths. Just a hint of perfume. My room has taken on the air of a boudoir and I'm feeling overwhelmed.

Edward has left me a message on my mobile so I ring him and tell him about *The Towers of Trebizond.* 'Isn't it weird?' I say.

'Just a coincidence.'

Then I ring Carole. It's funny not calling Mum. This must be the first birthday that I don't see her or phone her. I'm so glad she knew

I was writing this book. She had already read several chapters until she became so ill that I had to read the next ones to her, and even in her pain, she smiled and even laughed aloud on several occasions.

I am having a lazy day reading *True To Both My Selves* by Katrin Fitzherbert. It is about a child who was born in Germany in 1936 on the outskirts of Berlin and, ten years later, is repatriated to England and warned never to speak of her German origins and Nazi father. It is riveting and gives another side of the coin that you don't usually see. I realise it's not the usual book one would read in Germany and on one's birthday, but this doesn't bother me at all.

Wander in to have lunch, which is the usual salad display, and for the main course we have salmon and asparagus, with wild rice in the shape of a child's sandcastle, but only a trillionth of the size. We wouldn't want to get fat, would we? Dessert is a bowl of succulent cherries. It's all delectable and the menu couldn't have been better planned as far as I was selfishly concerned.

I do some writing in the afternoon, and then I feel I must have a cup of real tea…and would it be too awful if I have a piece of *Kuchen* to go with it? I walk to the village and over to Café Hubert, as I still feel guilty about Herr Hubert's car, but he's closed on Wednesdays. That leaves Café Stumpp for the next best cakes. I wander over and am enticed by the Bavarians sitting outside at tables enjoying the sun and their cooling drinks. The waitress, a pretty blonde girl with an enviable waist, comes to take my order. She is surprised that I want hot tea on such a hot day. She ushers me inside to choose a cake and I desperately look for the least fattening. Cheesecake. Yes, in Germany, cheesecake is probably the least fattening.

'Just a small slice,' I tell her, but she just smiles. Moments later she's here with a tray of tea and a piece of cheesecake the size of a breezeblock. Oh, no. But it's as light as candy-floss and the sharp lemon flavour persuades me that it doesn't contain much sugar. I eke it out over three cups of tea, savouring every mouthful. Café Stumpp, which used to be Barry's and my favourite café, hasn't lost its touch.

Just sitting down to supper when Daniella, the delightful waitress, comes to tell me that I have a phone call. It's Don to wish me a happy birthday.

'Do you know how long it is since you've phoned me at Tannerhof?' I ask.

'Must be all of thirty years.'

'Thirty-two.'

'Seems like yesterday,' he says.

After supper, the Heils and I open the Champagne and it froths as it slips down the back of my throat. There's nothing like it.

'Will you come with me to Bayrischzell later on?' I ask the Heils. 'There's a Bavarian group playing on the band-stand.' I know they are keen on classical music, like me, and not wild about Bavarian music but there is nothing else going on at Tannerhof this evening, and it is my birthday, so they readily agree.

The band has attracted quite a following, and the Heils and I take a seat a few rows back. Most of the people greet one another and I suspect they're nearly all from the village.

Ouch! A horrid nip. I'm wearing a sleeveless dress and that was a bite!

The music begins. The programme is all marches, which are pretty stirring, and you feel you can understand why youths in the thirties who were probably not that well-educated or bright, and were leaning towards being hooligans, would be swept along with Hitler's Youth regime.

I lean over to Herr Heil on my right to say something after several pieces of marching music, but he doesn't hear me. I say it a little louder and he takes an earplug out of his left ear. I get the giggles.

'I can't believe you're at a concert and wearing earplugs,' I splutter. He has to laugh himself.

'Sometimes it gets too loud for me. It is better when it is more quiet.'

'When it's blocked out, you mean. Well I can't say I blame you. Where did you say you bought your earplugs?'

I'm in bed at an early hour of ten o'clock with my book, but looking back over the day I think: I have had a fantastic birthday at Tannerhof. I was told by a guest this morning that I only looked forty-five (!!!) and was *beautiful* (more !!!), and not to ever tell anyone my real age (she was an attractive forty-two-year old); I'd had cards from my family and friends, I was sent a dozen red roses by an old flame, and I was amongst new and old friends here at my beloved Tannerhof. If that can happen at sixty then it can't be too bad. I've decided to enjoy every minute. *Happy Birthday, Denise!*

Chapter 33
Schlank-Tag

SHH

Schlank-Tag LITERALLY MEANS 'Slim Day' but Tannerhof describes
it as a health day. It's the day after my birthday so I don't feel I'm
missing out on anything by putting my name down on the list to
comply with the very light diet and strong exercise programme that
they have in store. I'm glad to see there are a few young ones on
the list, particularly a gorgeous firm-thighed Amazon, who speaks
excellent English.

She and I have become quite friendly but as the day proceeds
I realise trying to keep up with all this youth can be high risk. Let
me take you through this *Schlank-Tag* from the beginning and you
will see what I mean.

I was told yesterday evening that those of us on this special day
were to meet at 6.30 am at the front entrance ready to go jogging. The

trouble is… I've made the same mistake as the one I made thirty-two years ago on my first day in the kitchen. Frau Winklmüller said '*Halb seben*', which translates half seven, which to me is half-past seven. But in German it means half an hour *to* seven, that is, six-thirty. That shouldn't have mattered as I'm always awake at five, except, of course, this morning. I was writing my diary last night and didn't put my light out until a quarter to one. It never bothers me that I don't have a travel alarm clock as all I have to do is tell myself what time I want to get up and I always wake up a few minutes before the appointed time. So I told myself that a quarter to seven would be the time to get up.

What a nasty shock. The telephone shrieks into my ear from its position on the shelf above my head, and Frau Winklmüller says, 'We are waiting for you, Denise!'

I peer at my watch. It is 6.35. I remember. Bugger.

'I'll be down in five minutes,' I say. And I am. My five companions remind me of greyhounds ready to leap from their traps the second Frau Winklmüller says 'Go!' I feel guilty that I have held them up for ten minutes, but they hide any irritation and off we jog. I should tell you I have never been on an organised jog in my life. It starts off quite tamely, though I wish I was wearing a sports bra as I can feel myself bouncing up and down, and I don't think that's good for you. But I've never owned a sports bra, and am not quite sure even what they look like. I may have mentioned that I despise exercise with the exception of cycling, and can honestly say that I have never once looked forward to Chris, my twice-a-week trainer, turning up at 6.30 am. He probably feels the same way about me at that time of the morning when I'm bereft of make-up. Now, I'm trying to jog in a way to stop my breasts from jumping, but it's impossible. The other girls look properly restrained. They're obviously used to all this activity or else they're not so well endowed as me.

I look at my watch. Twelve minutes have passed and I'm proud that I'm not last. But I'm starting to puff. The others are chatting and taking no notice of the fact that we are travelling uphill. Bloody Hell! I expect we'll stop in a minute to have a sip of water. Why do I always fall into the trap of thinking that Germans take breaks? They never do. Ever. I take it all back. We're stopping. *What! Exercises?* Frau Winklmüller takes us through calf stretches, arm swings, neck arcs…on a public footpath where there are a few early-morning dogs with their walkers. No-one – least of all the dogs – takes any notice of anyone. If I was in England right now I would feel extremely self-conscious, but Germans, as I've said before, don't seem to feel that way at all where their bodies are concerned. Off we go again.

My heart is beginning to race but I'm not alarmed as I've had it all checked out and admired (for my age) by Dr Schröeder, though my lungs feel raw. I'm not gasping, but I know I won't be able to keep up this pace much longer. Everyone else is still chatting. How can they do that and jog at the same time? It's not normal.

A few more minutes creep by. We've been going now for twenty-five minutes and there's no sign of a let-up. I had managed to slurp some water whilst we were doing the exercises, but my tongue and throat are parched again. Heart's thumping in protest. I have to slow down to walking pace. I start lagging behind. I start feeling old. Not *old* old, but not as young as I like to think I am. Frau Winklmüller looks concerned.

'Are you all right, Denise?' she asks.

'Yes, but I think I'll walk for a bit.'

'That's okay. There's no hurry.'

You could have fooled me. Without a backward glance the others jog out of sight. I'm walking at quite an acceptable pace now and feel a million times better. Until I come to the crossroads. Which way? But there's Frau Winklmüller waving to me and I wave back. She immediately jogs off to join the other Schlankers.

I'm not that far behind the others after all. The Amazon, Liesl, admits that she, too, had to walk the last ten minutes and she's miles younger than me – exactly half my age, in fact. Suddenly, I don't feel so decrepit.

We're back at Tannerhof, and Frau Winklmüller directs us to the wading pool. I've always suppressed a giggle when I've seen people in the wading pool; they remind me of very solemn children, and I swore I would never subject myself to anything so silly. It's full of knee-high ice-cold water and you have to walk around it twice, which is supposed to be good for your circulation. I wish I had a camera. I try to imagine the English wading in single file, in perfect formation, oblivious to the freezing-cold water at 7.15 am. No, I simply can't imagine it, no matter how hard I try. Where's a towel to dry yourself? There isn't one. The dew hasn't even had a chance to evaporate in such a weak, early-morning sun.

Not more exercise? Grab left ankle from behind with left hand so you are balancing on one leg. Hurrah! Yoga and a personal trainer has paid off. I am perfectly poised while the much-younger-than-me ones are hopping about all over the place like one-legged penguins. I can't believe what Frau Winklmüller is doing! She is demonstrating the one-legged pose and is raising her right arm. Everyone follows suit. Before I can stop myself I also raise my right arm and blurt out, 'Heil, Hitler!' For an instant everyone turns to me, horrified. I have to laugh, and after three nail-biting seconds, they join in. Phew! I berate myself for my bad manners, but really – what do they expect?

Breakfast: slice of lemon in hot water. Three pieces of fresh fruit; the waitress looks away for a second so I whip four – a peach, a very small piece of melon, and two pieces of fresh pineapple. We're allowed to have a few nuts so I take ten almonds – and that is it! Stomach rolling, I leave the table. We have been told to rest through-out the morning. Just as well, as I'm not sure I've got enough energy to even pull the sun-lounger into the perfect spot. It's getting hotter and I can't wait to give up my body to the sun-god. Can't even get interested in book or mag. It's all too wonderful for words. I glance over at Liesl. She looks fantastic in her bikini – she's golden-tanned, and is oiling those long legs of hers. She throws me a smile and a wave. Everyone is so *nice* here.

Ten-forty-five. Didn't it say on the menu for the Schlankers that we could have a tomato juice mid-morning? I drag myself out of my stupor and wander over to the main house.

'*Ja*,' says Christa, one of the jolly waitresses, as I point to a jug.

I pour two. 'One for Liesl,' I explain. Christa nods.

'Oh, Denise, I had forgotten,' says Liesl delightedly, as I hand her a glass. We sip, making it last. It's glorious, considering I'm not that keen on tomato juice.

Doze again on my sun-lounger until it's time for my Treger massage. I am sure you will not have heard of this particular massage. It's American. A hands-on massage getting right into the joints, but it has a touch of the Alexander Technique in that an attractive masseuse places you on the bed with your weight spread in an incredibly comfortable way which you would never be able to do for yourself, and you are cocooned in a feeling of well-being when she's finished. Fabulous.

The lunch bell goes. It's like being at school – everything done for you, and no responsibilities at all. We form an orderly queue. I note that the ones on the Health Day are first. We're only allowed salad but there's a good salad bar. This doesn't mean potato salad in mayonnaise, or eggs or cheese, or anything containing more than 6 calories – it's just raw grated vegetables such as thinly-sliced cucumber in a yoghurt and dill dressing. We Schlankers can have as much as we like. I pile my plate high, and go and sit with the three sisters. I try not to look too enviously when their main course of salmon is brought to them. I refill my plate with a few more salad leaves.

Feel full of nothing. How do I take my mind off food? Well, there's always Nordic Walking. Have you ever tried Nordic Walking? Unless you're very fit and sporty… don't. They told me it would be a two-hour hike, which made me dubious from the start. Could I honestly walk two hours in the mountains fuelled only by lettuce leaves?

Two-fifteen. We all meet outside the main house and our instructor looks us up and down to gauge what size our two walking sticks should be. It takes me ages to get them clipped into the palms of my hands. Three chaps have joined us and one of them, blond and handsome, helps me. He can help me any time he likes.

'You all have water with you?' asks our instructor, a lean, dark-haired young woman.

It transpires that I am the only one with a bottle of water. She says she has enough for us all. I'm not surprised. Her rucksack is as big as a tea-chest strapped to her back. I'm curious to see what her posture is like once she gets going.

We all clamber into two cars and drive towards the mountains. The scenery is so beautiful it makes your heart squeeze with happiness. I get out of the car feeling as though I'm on a film-set. Any minute now I'm going to burst into 'The hills are alive...' but I manage to restrain myself.

We are given a short demonstration on how to handle the sticks and how to walk with their support – she makes it look simple and fun. I can't wait.

Synchronising the poles and your arms and legs is not so easy as it looks. I start off with the right leg (good start) and my right arm. Wrong. Immediately, I overbalance and fall over. But no-one jeers. They help get me back together again and off we go. After twenty minutes or so I'm almost getting the hang of it. I'm also getting thirsty as the sun is really beating down. We go on a bit further and stop. Good. A water break. No such thing. We're doing exercises – *again* – to stretch our calves...as if our calves aren't stretched enough already. A few walkers and cyclists pass, not even bothering to glance in our direction. I lose my self-consciousness and forget everything except the exercise in hand. We prepare to start walking again.

'I'm just going to have a sip of water!' I gasp.

'Good idea,' from our instructor, and the others follow suit.

I am doing so well that for the first time I become completely aware of my surroundings instead of having my eyes glued on the ground. The mountains are stunning today. The sun is so bright that the ones far away look misty, but those close to us are friendly and bursting with wild flowers, most of which I've never seen before. No-one stops to have a closer look. I'd like to but daren't as I'll get left behind as I did with the jogging. But the jogging route, I knew roughly where I was – this one gave no clues. We travel on for another half an hour. I can't take too much more. I must stop for water. They all stop and have a polite mouthful. If I hadn't stopped, they wouldn't have done. We've only been going just over an hour and all that is keeping me going is the thought of a goblet of soya milk mixed with crushed fresh fruit that Daniella promised me at the end of the walk when we are back at Tannerhof.

We have now been walking for three hours! I cannot go another step. Just as well that our cars are in sight. I slump into the back seat, dazed, and the others have to laugh at my distress, which they think I am exaggerating for effect.

We're home. Oh, no, not the knee-high-cold-water wade again. Well, I'm not going to be the only one who doesn't finish off the walk in the correct manner, so in I plunge, and have to admit that my legs instantly freshen up and I feel wide awake. Until I start walking and notice that my right leg is screaming. I think I've pulled a muscle. No-one else complains so I say nothing and hope it goes away. I don't want to go back to England a cripple after having spent two weeks at a health spa. If I can just make it up the steps to the front door of Tannerhof, and limp up the flight of stairs to my room…because that's where my delicious soya dessert awaits…

Supper – I head straight for the salad bar again and fill up my plate but Christa spies me.

'You must only have soup this evening,' she tells me. Blast! I don't really want soup, but obediently I give her my plate. 'Take a seat,' she says, 'and I will bring it to you.'

It smells rich. It's a Mediterranean fish soup and it wafts into my nostrils and soothes my throat. It's like invalid soup when you're recovering…which I am.

My last evening but one with Herr and Frau Heil. They go home Saturday morning. I'll miss our chats. They are so nice. I wish they were staying for the centenary, but they didn't know about it and are as disappointed as I am.

I go up to my room at nine o'clock. Do I do a bit more on the computer? Have I enough strength to switch on? And at the end of the *Schlank-Tag*, am I slimmer? It's too soon to tell, but still-puffy stomach doesn't give me much encouragement. Maybe today's regime has to work its way through the system. Well, I guess the scales will give me the answer tomorrow!

CHAPTER 34
THE LAST HUNDRED YEARS

Saturday, 25th June... Today is a very special day for Tannerhof. It's a hundred years since the von Mengershausen family founded Tannerhof as a sanatorium, or health clinic, as it's known nowadays. When the original von Mengershausens came across the house, it was more or less derelict but in such a fabulous spot, they knew it would be ideal for their alternative therapies and healthy regime.

It's not quite so sunny this morning as it has been but I don't think rain is forecast. I can hear the men banging and drilling under my window where they have erected three joined-together marquees. They have been working solidly for two days and still haven't finished. They only have a few more hours to go, and there's a lot of talking and laughter going on – can't decipher any swearing – so I guess it's going to plan.

I say my farewell to Herr and Frau Heil after breakfast. We promise to keep in touch.

'Don't forget to send us a signed copy of the book,' says Herr Heil.

'Definitely, as you do feature in it,' I say, 'but a signed copy won't be as valuable as an unsigned one.' I'm not sure they understand the joke, but they laugh anyway with me.

This morning I can relax with my book, *The Towers of Trebizond*, which I love. Actually, I can't completely relax as I am terrified of finishing it and I'm relying on Carole and the post to send me *Laurence of Arabia* in time. Being an addicted reader is fine when you have a stack of books lined up that you haven't read. I brought four with me, but obviously that wasn't enough. Good thing I'm off to Tai Chi. Instructor is so serious, it makes me want to giggle but I behave myself as everyone else is perfectly focused on the ballet-type movements. I hope all this will help my leg, which is still agonising from the Nordic Walking.

'*Und Wasser nehmen,*' (And take water) croons Herr Kohl, our Tai Chi instructor, as he sinks down, splaying his knees that crack like the whip of a circus trainer, and cups a pretend bowl of water, then rises like a genie, pushing the pretend bowl into thin air. His voice starts off quite high on the first syllable, and then it drops down an octave and the rest of the sentence is all on the same note, unless he says, 'Gut.'

Then he begins, 'Gu-u-u-u-u-t', which starts low and goes right up the scale. It makes me want to giggle again.

We all sink down with him, my knees cracking in harmony with his, and I'm feeling perfectly stupid with my pretend bowl of water, but the others accept his instructions with perfectly straight faces.

I think this was more of a joint session, as I don't really feel I've had much exercise, but it's very stress-busting, so I must try to remember it when I'm home.

Wonderful... cleaning lady has just recovered my earring, which must have fallen out of my ear last night. She says someone handed it in.

I have a shower and wash my hair – all perfectly straightforward until I attempt to dry it. I'm alarmed that the heating element inside my brand-new hair dryer is going to combust as it's gone an angry red inside. I check that I have switched the voltage over to the European 110. Maybe I shouldn't have changed it, but I've used it on this setting several times since I've been here and it seemed fine, except that the power of the air-flow was exceptionally strong and almost blew my scalp off the first time I used it. But I just thought it was because it was a modern travel dryer with more energy than my old heavy one. I turn it back to English voltage and the dryer immediately calms down, so I turn it off to let it cool for ten minutes before I attempt to switch it on again, leaving it on the English setting. Thank goodness – it's working and the power is not so fierce. No time now to style hair properly so it will have to be wild and natural.

I'm getting terribly excited. Gisela should be arriving at any moment. I'm reading out on the lawn. It's just gone two but already people are gathering, even though the celebrations don't officially start until three o'clock. I can't wait to see her again...

Can't wait for Gisela any longer. It's time to find my place. I've been told that we have a table near the front of the stage, especially reserved for those of us who are reading the Tannerhof poem. I'm one of that 'select' group. The elegant elderly lady who wrote the poem had asked several guests if they would read out the poem she wrote especially for today, but most of them politely declined, and she was relieved when I said I would take part. We only had a couple of rehearsals and everyone was so funny because they chanted this light-hearted poem completely poker-faced. In desperation, I mimicked them saying the line, '*That is fun*' in a dull tone with a deadpan expression, and after three or four seconds they got the message and laughed.

'You have to act the words,' I told them, and they promised they would.

'Here, Denise, over here,' the poet waves to me. Excellent. I'll have a perfect view. The others in our group join me and we admire the table, beautifully set with fresh flowers *and two sets of wine glasses*! It all looks promising until I remember that I am on antibiotics and not supposed to have alcohol. (Dr Schröeder spotted a mild kidney infection.) I don't suppose I'll die if I have a glass of champagne as my theory is that champagne goes with anything. I'm prepared to take the risk, anyway. Daniella comes round with a tray, but I play safe and choose a Buck's Fizz instead. 'It only has a dash of champagne,' I reassure myself.

Another waitress comes round with a delectable assortment of snacks, and I help myself to a morcelette of bread – the first I've had in ten days – and a slice of cheese no bigger than you'd put in a mouse-trap if you were being really mean. This is rapidly followed by a tray full of what looks to me like brownies. They can't be. Brownies are far too unhealthy. All that rich sticky chocolate. I'd better not have one but don't know how I've managed to resist. Everyone else tucks into theirs and tells me it is a famous Bavarian cake. It's too late for me to change my mind and I console myself with the thought: 'heaven on your lips – a lifetime on your hips', though there wasn't much consolation when I got on the scales the next morning after the *Schlank* Day and discovered I hadn't even lost an ounce.

Then Dr Mengerhausen comes onto the platform. It still seems strange not to see the mother, Anneli von Mengershausen, who I always felt, still do, *is* Tannerhof. But the daughter is just as charming and has admirably taken her mother's place in the running of the clinic. She makes a speech with no notes for over half an hour, speaking so clearly and slowly that I understand at least a quarter of it, and am extra proud when I get some of the jokes.

'I have always known Tannerhof is special,' she goes on, 'but I've never really known why. Is it because of the beautiful scenery – our wonderful mountains and the pure air? Is it because of the natural treatments, or the fresh healthy food? Well, I think it is a combination of all these things, but most of all, I believe, it is due to the people who work here.' At this, we heartily clap. I look round and see the smiling faces of the waitresses, cooks, cleaners, gardeners, therapists, office workers, all dotted around the marquee. 'They're the ones who really make it special. Then, of course, there are the guests…' she pauses, and beams at us, 'without whom there wouldn't *be* a Tannerhof.' We all laugh and clap.

Then *her* daughter, Burgi, also a doctor, takes the platform. She is tall and thin with short dark hair and a pretty face whose expression changes from gentle to vivacious depending on her subject. She explains the history of Tannerhof during the last hundred years, including both world wars. I find her more difficult to understand than her mother as she speaks rapidly, but her wide smile and quick burst of laughter is infectious, and I laugh along with the audience. She is followed by her husband, an incredibly tall, gangly young man with floppy blond hair who is a specialist doctor (not sure what in) who talks about the medicine and treatments at Tannerhof over the last hundred years, but again, I can't understand it all even though he gesticulates like an Italian. It's so frustrating. By the audience's response he is very amusing but much of it is lost on me.

Then a well-dressed elderly lady takes the floor. She speaks the slowest and clearest of all the speakers, and I understand her practically word for word.

'This is my forty-first time at Tannerhof!' she begins in modulated tones. We all clap. 'The first time was in 1968…' (so more than likely she'd been a guest during my time in the kitchen) and names like Ooffey and Maria turn up. She says how marvellous the staff were, and still are today. It's nice to hear about the people I knew, although she didn't mention poor Frau Weilland, who is now in a mental home with Alzeimer's, nor the kitchen staff all those years ago, and I know Emmi is here in the marquee at the back, and she has cooked at Tannerhof for the best part of forty years. I wish this nice guest would say something about Emmi, and, indeed, Anita, who is also here today. But she doesn't.

I wonder for the hundredth time if I can muster up the nerve to do a little speech in German. I think I can, as I've gone over and over it in my mind: the only thing that stops me is if Frau Mengershausen wouldn't want me to and yet wouldn't want to hurt my feelings if I asked her. Or should I do it without asking anyone after we recite our little poem? I'd love to tell these two hundred and fifty guests how I came to Tannerhof all those years ago, and here I am again as a guest. I would end with a joke and say that although I loved my year working in the kitchen, call me old-fashioned, but it's better to be a guest! They're all in such good humour today and prepared to enjoy every moment of this grand occasion. I'll play it by ear.

Talk about playing by ear. A man and a woman have just come onto the platform carrying a violin and a cello. Lovely. Some Mozart. We sit back and let his music wash over us. Germans do love their classical music and it makes me happy to share it with them.

The next speaker is an older gentleman who had had all kinds of ailments – high blood pressure, high cholesterol, diabetes and so on, and tells us how he was miraculously restored by visiting Tannerhof regularly, and now he doesn't have to take any blood pressure or anti-cholesterol tablets – he keeps everything under control by his diet.

It's our turn. Seven of us rise as one and make our way to the stage clutching our paper with the words. The two men stand behind us five women. The lady who wrote the poem counts *'Ein, zwei, drei'* and we're off in staccato rhythm. (Translation at end of chapter.)

'Tannerhof – Mengershausen – Hundert Jahre – Wun-der-bar.'

The men now have to say *'Tan-ner-hof, Tan-ner-hof, Tan-ner-hof'* in an undertone to coincide with our words. I don't know how I stop myself from giggling as everyone's po-faced. It is heavily recited and the last three words of each line have a pause in between every word, which sounds laborious:

Morgens Müesli – Obst und Käse – Mittags Bio / das - tut - gut.
Fastenstube – Fastenbrühe – Fastenbrechen / das - macht - schlank.
Frühgymnastik – Nordic walking – Meditieren / das - macht - schwer.
(next line chanted very quickly)
Wird schon besser – wird schon besser – wird schon besser – (slow up)
Im – mer – mehr.
(back to normal rhythm)
Wechselgüsse – Ganzmassage – Moor und Fango / das – be - lebt.
Volkstanzschreiten – Yoga üben – Kochen lernen / das - macht - spass.
Schwimmbadfreuden – Saunabaden – Bilder Mahlen / ein – Ge - nuss.
Ärzten Schwestern – Haus und Küche – allen Helfern / viel - en - Dank.
Tannerhof – noch viele Jahre – Gottes Segen / im – mer - dar.
(next line very quickly)
Tannerhof – Tannerhof – Tannerhof – er lebe drei mal hoch! Hoch! HOCH!'

After every *Hoch!* fling hands up in air to demonstrate height to which Tannerhof can rise and encourage audience to join in.

They do. They obviously love it. We make all the right gestures at the right time (just as I coached them) and everyone is laughing and clapping at the end of every verse. Maybe they hope each time a verse ends that that must surely be the end of the poem.

It seems to be a huge success and we take a mock bow and totter down the steps to our table. I blow my chance to give my little speech – it's probably just as well.

One of the ladies I pass stops me and says:

'I watched your actions – you should be on ze stage.' Little does she know.

Time for a break. We troop outside where it's sunny but there are clouds gathering. I spot Anita in a very girlish dirndl. I give her a hug, which she doesn't seem to mind too much and I ask her how she is, as Frau Mengershausen told me Anita has breast cancer. She tells me she has had the 'all clear' from the doctor, which is marvellous news.

'*Und wo ist dein Sohn?*' I ask her. (Where is your son?)

'*Er ist hier,*' (He is here) and she beckons me to follow her. I am introduced to a stocky, dark-haired young man, not quite the seven footer that Anita had once demonstrated.

'The last time I saw you, you were a baby,' I say in German, rocking a pretend baby in my arms to make sure he understands, and he laughs, which lights up his plain features, but he disappears pretty smartly, no doubt running out of conversation with this dotty Englishwoman. Anita's gone too. It's difficult to have much of a conversation as my German is limited, never having any practice at home, and I have little in common with the old kitchen crew any more. But I don't give up. Emmi and her husband are a few feet away so I stroll over.

'I'm sorry I had to rush the other day at the station,' Emmi says (in German, of course). She promises to make me some of her famous *Apfelstrudel* and I am to go over to her house the following Tuesday. She'll send her husband to escort me. He is laughing and nodding. He's terribly sweet, shorter than Emmi and looks younger. The years haven't been so kind to Emmi. She's been such a hard worker all her life.

The sky suddenly blackens only to be blasted by a flash of lightning. Thunder growls and rain stings the backs of my legs like a hundred wooden spoons as we stumble back to our tents. Only just in time. It's like a monsoon bursting through the canvas where two of the tents are joined, obviously not very well, near the stage and right where I'm sitting. Someone rushes with a towel but it's like using a face-cloth to stem a flood. I worry about all the wires for the microphone and lights as the rain is splashing onto them. Everyone at our table is getting wet, including me, but no-one moves. They take no notice at all.

After another soaking minute I get up and stand a few steps away at the side to watch a scene being set for a play that some of the staff are putting on. It's a send-up of Tannerhof in 1905 and its patients (as they would have been called in those days). The 'actors' enter one by one in their comic period costumes, all instantly recognisable as waitresses and therapists, and several of the Mengershausens. Their first lines are drowned in the noise of the downpour and one or two people call out that they can't hear so the 'doctor' (who really is young Dr Mengershausen) has to take the microphone. As there is only one, it becomes the roving microphone, and whoever has it has to remember who speaks next and get it over to them in time. The play is very funny anyway but it becomes hysterical as the actors never remember who needs the microphone next and sometimes it has to be thrown over, or rammed almost down the next speaker's throat. Even so, you can't hear the words properly, so any worry I had about not understanding what was being said is dispelled as no-one else can hear either. Afterwards, when we've clapped ourselves silly, I hear one woman laugh to another how the rain and the microphone made the play, and I realise (not for the first time) Germans *do* have a sense of humour.

Supper at 8 pm, and the cooks have surpassed themselves. We troop out in orderly fashion, table by table to the salad buffet, which is a magnificent spread. Because we'd had a cooked lunch, I thought this was to be our main meal so pile my plate. Oh, no, the waitresses are bringing everyone a hot supper with a choice of three dishes. I choose salmon, new potatoes, broccoli and delicious sauce and fall on the potatoes as I haven't tasted a potato, or carbs for ages. I accept a glass of white wine, knowing that I'm not supposed to, but what the heck.

The food is great, but the desserts are to die for. There are at least a dozen to choose from and greedy, deprived me wants some of everything. I settle on three (very) small helpings: fruit tart with home-made vanilla custard, apricot whip with dark berry sauce and one home-made truffle. During all this wonderful eating, the Bavarian band sets itself up on the platform: there are ten musicians, all in *Lederhosen* complete with Tyrolean hats, looking very jolly and colourful.

No sooner have we finished supper than our table, being in the front, is chosen to be pushed to one side, along with a few others, to create a dance floor. Ruth asks me to dance, but I *loathe* dancing with a woman, so meanly refuse and then feel guilty. She's such a nice person, but I see she soon finds a willing partner. She's twirling the other lady round and is as flushed as a schoolgirl. The floor becomes jammed with guests and waitresses and cooks and Mengershausens dancing like there's no tomorrow; the older ones giving it every bit as much energy as the younger. I feel envious and wish I hadn't been quite so quick to refuse Ruth's offer. It doesn't look as if I'll even get to dance at this rate. I particularly watch the young Dr Mengershausens dancing. They never stop smiling at one another, he so tall and gangly looking down on Burgi's neat dark head and sweet face. How wonderful to be so much in love.

Another song ends, and I hear some unbelievably magic words from one of the members of the band who I had briefly spoken to when they were setting up their instruments.

'I will dance wiz ze English girl.' (Girl... GIRL!) And he jumps off the platform to claim me.

I stutter that I've forgotten how to do Bavarian dancing, that I'm not wearing the right shoes, and that they're bound to slip off and trip me up.

He grins. 'I will hold you,' is all he says. *It's all he need say*, I think, as I look into those young brown eyes, and smiling lips. I'm clumsy on the floor, but he's so good that he compensates, and then I have flashes of rhythm and step perfectly in time with him, just like in the *Heuboden* days, which lulls us both into a false sense of security, before I dance right out of my shoe, and he has to catch me from slipping through his fingers. (I truly didn't do it on purpose.) He doesn't give up. I'm whirled straight into the next dance and the next, waltzing and polkaring and square-dancing, till laughing and spent, like the *old* girl I really am, I plead to sit down.

'I will come for you later,' he promises. I can't wait.

I realise how much I enjoy dancing, and how rarely I do it at home, and how bad I am at it unless I have a superb partner. The Bavarian was good, but no-one will ever match Marijan, from Yugoslavia, as it was then called. I met him at the Goethe Institut (where I went in March '74, if you've kept up with these adventures, after I left my cooking job at Tannerhof). He was tall and slim and muscular, with black hair, dark brown eyes, and gorgeous. He had no idea how handsome he was; but he knew he was an excellent dancer.

At the first party a few days after we all arrived, Marijan asked me to dance. I fancied him like mad and he was asking the worst dancer in the room to partner him. As I warned the Bavarian in the dance band, I told him I was a lousy dancer and he said, in an irresistible Slavic accent:

'You won't be with me.' Well, what would *you* have done? After only a few steps of a waltz, I knew I was with a pro as we dipped and bobbed and twirled. I was in fantasy-land until I realised we were the only ones dancing, and if it hadn't been for Marijan's strong arm I might have lost my balance as well as my head. *They had cleared the floor!* You see that sort of thing in films, but never in my wildest dreams could I have believed it would one day happen to me. And when he threw my body over his arm as though I weighed nothing more than one of the snow-flakes falling outside, and with his face so close to mine I could feel his breath, I knew exactly how Ginger Rogers must have felt when dancing with Fred Astaire, except that I never complained (as *she* did) that I did everything Marijan was doing except backwards in high heels!

But I was thirty-one years younger in those days, and today I'm just grateful to have *any* male dancing partner!

I'm sitting on my own now, as everyone at my table has gone off to dance. Frau Mengershausen comes over with a handsome blond young man, whom she introduces to me as Michael, one of her two sons. He's dressed in *Lederhosen*, and manages to make suede over bum look sexy – not to mention his English, which is practically perfect. He was born during the time I worked at Tannerhof and has his PhD in Psychiatry but doesn't practise at Tannerhof – otherwise I would definitely have booked a few sessions. A bit of psychiatry never goes amiss! We talk and talk, and he gives me his full attention. *That* is when a man is charming. When they *really* look at you and don't let their eyes rove over your shoulder trying to spot someone younger and prettier, and pay you attention and laugh in all the right places – that's charm. This boy will go far. He's asking me to dance! I can't believe my luck, being led onto the dance floor with this young Adonis.

We change partners a few times, as you do in Bavarian dancing, and Michael claims me again.

'No more,' I pant, as though I've been making love all night, and he guides me stumbling to my table, dizzy, thinking it's time I left and got to bed before I turn into one of the ugly sisters.

'You must have one more dance before leaving, so I will come back for you.'

I don't want to push my luck, and besides, there are some lovely women his own age out there for him to dance with – he doesn't need to be saddled with a sixty-year-old! But thanks for asking, Michael – it was the perfect ending to a perfect day.

Our Centenary Poem

Morning müesli - fruit and cheese - midday salad / that-is-good
Fasting Room - Fasting broth - Fasting break / makes-you-slim
Early morning gymnastics - Nordic walking - meditation
     / that-is-difficult
We'll get better - etc.
Continually improving.
Hot and cold treatments - full massage - mudbath / that-we-love.
Swimming - sauna - painting / a-de-light.
Doctors, sisters - house and kitchen - all help / ma-ny-thanks
Tannerhof - for many years - God's blessings / al-ways-there
Tannerhof... it proudly lives...

This is the best translation I came up with.

Chapter 35
A Serendipitous Meeting

TODAY, TUESDAY, IS A*pfelstrudel* day. Emmi is sending Karl, her cheerful little husband, to Tannerhof to take me to their apartment on the edge of the village. But first things first. It's 6 am and I have to give up another pee-pee to make sure the antibiotics are working. Then a lovely blueberry müesli breakfast, gymnastics, swim, lunch, and now I'm waiting for Karl, and reading my book on one of the sun-loungers pulled half-way under a tree so as not to get sunburnt. The sun's in full force again after a sample of mountain storms, and it skims over my bare arms like an invisible masseur.

'*Gruss Gott!*' Karl has appeared from around the laundry rooms. From now on, the conversation will be all in German, but he is careful to speak slowly in *hoch Deutsch*, enunciating each syllable, and making sure I understand. He asks if I'd like to walk the scenic route; he says it's shadier. I don't know if I'm familiar with the scenic route. Shady, it definitely is; shorter, it isn't. We trudge through a leafy path, over little bridges that will only support one of us at a time (I only know this by Karl's wild miming), past pretty little cottages adorned with painted walls and flowers in window-boxes, dip down through the trees again, stop to admire a statue of Madonna and her child, hover by the small man-made pool anyone can jump into if they are overcome with heat, and what looks to me like animal troughs, which Karl explains are arm-coolers – for humans – you lay your arms in the ice-cold water to cool off, rather like the wading pool; finally we come out into a clearing where there are some plain looking, low-rise apartment buildings. I wonder if they are council flats. Emmi and her husband live in one of these. I have been before when Carole and I were invited ten years ago, but would never have found it this time without Karl.

Emmi appears at the top of the steps.

'Where on earth have you been?' she demands of her husband, sounding like every other wife in the world, only she speaks with a strong Bavarian accent. Karl also lapses into Bavarian, explaining why it's taken us over half an hour for a ten-minute walk, and I struggle to keep up with the conversation.

'*Kommst Du mit mir.*' (Come with me.) Emmi leads me into the living room, which doubles as a dining room. I remember the room. She has thrown open the French windows that lead onto a long L-shaped balcony where pots of geraniums add a splash of colour, and the warm air gently blows over the living-room table, which Emmi has already laid with a crisp white embroidered cloth. A large silver pot of coffee (oh, dear, I'm not supposed to be drinking coffee) stands alongside all the best bone china, and I spot a jug of what I hope isn't real cream. Now I smell what I've come for – Emmi's *Apfelstrudel*. It's over there, on the opposite table, spread out in spicy sweet-smelling tantalising loaves, the same waft as Tannerhof when you open the front door.

A few weeks ago I treated myself for the first time to a tea at Fortnum & Mason. I ordered a pot of Assam and a slice of apple strudel from a lovely smiling waitress, and settled to read a book I'd just bought. My waitress came with the strudel and a little jug of cream. I have to tell you, it was delicious. Light flaky pastry, gently warmed through, fresh apple, not too sweet, plump raisins…we'll see how Emmi's strudel shapes up.

Fortnum & Mason – eat your heart out.

She pours coffee and sees my worried expression.

'Decaf,' she assures me.

I savour every mouthful, listening to Karl and Emmi. She cannot speak *hoch Deutsch*, so Karl translates for me. It's the weirdest thing, having a translation from Bavarian into normal German, but I find I can understand nearly everything. I ask Emmi lots of questions about the people we used to work with, and she fills me in with almost everyone, swallowing her Bavarian vowels, and not bothering to slow up, so I lean forward in concentration. She's amazed when I tell her that Irene was a guest during the first three days of my visit. It's fun that I can give *her* an up-date.

We talk about the old days in the kitchen and the various changes. Emmi is surprised that the kitchen closes for a couple of hours in the morning. We remember how we used to work right the way through that long morning shift, and only I, out of the kitchen crew, who would have the nerve to stop for ten minutes with a pretend coffee. Emmi shrugs. Then brightens.

'Would you like to see some photographs?'

Most people, on hearing this, would be looking at their watches and asking *'Is that the time already?'* but I am delighted. Why, she might even have a photo of me! As she is digging them out of a cupboard, Karl asks if I'd like to sit outside on the balcony in the sunshine.

Emmi has found several albums. There she is, an attractive young German woman in white apron and cap in 1959.

'Good legs, Emmi,' I tell her, pointing to the photograph.

'*Ja*,' she agrees, with no modesty, '*schöne Beine*.'

We pore through four albums, as heavy as Yorkstone slabs, and finally get to the year of 1973. I'm excited.

'Lorraine,' I cry, pointing to a black and white photo of a pretty girl with mane of hair, laughing out at us. 'Do you remember her, Emmi? One of the other English girls.'

Emmi looks blank and shakes her head. I'm on the right trail now, but although Emmi seems to have kept a diary-like sequence of photographs of all her years at Tannerhof, there are no other photos of we English girls, or Barry. The only other person I recognise is Suna. There are several of her; one or two of them where she is looking glamorous at someone's birthday party at Tannerhof.

I'm disappointed, but at least I've given Emmi my full attention and been genuinely interested to see how Tannerhof has evolved over the years. The kitchen went through three major updates, one of them immediately after I left in February 1974. Our two hours together have flown by and it's time to leave. Emmi puts two huge slices of strudel into a plastic container for me to take back. Bang goes my careful diet for the next two days.

'Emmi is going to walk back with you,' Karl says. 'She has to water the plants in the greenhouse at Tannerhof.'

We say our goodbyes to Karl and set off. The sun has already gone in and it looks dull so we hurry along the non-scenic route, which is still scenic. We just make it to the main street of Bayrischzell when the sky bursts and chucks down rain with the force of Victoria Falls. We join several other unprepared Bavarians who have rushed under the canopy of the Café Königslinde (where I often have my afternoon cup of real tea). Neither Emmi nor I have an umbrella or raincoat, and there's no question that we can attempt to continue to Tannerhof in this deluge. A car draws up, and a woman opens the window and calls:

'Taxi!'

The car doesn't look like a taxi, but in this torrent, I'm not going to argue. Emmi seems to recognise the voice and she braves the storm to get a closer look at the driver. She beckons me, and opens the door and gets in. What luck. Someone Emmi knows. I climb into the back seat, soaked from running those few feet, and listen as the two of them talk. I can see the woman's face in the driver's mirror. It's attractive and I have the odd feeling I've seen her before. Thick shiny chestnut hair, merry hazel eyes and wide smile. I hear Emmi explain who I am, and then I hear her say 'Traudl.' It can't be…it can't be *my* Traudl.

'Haben Sie einmal im Tannerhof gearbeitet?' I ask her in my best German. (Did you once work at Tannerhof?)

'Ja,' she replies.

'Wann?' (When?)

She tells me from 1969-73 working as a waitress.

'Traudl!' I'm almost shrieking. 'Do you remember me? I'm the English girl who you taught how to pronounce *"München"*. You made me repeat it fifty times until you were satisfied that I'd got it right.' In my excitement I'm lapsing into English. Traudl laughs and answers me also in English.

'Yes, I do remember you, English girl. I recognise your voice.' (What about my face?) She pulls up to the front door of Tannerhof and says, 'You must come to tea and we can talk. Can you come tomorrow afternoon? I will come over to Tannerhof to collect you at 3 o'clock.'

Tonight I'm inspired by Emmi's photo albums so I decide to try to find the archives at Tannerhof. Daniella told me yesterday that one of the guests showed her a poem I'd written about the clinic when I was here with my sister ten years ago. She said there were loads of albums in the painted wardrobe right outside my bedroom door. I nose around and find the guest-book with my poem, and a dozen photo albums. I retrieve the ones for 1973-4, make a cup of ginseng tea and take everything to the fasting room, which is also next door to my room. No-one's in there and I can sift through it all without disturbance.

So I *did* work at Tannerhof – it wasn't a dream, for there I am. Sitting at a table in the library (makes a change from the kitchen) with Irene and Suna and some of the others. It was taken on 9th July and as there were cakes, it must have been someone's birthday. My name was written underneath with G.B. in brackets. My hair is shoulder-length and pulled back with a slide. Mouthful of food. I do hate it when people take a photo of me eating. My lips double in size and it's most unbecoming. I'm sitting next to someone with blonde hair in a French pleat. I wonder if it's Del, but I'll never know as I'm completely blocking her.

I come across a photo of Barry. They have called him 'Berry'. He's in profile standing with Emmi, Anita, Irene, Frau Mengershausen and several others at what might be the station. Frau Mengershausen has a rucksack (she would never go on any trip without one), and Barry is carrying a bag – in fact, they've all got bags. Where are they going? It looks like some kind of staff outing.

I find a few more of Barry, one of them taken when Tannerhof was having an indoor swimming-pool built. Barry is climbing the scaffolding to help put the new roof on. It looks highly dangerous to me, but he's laughing. He is wearing jeans rolled up at the ankle in a deep cuff (teenagers today think they are so fashionable with this look, but we had it way back then), and a sweater with a white stripe round the neck and cuffs, and he's carrying a hammer. I turn the page. There's one of Mieke sitting next to Frau Mengershausen who is playing her guitar. Suna is with them. Here's another one of Suna in a very short skirt, her arms disappearing under a mountain of soap-suds. It was taken in her old position in the scullery. I feel like I'm being beamed from 2005 back to 1973 in the space of seconds. Oh, here's a nice one of Mieke and me sporting our Vidal Sassoon hairstyles. But I never come across one of Del. I'm glad I have a picture of her at home.

And finally, there's Gisela, looking stunning as usual, even though she is in her therapist's whites. Well, she didn't make it to the centenary, but I've been told that she is definitely coming tomorrow in time for supper. I've even seen her napkin holder with Schwester Gisela written on it. She will be in my dining room at the next table. What fun it will be showing her all these photos. Can't believe I will be seeing Traudl and Gisela tomorrow; both I never dreamt I would see again, especially after thirty years.

It was awful at lunch today. Monika, the little red-headed Barbie doll, came into the dining room with her face in a terrible state. She had an eye that looked as though someone had rammed a fistful of blackberries at it, a long angry cut on her forehead, which was stitched, and her normally pale complexioned face was the colour of a Geisha. I could tell she was still in shock as she explained what had happened.

'I had cramp in ze night,' she said, in her halting but perfect English. 'I jumped up, and because I have low blood pressure, I faint… fainted?.. and hit ze floor on my face. I don't know how long I was there. Then I woke… awoke?… and went to ze next door, but nobody was in. I went to another door, and a lady helped me and called ze doctor. I have been in hospital for ze last two days.'

I wondered why I hadn't seen her lately, but just thought that our appointments and mealtimes weren't coinciding. Poor Monika. She was so worried that her face would be scarred, but we all assured her it wouldn't be noticeable after a few weeks. I hope we're right.

A knock on my door and it's Traudl. I can see her clearly now she's not just an image in her car mirror. And it definitely *is* my Traudl. We hug and kiss, both of us laughing with the delight of it all. Before we go, I show her the photographs, and she is suitably intrigued. Then we walk back down the hill to her house, which she and her husband had built eight years ago. All my estate agency instincts

return and I am thrilled with the chance to see the interior of a real
Bavarian home. She's pleased that I like it. Shiny wooden floors and
ceilings, with Tyrolean touches such as the shutters and balconies
with their colourful window-boxes, and everywhere spotless.

'You must spend all day cleaning,' I say, thinking how Herman
would have approved. The table groans under a massive teapot,
beautiful china tea-service, water and wine glasses, and enough
cakes to start a bakery.

'Herr Hubert's?' I guess. She laughs and nods. She laughs even
more when I tell her the story of Herr Hubert and his smashed car.

'Poor Herr Hubert,' she says. 'He is such a good man.'

'Not to mention that he makes the best cakes.' I greedily eye the
platters.

Then we reminisce. She doesn't remember our wine evening to
celebrate that we could call each other *'Du'*, but she *does* remember
giving me my one and only lesson in the *Rohkost* Room.

'I didn't think at the time you'd be the right person to show me,'
I admit. It's such a relief that we can speak in English.

'It was all part of my hotel training course,' she says. 'But I left
before you.'

'Yes, just as we were becoming friends,' I say, through the last
crumbs of one of Herr Hubert's delicious pieces of quark cake. 'I was
sorry to see you go. You were always so cheerful around the place.'

'I *loved* my time at Tannerhof,' she says. 'They were four of my
happy years working with Maria and Mena.'

We are only able to polish off two cakes between us with two
pots of tea and soya milk – Traudl is allergic to cow's – as we are
talking so much. It's such fun sharing memories of those days, and
I realise Traudl has hardly changed. Then we go on to tell each
other what we've been doing in the thirty-odd intervening years.
Neither of us had children, but, unlike me, she has kept the same
husband. She says not much has happened to her as she has been
living in Bayrischzell all this time, and nothing much happens in

Bayrischzell. She's amazed that I am writing a book on Tannerhof, and even more so when I tell her that one of the chapters is practically devoted to her.

'I open a bottle of sparkling wine to celebrate our meeting and your book,' she says, 'and we must talk in German. You see, I am still bossy – I don't change.' We both laugh.

She fetches two champagne glasses, the wine, and a bottle of elderflower syrup. She pours a little of the syrup in the bottom of the glasses and fills it with Sekt, the bubbles almost ready to spill over the edge and hands me a glass.

'*Prost*,' we say, clinking our glasses. It's divine. Fresh and slightly sweet and the elderflower syrup has enhanced the flavour of the champagne.

When I ask her for her email address she confesses that she's not on the Internet nor does she have email. She hates the computer. I try to encourage her to get going with it. She says it's too late and I remind her I'm older than her. It's strange, as she doesn't look anywhere near her age, which must be about fifty-five; neither does she act it, but she is not bothering to become part of the modern world.

I meet her husband who has just come in from work. He seems pleased that Traudl has a friend for tea. He's nice. Nice face, lost his hair, but Traudl had showed me a photo of him when he was young and he was really handsome. Why, oh why, do we all have to get old?

It's time for me to leave, but we've exchanged addresses and have promised to keep in touch. Another hug and kiss and I'm walking back up the hill to Tannerhof. I'm sad that I've said goodbye to Traudl but astonished that by the most incredible serendipity (I suppose serendipity is always incredible) we have met again. And I've still got Gisela to look forward to.

Supper: there's someone in Gisela's place. It's not Gisela. Are you sure? I ask myself. You know you're short-sighted in one eye. I squint again.

Well, unless Gisela has over-shot me by some twenty-five years, and shrunk about a foot, it isn't her. This is a little grey-haired feisty old lady. Maybe she's got into the wrong seat. She turns to the lady on her right as she forks down a plateful of salad. They talk, and I hear her companion call her 'Schwester Gisela.' I've been told about the wrong Gisela! I'm so disappointed. She looks across at me several times, rather sternly, I feel, and then carries on with her conversation. Oh, well. I've had plenty of excitement in one day.

After supper, not my Schwester Gisela gets up, hesitates, and to my surprise comes across to me. She's even older than I had first thought, and rather bent, so I gesture her to take the empty seat by me. This is our conversation (in German):

'Are you Frau Barnes?'

I admit that I am.

'I am Schwester Gisela.'

'I know.'

'Did you telephone me at my house about three weeks ago?'

'Yes, I spoke to your friend. She was very helpful and said you were away and that you'd be going to Tannerhof at the same time as I told her I was going.'

'You spoke to my husband.'

'No, it was a woman.'

'There is no woman in my house. It was my *husband*.' By this time she was looking positively fierce. I backed down. Obviously her husband has a high-pitched voice and she must get fed-up with hearing people say this.

'How do you know me?' she demands.

I explain that I had worked here thirty years ago and had been very friendly with a Gisela who was a masseuse. And I had rung Tannerhof before this visit to get her telephone number to let her know I was coming. Schwester Gisela raises a spiky grey eyebrow, but I can see that she is listening intently for me to continue.

'But they gave me the wrong Schwester Gisela!'

She looks at me and bursts out laughing. She has to wipe her eyes. I'm delighted to see her so merry as I had completely misjudged her. She gives me a little tap on my arm and laughs all over again and of course I join in. 'The wrong Schwester Gisela. Ha, ha, ha.'

Chapter 36
An Evening with Bach

I've made a new friend, Uschi, who owns the only shop at Tannerhof. She has an eclectic mixture of goodies: clothes that are ethnic in style and fabric; accessories, including a range of brightly-coloured felt flowers to be worn as necklaces or brooches; all sorts of health foods, some of which I've not seen in England, such as dried mango balls (I can't resist a packet of those); health and cookery books, including, of course, Frau Winklmüller's; cosmetics and skin treatments that are herb and flower based; pictures and posters and a few ceramic items. There are always several guests browsing, and I think it's a real winner as I don't know any woman who is not keen to shop.

I was wandering around Uschi's shop the other day and chatting to her, telling her I'd been to Bayrischzell a few evenings ago to hear a Bavarian band, but that I really loved classical music and noticed there was a concert at the next village this coming Sunday. She immediately said she would take me. It's now Sunday evening, and after a day of pouring rain and burning sun, it's calmed down and I'm dressed ready to meet Uschi. She's looking glamorous in a floaty skirt and jacket with two of her own bright pink and cream felt flowers at her neck.

'Nele is coming with us, if that is all right,' she says, and I'm delighted. Nele von Mengershausen is an artist who takes the painting classes at Tannerhof. She is also dressed up and looking most attractive. I make Nele sit in the front so they can chat together but I don't feel at all left out as they're easy to understand, probably because they keep turning round and translating for me. The concert is to be held in a baroque church, or is it rococo, full of exuberant extravaganza, as churches often are in Bavaria, but you still can't help enjoying all the razzmatazz.

Tonight it's an evening of Bach. He's not my favourite composer as I am not a fan of the organ, but I would rather listen to that than go through another evening of more Bavarian marches. According to the brochure it doesn't look as if the organ is featuring, which is excellent. A crowd is gathering outside as we go in to buy our tickets and when we come out again – we're early – I can't help noticing that nearly all the older women are wearing their best dirndls. They look very sweet, but I can't see how a dirndl has any sex appeal whatsoever. That apron screams domesticity and the skirt covers every bit of their legs. Do German men find their women seductive in these dirndls? Can they not wait to rip those aprons off their women's hips? To me, they just don't look like grown-ups' dresses. But I suppose it's what you're used to, and seduced to.

An Indian chap strolls over and starts speaking to me in English, or rather American. He nearly comes up to my neck, but that doesn't deter him in the least. I think he thinks I'm alone as Uschi and Nele have already gone inside. He tells me his life history, which is incredibly boring, barely asks *me* anything, and as the bell goes for us to take our seats, he says: 'Did anyone tell you what beautiful eyes you have?'

'They never stop,' I reply, thinking he must be really desperate if he can't see that my eyes are bloodshot today through no sleep last night.

Thankfully, I escape him and find my seat next to the two Tannerhof women. Then I see something that makes my heart drop. A young mother is strapping her little tot, who can't be more than two-and-a-half, into a small chair in the aisle. Bugger. Well, at least the mother has the pram facing towards the church door so when (and not *if*) the kid cries, at least she can make a fast get-a-way, after the kid's ruined the music for everyone. I watch, fascinated. No-one looks perturbed. She is a dear little girl to look at, wearing a navy blue sailor dress and navy straw hat trimmed with flowers turned up around her face. The mother ties a Teddy bear onto the child's wrist, and gives her a bottle of juice. Wonder how long it will last before the first scream bellows out. The mother keeps talking to her daughter and then the concert begins. We all clap, including the child, when the musicians appear, and then there's that expectant hush that precedes any live performance.

The concert begins. Bach carries me away and I forget about the child until nearing the end, when I realise she hasn't fidgeted at all. Or made a peep. She claps when we do, and in between the movements, when people often mistakenly clap, she is silent, until the finale. The child had sat as quietly as the statues of the *putti* around her, not even having a swig out of her bottle until the interval. Amazing.

During the interval I can't resist saying something to the mother, who is gorgeous with her thick naturally-blonde hair pulled back in a long elegant pony-tail. She is talking to her daughter – not fussing over her – but offering her a drink and asking her if she wants the toilet.

'I can't believe that she was so well-behaved,' I say in English, sure that the mother will understand me. 'Even *I've* been known to have a fidget during a long piece of Bach.'

The mother smiles. 'It's an experiment.'

A dangerous one, I think.

The kid's normal after all. Five minutes into the next piece, she starts to cry and the mother immediately whisks her out. But half-way through the concert she brings her back in again, and the child is faultless. I wonder if the child belongs to one of the three handsome young violinists, and that's why she is so connected to the music. But then you'd think she would be running down the aisle shouting 'Papa'.

The music comes to an end. Oh, there goes the little girl, flying down the aisle to the stage, her mother following with a bouquet of flowers that she presents to the lady who played the harpsichord, which to *my* ear is so much nicer than the organ. There are lots of hugs and kisses on the stage, and by the looks of the programme they are a famous family who travel the world with their performances. Yes, I was right. One of the violinists picks the tot up and flings her about in the air as fathers do. What a marvellous grounding for the child. She'll grow up with classical music, and more than likely learn an instrument herself that she'll excel in. As my Dad used to say, 'It's the house you get dropped off at that has the most bearing on your future.'

Uschi and Nele are big Bach fans and I tell them it's the best Bach performance I have ever heard — and mean it. They glow as if they'd discovered the very man themselves!

CHAPTER 37
Auf Wiedersehen

It's TIME TO pack. I can't believe I'm going home tomorrow. This is the worst part. I feel I could live here for ever, as Tannerhof feels like my spiritual home, but I know that's irrational. The first person to say goodbye to is the earringed owner of the Café Königslinde so I trot down the hill for my last cup of Asaam. Why is this café so super? Okay, it's a beautiful day, the mountains still back-drop, the villagers who stop for a drink and gossip look so relaxed that they might be taken for holiday-makers themselves, the café bathes in sunlight like a Cézanne impression. Can it be the inviting basket chairs with their plump red-and-white-checked cushions, some of them placed outside to make the most of the sun, even in winter, and others pushed back under the verandah in case of a downpour? Is it the tubs and baskets brimming with flowers? The Tyrolean building?

But most of the cafés look similar. Then is it the excellent tea they serve here – a variety of teas rather than only Liptons, which most European cafés offer and which tastes like oil when it's made with foreign and not very hot water?

As usual, it boils down (!) to the people. This particular owner gives excellent service with a welcoming smile, and sets everything out so neatly on the little silver tray that you feel Ritz pampered.

'It's my last day,' I tell him. 'I'm leaving in the morning.'

He looks suitably sad.

'You must come back soon.'

When my tea arrives, he's put a chocolate on the plate alongside the minuscule macaroon. I'm really going to pig out and ruin my fortnight's diet now.

My waiter has got to know me, and I don't have to remind him to bring cold milk instead of the jug of frothy hot (hot milk in tea – ugh!) that he first brought me. I sit at one of the outside tables with *Laurence of Arabia*, sometimes deigning to raise my head to look at the Bayrischzellers who come wandering in for a *Pause*, feeling perfectly and utterly content.

Then I think, it's not just this café. What about Café Stumpp and Café Hubert? Café Stumpp with the best cheesecake and intelligent waitresses who speak English when my mind goes blank (a not infrequent occurrence but only since I've turned sixty, I tell myself). Kind-hearted Herr Hubert who rescued me on my arrival and smashed his car up by doing so, and wouldn't allow me to feel guilty… good-humoured Volker and his gentle wife Jutti, with whom I've had such great conversations, talking about everything, including the war, without feeling the slightest bit uncomfortable, and sharing many laughs… my new friends, Monika (whose bravely made-up, scarred elfin face is improving by the day), and Brigitte, whose life, she revealed in our girlie chat yesterday evening, has often run parallel to my own…my old friend Traudl, and Emmi, Anita and Irene… I wish I could have seen Suna again… and dear Gisela was also missing, but she was probably still with Herman!... numerous other lovely guests at Tannerhof who all know who they are if they have picked up this book...the waitresses, cleaners, cooks, gardeners, office staff, therapists, doctors...all the family von Mengershausen...they have made this visit incredibly special by making me feel special.

I'd held plenty of pre-conceptions about Germans. That they were serious, disciplined, law-abiding, obsessively hard-working, religious... Yes, they are all those things. But they can also play hard, are kind, cultured, intelligent and interesting. And they do have a sense of humour. Thank goodness for once I didn't listen to my big sister that bitter day in March, all those years ago, as we stood on the platform at Bayrischzell, waiting for her train...

This little reverie is interrupted by my cheerful waiter who sets down a fresh pot of boiling water without my having to ask.

I feel obliged to give you the real Bircher-Benner müesli recipé as we were told it was the best start to the day, summer and winter. It's a delicious Swiss recipé, nothing like the way most people in this country serve it—just with milk. I do, however, break away from tradition where at Tannerhof I used to make up my own müesli from several different cereals; now I use a good-quality basic müesli mix of oats, barley and wheat etc as life's too short.

MÜESLI X 2

3 tablespoons good müesli mix with raisins, nuts etc but no added sugar or salt
2 tablespoons plain live yoghurt
1 apple, peeled and grated
1 or more other fruits such as banana, orange, melon, and any seasonal fruits, chopped
1 teaspoon honey (if desired)
pumpkin seeds/pine-nuts/grated nuts as a topping (optional)

The most important bit is to soak the müesli mix overnight in 4 tablespoons water or apple juice. In the morning mix in the yoghurt, grated apple, other chopped fruit, and honey. Sprinkle with the grated nuts or other topping. A spoonful of *quark* or very low-fat *fromage frais* is lovely on top.

If you can't face a cold breakfast in the winter, this next recipé would be a warming start, even though we used to have it as a supper dish in the old days at Tannerhof.

SCHROTBREI (LUXURY PORRIDGE TO YOU AND ME) x 2

5 tablespoons of pinhead oatmeal (if possible—if not, porridge oats)
pinch salt
grated lemon and orange peel
juice from 1 orange and half a lemon
1 tablespoon raisins
half a pint milk
quarter pint water

Allow oatmeal to cook gently in the water for a few minutes. Stir occasionally. Add the other ingredients and enough milk (you may need to adjust the liquid) to make a thick creamy mixture, all the while stirring. Serve with a dollop of *quark* or low-fat *fromage frais*.

HAFERSCHLEIM (EXCELLENT FOR AN UPSET STOMACH) x 1

2 - 3 tablespoons oats and baby oats mixed
Water

Mix oats with quarter to a third pint water and gently bring to the boil, stirring occasionally, until the mixture thickens. If this is not for an invalid but for a low-calorie breakfast, it can be served with a pinch of salt, fruit and very low-fat yoghurt, *quark*, honey etc.

ABOUT THE AUTHOR

Denise Barnes has travelled the world, unpacking her suitcase in a score of countries and working at more jobs than she cares to remember. Mentionable ones include selling lipstick in a Denver department store, cat-walk modelling in Atlanta, assistant to the UN Narcotics Director in Geneva, cooking at a Bavarian health spa, chauffeuring a Swiss Gnome in Zurich, and acting as production assistant to an internationally-famous film producer.

Back home in England, Denise took up Britain's third most reviled profession – as an estate agent! Juggling the running of her own chain of eight offices in south-east England with taking an Honours Degree in the Arts from the Open University, Denise also managed to find time to pursue her lifelong passion for writing. Her articles have been published in magazines that include *The Lady* and various life-style magazines.

Selling her business in 2005 has meant Denise can concentrate on international travel (most recently on the Silk Road through Russia and China, and a trans-continental train journey across Australia) and writing full time. *From Bad to Wurst* is Denise's first non-fiction book and she is currently working on a novel.

www.denisebarneswriter.com
www.tannerhof.de

ORDER FORM FOR FURTHER COPIES

Name:

Address:

Postcode:

No. of copies (up to 5):

Total amount: £

Price £8.99 plus £1.50 p&p per copy. Send your cheque and completed order form to:

Pen Press Publishers Ltd
25 Eastern Place
Brighton
BN2 1GJ

For orders greater than 5 copies and trade discounts call 08451080530 or email info@penpress.co.uk

Please tick here to recieve information on Pen Press' services and other publications ☐